Vibe Coding with Cursor, Windsurf, and Lovable

Build Apps Fast with AI-Assisted Software Development and Testing

Greg Lim

<packt>

Vibe Coding with Cursor, Windsurf, and Lovable

Portfolio Director: Ashwin Nair

Relationship Lead: Nitin Nainani

Content Engineer: Kinnari Chohan

Project Manager: Ruvika Rao

Technical Editor: Rohit Singh

Indexer: Rekha Nair

Production Designer: Shankar Kalbhor

Growth Lead: Anamika Singh

First published: February 2026

Production reference: 1060226

Published by
Packt Publishing Ltd.
Grosvenor House
11 St Paul's Square
Birmingham
B3 1RB, UK.

ISBN 978-1-80730-163-7

`www.packtpub.com`

About the author

Greg Lim is a technologist and author of several programming books. Greg has many years in teaching programming in tertiary institutions and he places special emphasis on learning by doing.

Contact Greg at `support@i-ducate.com`.

Table of Contents

Preface

In this book, we take you on a fun, hands-on, and pragmatic journey to Vibe Coding with Cursor, Lovable, and Windsurf. You'll start building your first app within minutes.

We will discover how to shift from traditional programming to a 'vibe coding' approach, where we will prompt AI Agents using natural language to build, test, and deploy our applications.

We will use AI tools like Cursor and Windsurf to guide and refine AI output rather than wrestling with every line of code manually.

In the course of this book, we will cover:

- Introduction to the Vibe Coding Approach
- Vibe Coding with Cursor
- Software Development - Traditional vs Vibe Coding workflow
- Iterating with New Features
- Adding Automated Tests
- Rules for Controlling the AI Behavior
- Providing Context by Referencing Resources
- GitHub Integration and Deployment
- Building Apps with Lovable (No-code/Low-code)
- Creating the Software Specifications Document
- Supabase Integration
- Domain and External Hosting Options
- Working on Existing Code Bases with Windsurf
- Windsurf Rules and Workflows

  and more..

Whether you are a complete beginner, curious to build your own apps with AI, or an experienced developer eager to speed up prototyping and learn to guide AI output, this book is for you.

What will you learn

- Build apps from scratch by describing ideas in plain English and turning them into working code
- Identify, debug, and refine AI-generated code
- Version control, track changes, and roll back safely with Git and GitHub
- Add automated tests to check your app functions well
- AI-guided deployment to launch your app

Working through this book

The book takes a practical hands on approach to learning through practice. You learn best when you code along with the examples in the book.

Get in touch

Feedback from our readers is always welcome.

General feedback: If you have questions about any aspect of this book or have any general feedback, please email us at `customercare@packt.com` and mention the book's title in the subject of your message.

Errata: Although we have taken every care to ensure the accuracy of our content, mistakes do happen. If you have found a mistake in this book, we would be grateful if you reported this to us. Please visit `http://www.packt.com/submit-errata`, click **Submit Errata**, and fill in the form.

Piracy: If you come across any illegal copies of our works in any form on the internet, we would be grateful if you would provide us with the location address or website name. Please contact us at `copyright@packt.com` with a link to the material.

If you are interested in becoming an author: If there is a topic that you have expertise in and you are interested in either writing or contributing to a book, please visit `http://authors.packt.com/`.

Download a free PDF copy of this book

Thanks for purchasing this book!

Do you like to read on the go but are unable to carry your print books everywhere?

Is your eBook purchase not compatible with the device of your choice?

Don't worry, now with every Packt book you get a DRM-free PDF version of that book at no cost.

Read anywhere, any place, on any device. Search, copy, and paste code from your favorite technical books directly into your application.

The perks don't stop there, you can get exclusive access to discounts, newsletters, and great free content in your inbox daily

Follow these simple steps to get the benefits:

1. Scan the QR code or visit the link below

   `https://packt.link/free-ebook/9781807301637`

2. Submit your proof of purchase
3. That's it! We'll send your free PDF and other benefits to your email directly

1

Introduction

Welcome to this book where we'll explore this new and exciting way of building software called Vibe Coding. Vibe coding lets you build apps by simply describing them in plain English. No need to worry about programming languages like JavaScript or Python.

If you've ever copied code from ChatGPT, pasted it into your editor, and then sent back the errors that occurred—congratulations! You've already done some coding. But in this book, you'll be blown away by what else is possible.

Vibe coding isn't just a new tool. It's more of a mindset—an approach to writing code and building applications. The term was coined by Andrej Karpathy, who describes vibe coding as fully giving into the vibes, embracing exponentials, and forgetting the code even exists:

Andrej Karpathy
@karpathy

There's a new kind of coding I call "vibe coding", where you fully give in to the vibes, embrace exponentials, and forget that the code even exists. It's possible because the LLMs (e.g. Cursor Composer w Sonnet) are getting too good. Also I just talk to Composer with SuperWhisper so I barely even touch the keyboard. I ask for the dumbest things like "decrease the padding on the sidebar by half" because I'm too lazy to find it. I "Accept All" always, I don't read the diffs anymore. When I get error messages I just copy paste them in with no comment, usually that fixes it. The code grows beyond my usual comprehension, I'd have to really read through it for a while. Sometimes the LLMs can't fix a bug so I just work around it or ask for random changes until it goes away. It's not too bad for throwaway weekend projects, but still quite amusing. I'm building a project or webapp, but it's not really coding - I just see stuff, say stuff, run stuff, and copy paste stuff, and it mostly works.

7:17 AM · Feb 3, 2025 · **5.1M** Views

1.3K 5.2K 30K 15K

On the front lines of this movement are tools like Cursor and Windsurf. Let's briefly walk through a simple project.

In Cursor (which is based on VS Code), to create a new project, you simply chat with Cursor. Behind the scenes, it uses an LLM and immediately gets to work. I can ask it to recreate my favorite childhood game, a car dodging game where a player drives a car down a highway and dodges oncoming traffic.

So I can prompt it:

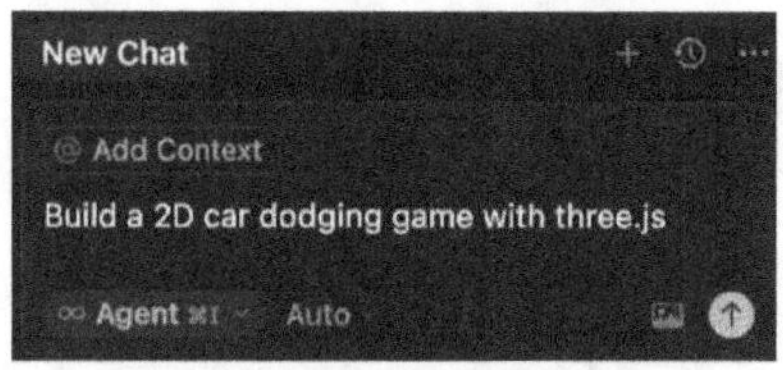

Here's the cool part: because it's an agent, it can take a lot of actions on its own—creating files, executing commands, installing dependencies, deploying, and more:

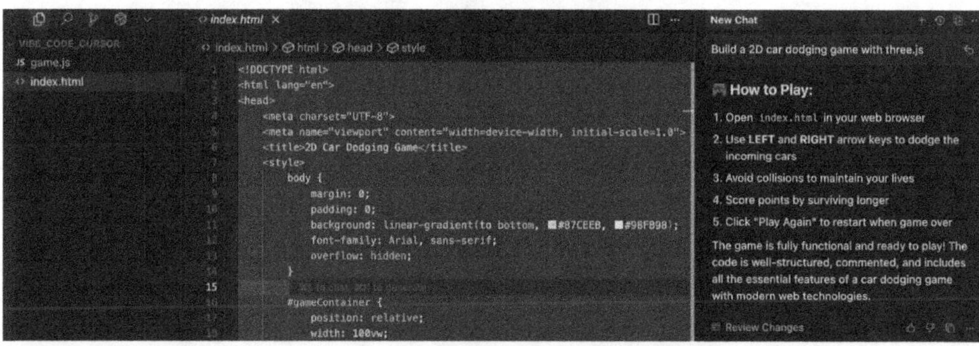

In less than a few minutes, you'll have your first working iteration:

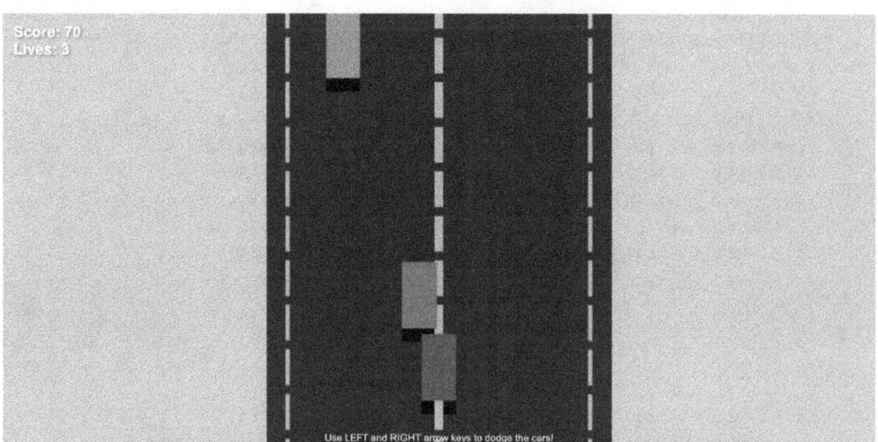

It might not look great at first, but still, it's amazing what you can do in just one minute.

In traditional programming, you need to know every line, every file. But today, the way we build software is changing fast. Writing code itself isn't the main skill anymore. AI can do that. Instead, the most important skills now are being able to experiment, understand, debug, guide and work side by side with AI.

This book is for anyone curious about how AI is changing software development. Whether you're a complete beginner or already a developer, we will see how AI can help us build faster—and how to do it right.

We'll explore different tools and build multiple projects. We'll talk about prototyping apps, spotting bad code, and which skills matter most in this new era.

We'll also see firsthand why strong fundamentals are still important—especially if you want to build advanced, production-ready apps.

By the end of this book, you'll be able to describe your app ideas in natural language and turn them into working prototypes using AI-powered tools.

Essential software development practices such as using Git for version control, organizing projects into clear and maintainable structures, writing and running tests, and automating parts of the process such as deployments.

This isn't just about writing code faster—it's also about learning how to build real-world, production-ready apps with confidence.

Even if you're just starting out, it still takes time, practice, and patience. But with the right mindset and the help of AI, you can go from idea to working prototype—and potentially a product—in record time.

That said, don't expect magic from a single prompt. It's like telling a builder, "Build me a house." You still need to specify the size, style, and materials. The clearer your instructions, the better the result.

This is how software development works realistically. Except now, English—or your native language—becomes your programming language.

Requirements

Now, if you've never written code before, following this book will be a bit challenging. There's a lot to learn, and running into hiccups is part of the process. Having basic programming experience will help you understand the code that the AI generates and able to debut when issues arise. Email me at `support@i-ducate.com` if you need introductory programming resources.

AI-Powered Coding Tools

This book aims to teach you the skills you need, regardless of which AI coding tools you choose to use. Right now, there's an explosion of such tools in this space, and it's difficult to keep track of them all. In this section, we will give you some orientation so you know which tools might work best for you.

If you're just starting out and don't have much experience installing Development Tools on your computer, you can use web-based tools like Lovable, Firebase Studio, Bolt or Replit.

For example, here's Lovable:

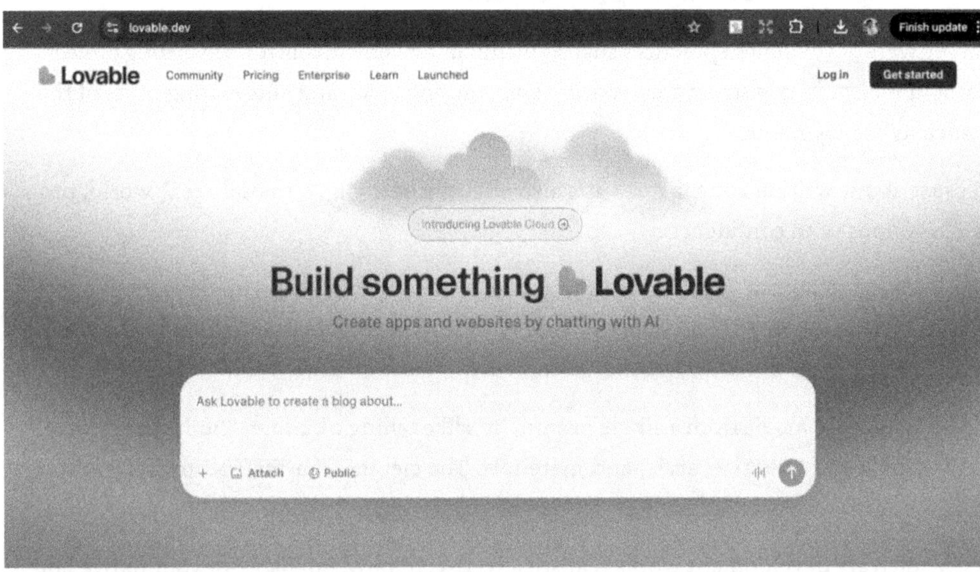

Web-based tools are user-friendly for creating beautiful front-ends without needing to install anything or leave your browser. We just provide a prompt (optionally attach an image or a Figma design) and it can generate a working app.

For instance, I created a small app that helps my child with Math Practice. I simply wrote a short prompt:

```
I want to build a math practice app for students. Each card should display
a simple arithmetic problem, such as addition or multiplication. When
flipped, it should show the correct answer. The app should randomize
problems and track how many were answered correctly.
```

And Lovable generates an interface that would have taken us much longer to build from scratch:

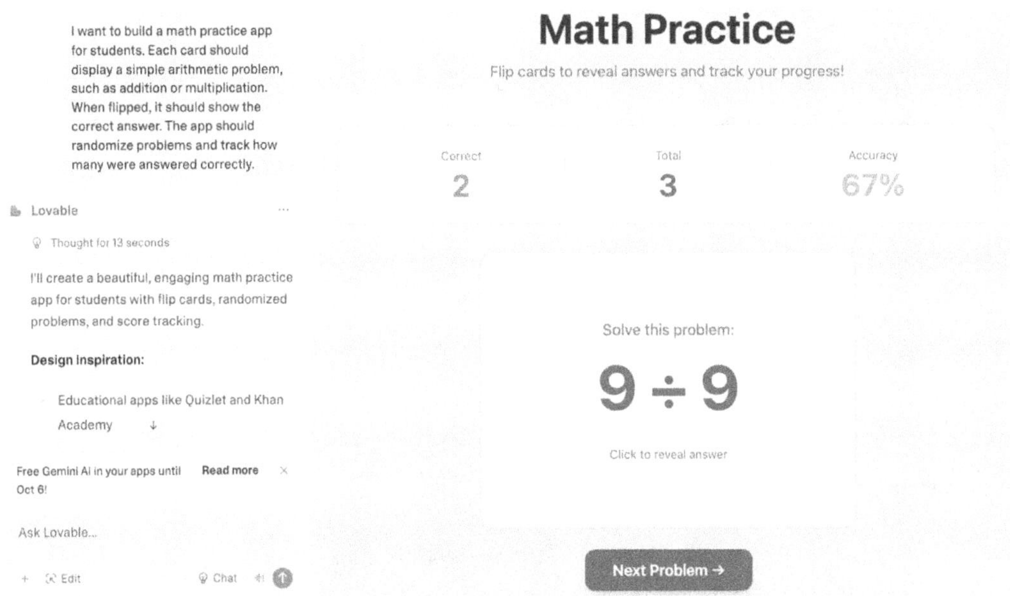

From there, we can continue refining the app and improving it through conversation.

Lovable even handles deployment—you can use a domain directly from them:

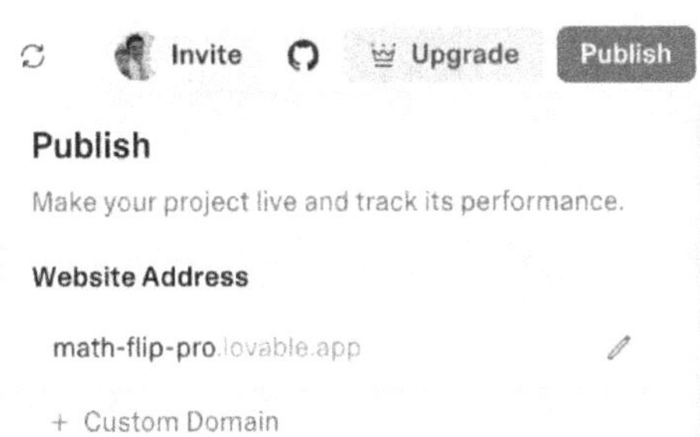

You can also view the generated code if you're more technical:

We can even sync it with GitHub:

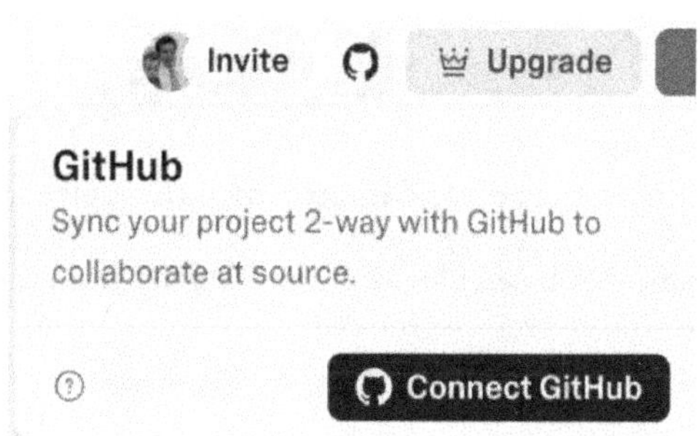

Beyond that, we can integrate with services like Supabase for data storage and backend functionality.

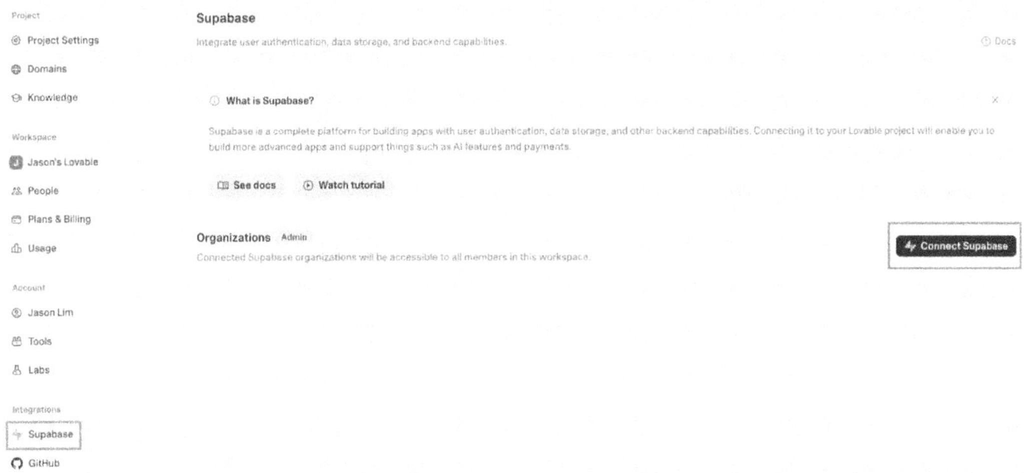

This makes Lovable a great starting point, especially if you don't want to leave your browser. We will cover Lovable later in this book.

If you want something a little more advanced, Firebase Studio (launched by Google) provides more functionality. Though remember that for beginners, "more" isn't always "better."

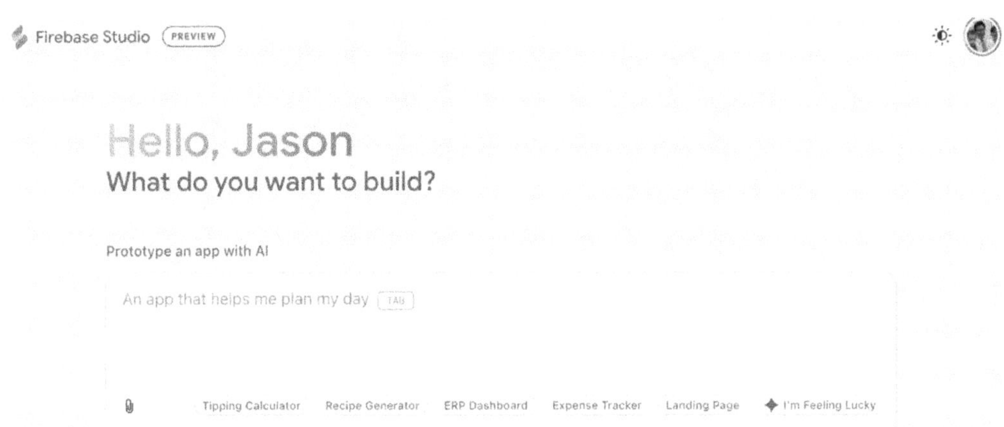

In short, if you're a beginner and want to build entirely in your browser, start with one of these apps. Lovable is an excellent entry point.

Apart from web-based tools, we have **Integrated Development Environment** (**IDE**)s where popular ones include Cursor and Windsurf. Both are Visual Studio Code forks and we will cover them in this book.

Next, we have a small category of CLI tools, like OpenAI's Codex CLI but it's not something we'd recommend if you're just getting started.

The advantage of IDEs is control—you're not locked into a single platform or technology. But with more control comes more responsibility. So we recommend IDEs for those with some programming experience or for learners eager to dive deeper into software development.

Regardless of which tools you use, the skills you develop are transferable. Even if this book demonstrates a specific tool, the concepts apply broadly. Don't skip a section just because it uses a tool you're not planning to adopt. For example, lessons shown with Cursor can still be useful if you prefer Lovable.

Let's look at installing Cursor and building our first app in the next few chapters.

2

Installing Software (Cursor, NodeJS, Git)

Let's dive right into building our first app. For that, we'll need a few tools: Cursor, Node.js, and Git. We'll explain the role of each in this chapter. All of these tools work on Windows, macOS, and Linux, so no matter what computer you have, you're good to go.

Opening the Terminal

Throughout the book, you will be asked to open a terminal. If you've never used it before, it's quite simple. On macOS or Linux, search for a program called **Terminal**:

On Windows, search for **CMD** or **PowerShell**.

What you'll see might look slightly different depending on your system, but the idea is the same: it's a place where we can type commands and communicate directly with the computer. We'll show you exactly how in a moment.

Tool 1: Node.js

The first tool we'll install is Node.js (`nodejs.org`):

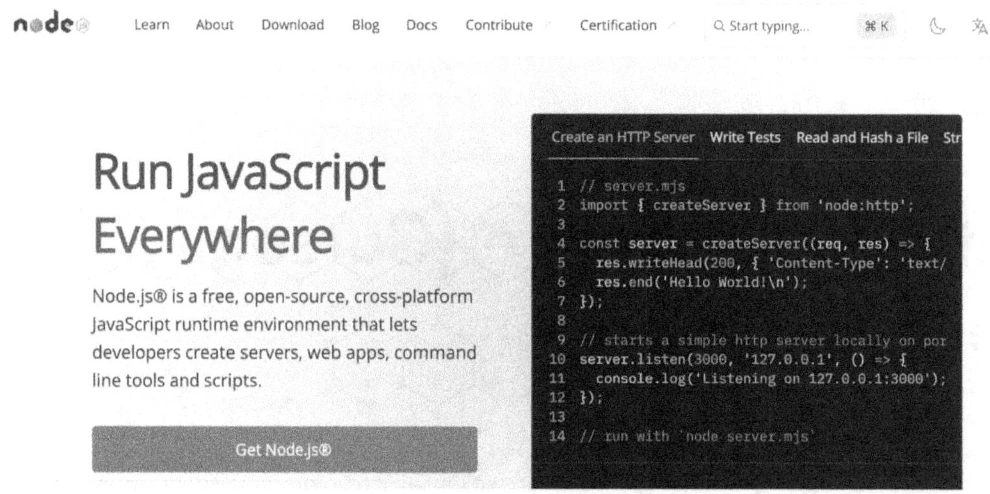

Node.js allows us to run JavaScript on our computer—it's like the engine running behind the scenes. Follow the download instructions in `nodejs.org/en/download` to download and install Node.js.

To check if you have Node.js installed, open your terminal and type:

```
node -v
```

It should print something like `v22.20.0` or another version number. If a version number appears, you're all set.

Tool 2: Git

The next tool is Git. Git helps us track changes in our code, save different versions of it, and collaborate effectively. We'll use Git frequently during the book, so it's important to have it installed.

To check if you already have Git installed, type this into your terminal:

```
git -v
```

If you see a version number, you're good to go.

Tool 3: Cursor

The final tool we'll use in this section is Cursor (`cursor.com`):

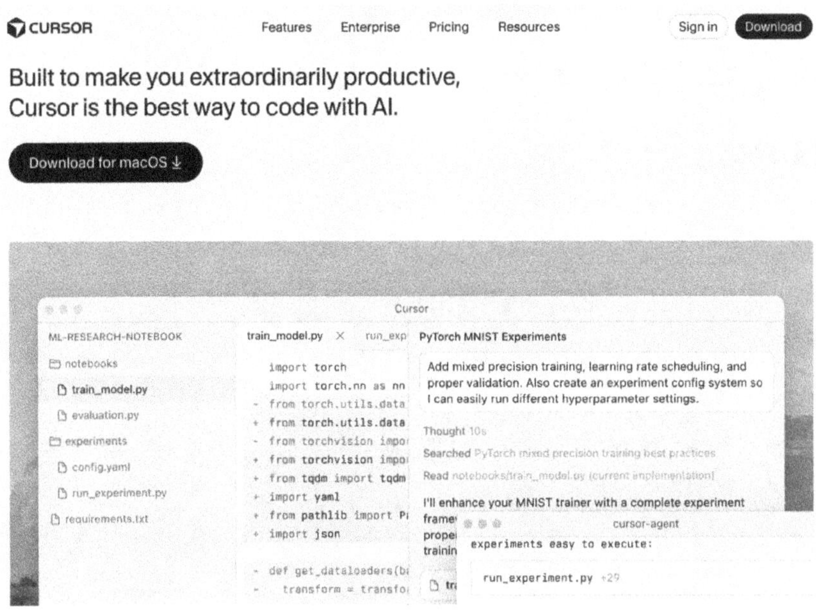

Cursor is an AI-powered code editor, built on top of VS Code, so if you've used VS Code before, Cursor will feel familiar.

To get started, visit the Cursor website (`cursor.com`) and download the version for your operating system. After installation, when you open Cursor for the first time, you'll be asked to go through a quick setup:

1. **Language** – Choose English or the language you're comfortable with.
2. **Terminal integration** – Optional, but I recommend enabling it.
3. **Extensions** – I suggest starting from scratch so Cursor doesn't get cluttered with unnecessary extensions.
4. **Privacy** – I prefer enabling Privacy Mode so my private code isn't shared.

Finally, you'll need to create a Cursor account. Sign-up is quick, doesn't require a credit card, and once you log in, your account will be connected to your local installation.

When Cursor first opens, the interface can feel a little overwhelming. But don't worry, we will guide you along. If you look for the small buttons in the top-right corner:

They open and close different panels. Spend a moment exploring these so you feel comfortable.

Pricing Note

Node.js and Git are completely free. Cursor, on the other hand, offers both free and paid plans. At the time of this book's writing, new users get a two-week Pro trial:

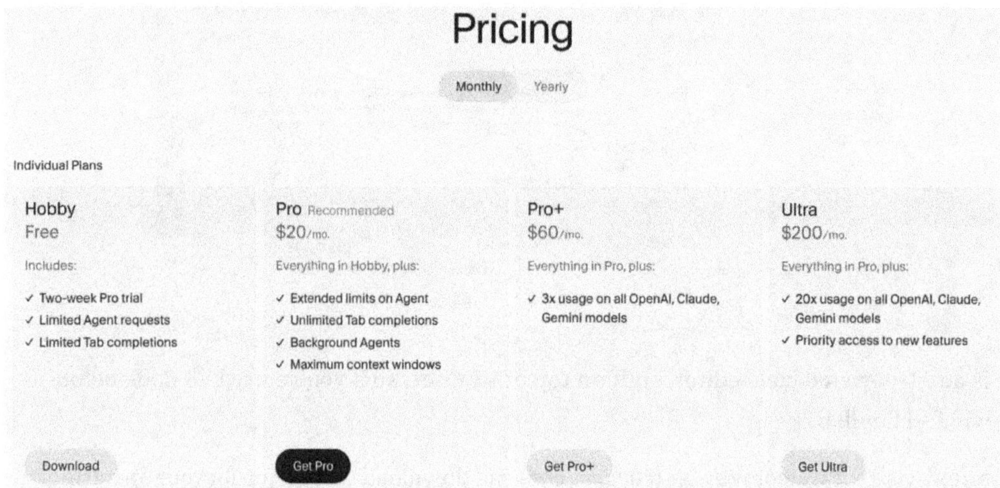

The free plan works well but has some limits, while the Pro plan unlocks more features. For now, we can enjoy the free trial. But if you really want to invest in a good learning and coding experience with Cursor, it is worth signing up with a **Pro** plan for one month first, as the free plan quickly runs out.

Having installed Node.js, Git, and Cursor, we now have all the tools you need. Let's get started building our first app.

3

Vibe Coding with Cursor

Let's build our first mini-project using Cursor. Create a new folder on your computer and give it your project name, e.g. `2d-car-race` (I am building my favorite childhood game):

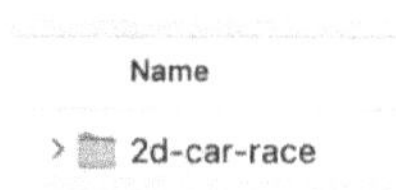

Once you create the folder, click **Open project** in Cursor and select the newly created folder:

There won't be much stuff appearing at first since we are opening an empty folder. But on the top-right, click on the **AI Pane** icon:

You can toggle it on or off. Similarly, you can open or close the Terminal panel with its icon:

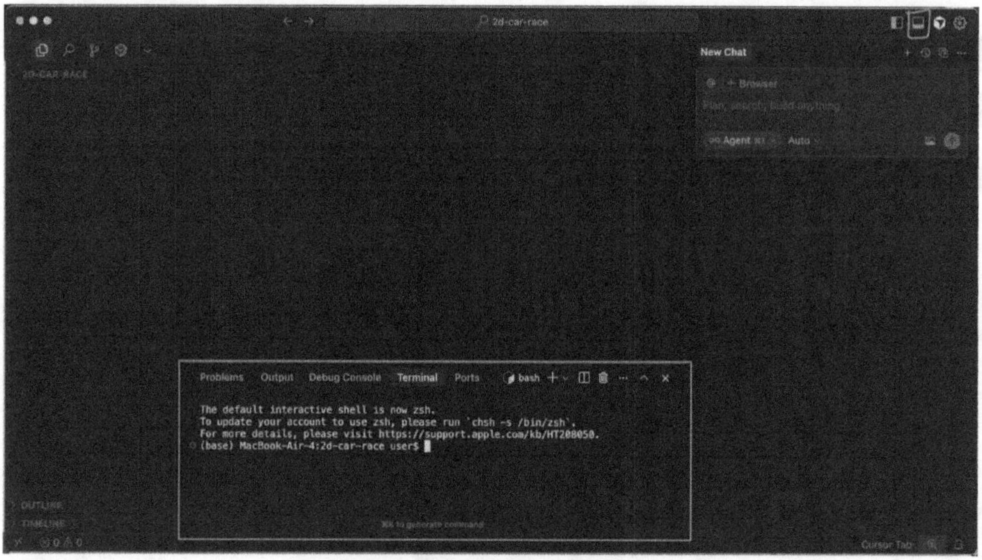

In the Chat panel, by default, the mode should be set to **Agent**:

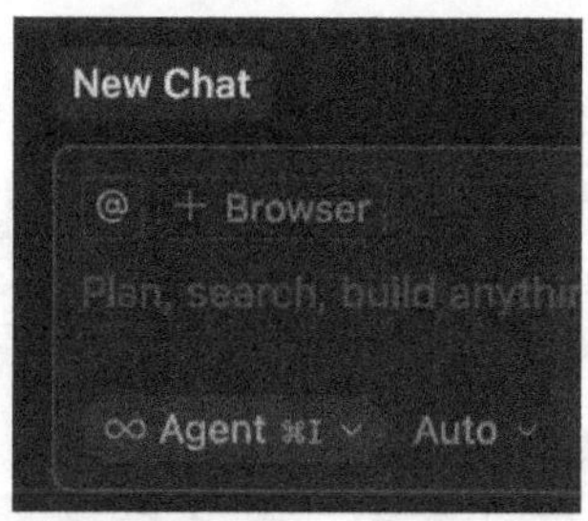

An AI agent is like a smart assistant. It can:

- Read your code
- Understand what you're trying to do
- Write or fix code automatically
- Create files
- Run commands

Let's see it in action. In the chat panel, I type the instruction:

```
Build a 2d car dodging game with three.js
```

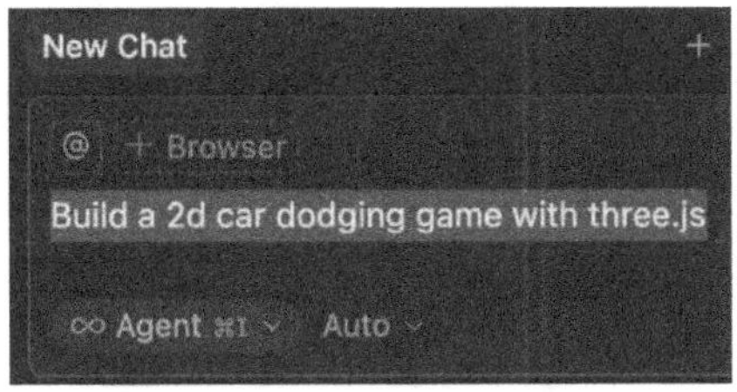

Press *Enter* and Cursor begins generating code step by step. Files start appearing as the agent works, such as:

- `main.js`
- `index.html`
- `style.css`
- and other source files needed for the game

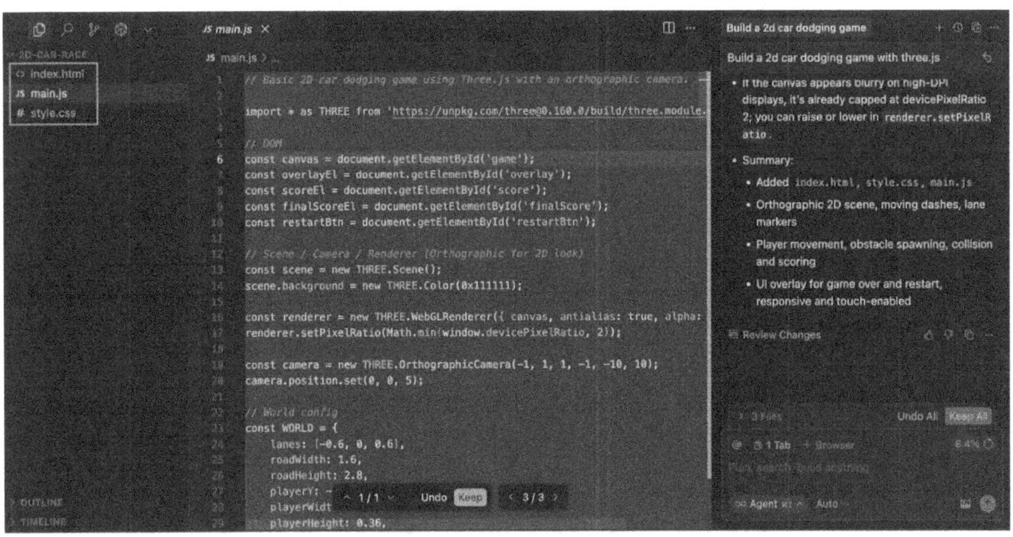

Reviewing and Accepting Changes

When the agent has created the files, you can check the Chat history to see what was added and why:

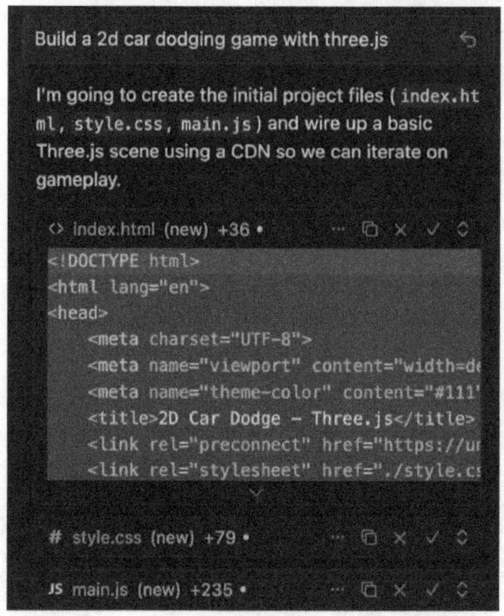

You can also ask follow-up questions, like `Why do we need main.js`:

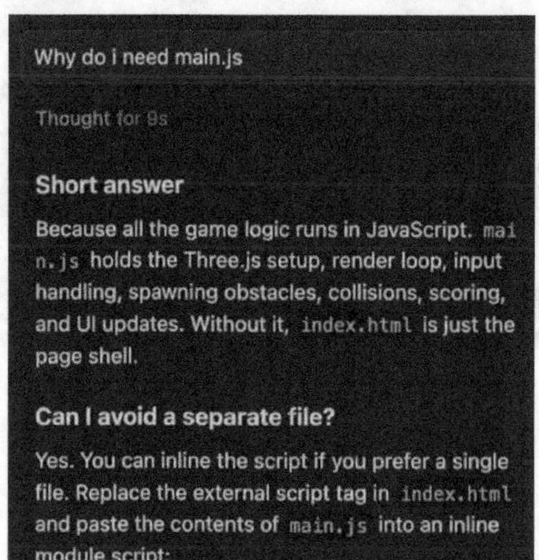

Asking the AI to explain files or code is a great way to learn.

If you're happy with the changes, click **Keep All**, and the files will be saved into your project:

When I try to open my `index.html` in a browser, I see the UI:

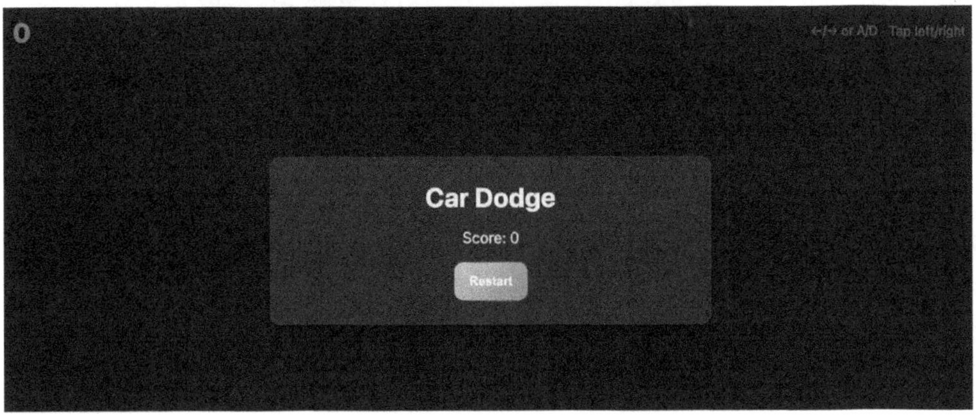

But the game fails to load (Your version might behave differently and might produce a working game).

I prompt it again `how can I run the game`:

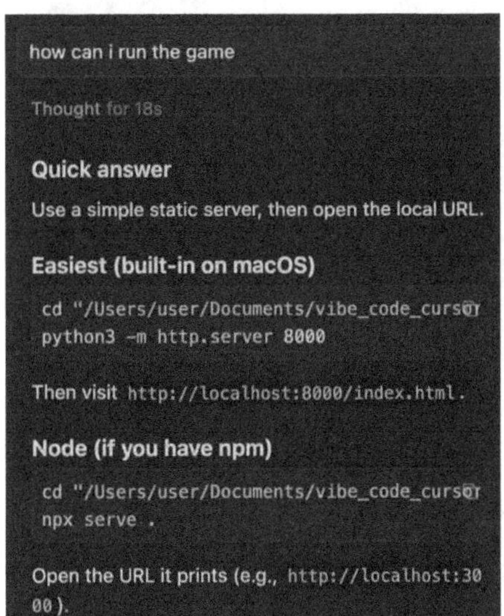

It tells us that we have to use a simple static server. So let's follow the easiest method, run the Python server (as per the instructions – or the AI might ask you to run a Node server). Visit the localhost URL i.e. `localhost:8000/` in a browser:

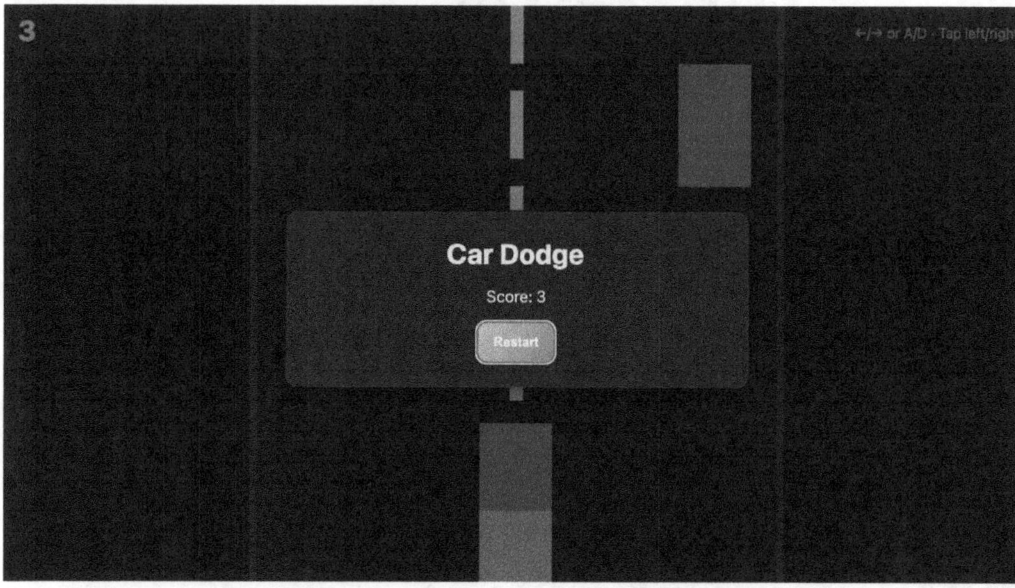

In my version, the game starts but is blocked by the score popup. We can simply ask the agent: `the score popup is blocking the game`. The agent recognizes the issue and updates the code:

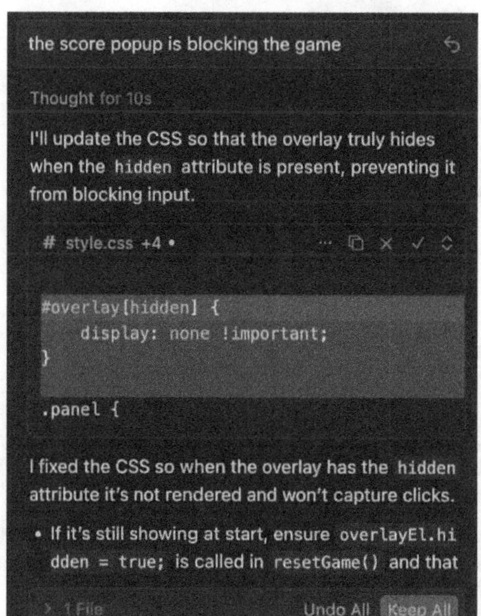

I **Keep All** the changes. And when I open the browser again (you might be prompted to restart the server)— the score popup doesn't block the game play:

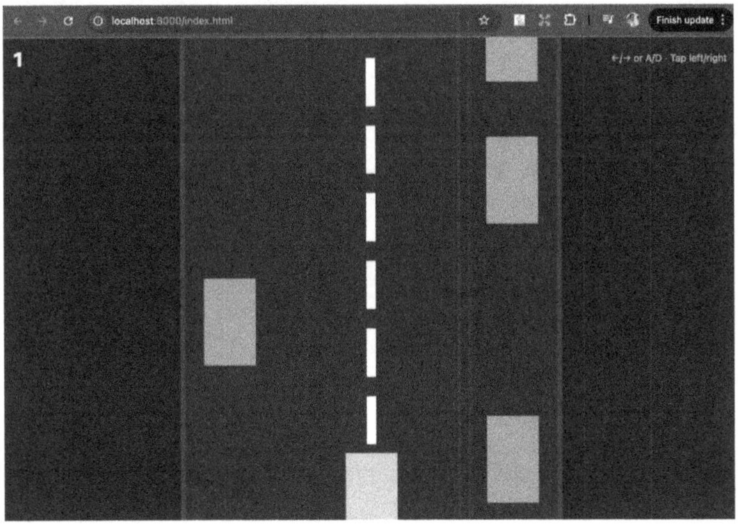

As you can see, the agent is quite independent. It actually generated a To-do list of features to figure out what needs to be done and makes changes automatically:

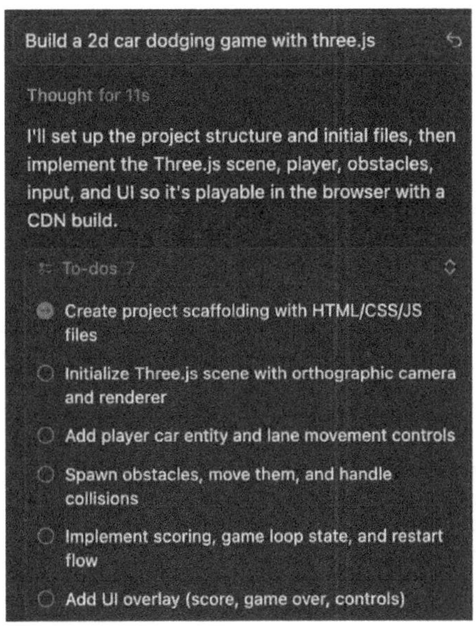

This example might seem simple but it shows you what coding with an AI agent is really about. You can continue experimenting, fixing bugs, and adding features simply by talking to the agent.

Understanding that LLMs are Non-Deterministic

Now, your version of the game generated will look different from mine even though you might use the exact same prompt. That's because the large language models that we connect to from Cursor are non-deterministic.

One reason results vary is something called **temperature**, a setting that controls how creative the model can be:

- A higher temperature makes responses more random and creative.
- A lower temperature makes them more focused and predictable — which is usually better for tasks like writing code.

Most tools don't expose the temperature setting, so don't worry if you can't find it. But it's still helpful to understand temperature exists.

Another reason for variation is that each large language model has its own "personality," shaped by its training data and design. Even if you send the same prompt to two different models with the same temperature setting, their responses can still differ.

Embracing Randomness

This small amount of randomness is actually useful. It can lead to fresh ideas, alternative solutions, and new ways of solving a problem.

So if you're not satisfied with a result, don't be discouraged. You can simply delete everything, try the same prompt again, and see if the new answer works better. It's like rolling the dice — and sometimes, that's exactly what sparks the best solution.

Choosing a Model in Cursor

Cursor allows you to use various models, and by default, this setting is set to **Auto**.

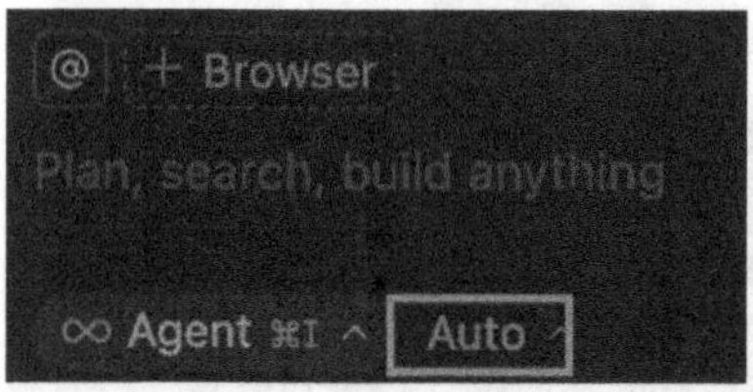

If you toggle **Auto** off, you'll see a list of available models:

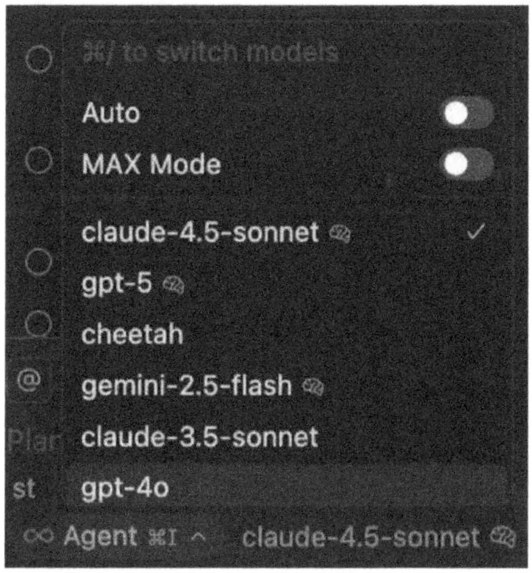

> **Note**
>
> This list will continue to change — some models may disappear while new ones appear over time.

Auto simply tells Cursor to automatically choose the best model for you. For most users who don't care about which model runs in the background, this option works perfectly fine.

However, there are differences between models, and if you know exactly what you're looking for, you might want to manually select the model that best suits your needs. For now, just keep **Auto** enabled.

We have built a simple app with a single prompt in this chapter. But for bigger and more complex projects, it makes a lot of sense to incorporate software development life cycle principles in our app building process. More on that in the next chapter.

4

Software Development - Traditional vs Vibe Coding workflow

Software development is not just about writing code. There are steps before and after the coding itself. If you want to build real, production-ready applications, you need to understand all the steps required to bring an idea to life and deploy to users. This entire process is known as the **software development lifecycle** (**SDLC**). It might sound boring at first, but it's important in the long run.

Some parts of the SDLC can be done entirely by AI, but in most cases, you'll get the best results when you stay in control and guide the AI — and not the AI guide you. Let's briefly go over the main stages of the lifecycle and understand why each one matters.

1. Planning

We start with a plan — understanding what we're trying to build. We move from an idea to figuring out who will use the software and what they need from it. We gather requirements, break the project down into smaller, more manageable tasks, and estimate costs, timelines and team availability.

Don't underestimate the effort involved in planning. It's the foundation for everything that follows.

2. Design

Planning naturally flows into design where we think about the architecture — how we want to structure the application. What technologies and frameworks will we use? What does the tech stack look like?

We also plan the **user interface (UI)**: how it should look and feel, and how users will navigate through it. On the backend, we decide where data will be stored and whether we'll need to rely on external APIs. A lot of thought goes into this stage before a single line of code is written.

3. Implementation (Coding)

Once the planning and design are in place, we move into implementation — writing the actual code. Here, we can rely heavily on AI to speed things up. But having humans review the code to ensure quality is still very important.

During this phase, documentation of the code is also essential. It allows us to track decisions, explain logic, and make future maintenance easier.

4. Testing

Next comes testing, which ensures that quality is maintained, bugs are caught early and everything works as expected. We will go into more detail like Unit testing and End-to-End testing later.

5. Deployment

Once testing is complete, we're ready to deploy the application — to launch it into the real world.

We usually go through multiple environments first, such as staging or testing environments, before deploying to production.

We also use version control to track all changes and maintain a clear history of the project.

6. Maintenance & Iteration

After deployment, the lifecycle doesn't stop. We continue to iterate as quickly as possible:

- Fixing bugs as they arise
- Adding new features
- Updating dependencies
- Monitoring performance metrics

We also track how users interact with the application, ensuring everything runs smoothly and identifying opportunities for improvement.

Summary

This, in a nutshell, is the software development lifecycle. Throughout this book, we'll implement many parts of it in practice. Understanding these concepts now will make everything we do later clearer and easier.

Don't worry if some of this sounds new or overwhelming. We'll dive deeper into selected stages as we progress through the book.

Choosing a Tech Stack

Before we dive deeper into vibe coding, let's understand what is a tech stack. A tech stack is a combination of technologies used to build a software product. It typically includes:

- **The front end** – what the user sees and interacts with
- **The back end** – where the processing and logic happen
- **A database** – where data is stored
- **Plus various tools and services** – for deployment, hosting, and infrastructure

If you already have a favorite tech stack where you can create an app quickly, that's your answer! Don't bother with the latest shiny tech stack, just stick to the one you are most confident in and can chunk out your best code in the shortest amount of time!

Having said that, here are two great tech stack choices for beginners.

1. JavaScript (Full Stack)

JavaScript is a great choice because it can be used for both the front end and back end:

- **Front end**: Combined with HTML and CSS for building user interfaces. Includes popular frameworks like React and Vue.
- **Back end**: With Node.js to handle server-side logic.

The advantage of JavaScript is that you can build a complete app using just one language. It's efficient, has a massive community, tons of free resources, and is beginner-friendly — especially for web applications.

2. Python (Backend-Focused)

Another excellent option is Python, which is often used for backend development.

Python is easy to read, write, and learn. It's widely used not only in web development but also in AI, data science, and automation. While it's less common for front-end work, it's flexible, has a clean syntax, and is extremely popular.

5

Vibe Coding Fundamentals with Cursor

In this chapter, we'll build and deploy a Math Practice application using Cursor:

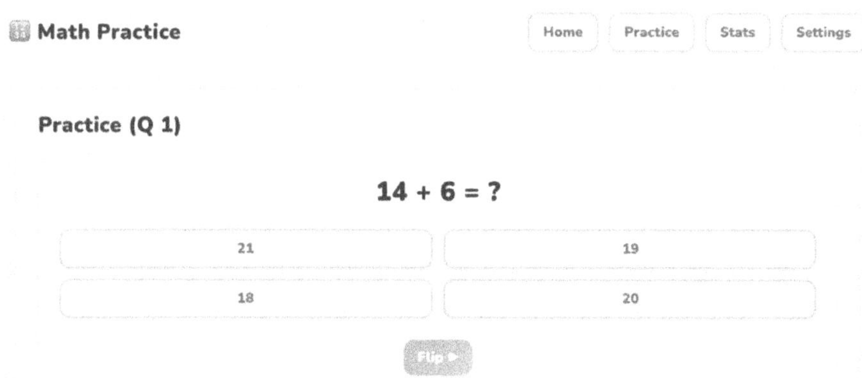

To follow along, you'll need to be on the free Cursor Pro trial (which lasts two weeks) or have an active Pro plan.

This chapter is designed to help you build a strong foundation for working with AI coding tools. Even though we're using Cursor, the concepts you'll learn, like working step by step, writing clear specifications, and testing your code — can be applied to other tools as well. So if Cursor isn't the right fit for you or feels too expensive, don't worry, what you'll learn here will still be valuable.

In the next few chapters:

- We'll start by creating a software specification to guide our project as we build the Math Practice app.
- After that, we'll make a features to-do list to help us develop the application iteratively, improving it step by step.
- To make sure we don't lose any work, we'll use Git for version control.
- And since we don't want to run manual tests every time we make a small change, we'll write and run simple automated tests to ensure everything is working correctly.
- We'll also learn how to write rules for the AI to follow.

Building this app will be fun, but it can also be challenging at times. So if you ever get stuck or have questions, email me at `support@i-ducate.com`.

Before we begin, make sure you have Cursor, Node, and Git installed and ready.

Writing a Software Specification

How do we get started building a new app? First, let's create a new folder e.g. `math-practice` and open it in Cursor.

In Cursor, we could jump straight and say, `Build a Math Practice app.` Cursor will probably produce something decent, but it's unlikely to match our expectations without a long back-and-forth to nail down details.

A better approach is to invest time up front in a proper specifications document. This is a key step in building good software, where we specify exactly how the app should look and behave.

If you're unsure what to build or which technologies to use, use a general-purpose LLM (e.g. ChatGPT, Gemini or Claude) to ask questions first. Treat it like a consultation: explore options, outline requirements, and shape what the specification should include. Avoid trying to do everything in one "zero-shot" prompt; that rarely works well.

For the Math Practice application, I can ask ChatGPT to draft a specification in Markdown with a prompt something like:

```
Help me come up with a software specification in markdown.
I want to build a Math Practice app for children 7-12 years old with
addition, subtraction, division and multiplication operations.
I want to use React.
The practice questions should come in cards which have multiple choice.
```

```
There should be a function to flip the cards to reveal the answer.
After flipping, I should have two buttons asking if I got it right or
wrong.
Remember which questions I got wrong.
There should be a statistics page to track how many questions attempted,
and how many correct vs incorrect answers.

Ask follow-up questions if something is unclear before you start
generating the specification.
```

I added the last line in that prompt: `Ask follow-up questions if something is unclear before you start generating the specification.` to make generating the specification more efficient, as clarifications produce a better specification:

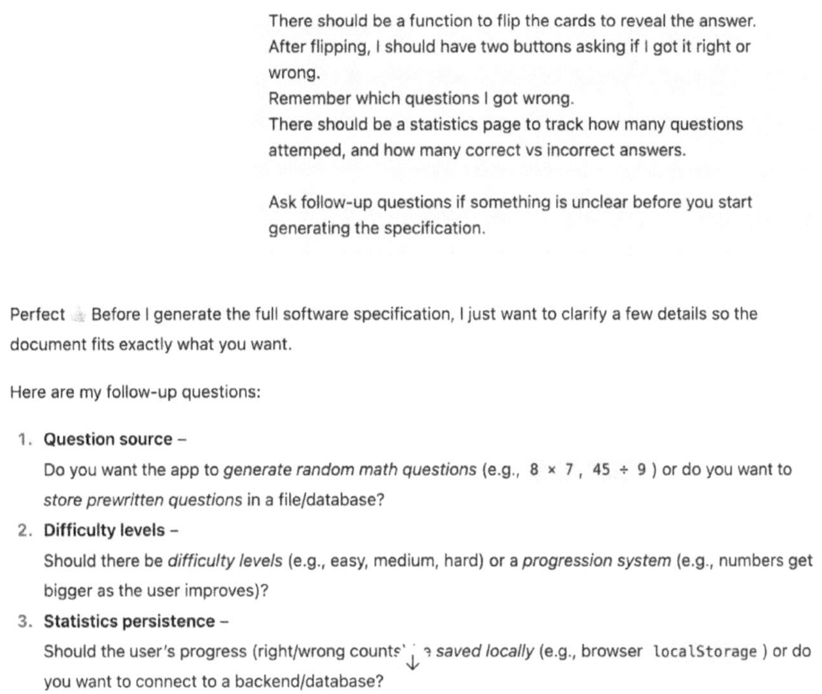

There should be a function to flip the cards to reveal the answer.
After flipping, I should have two buttons asking if I got it right or wrong.
Remember which questions I got wrong.
There should be a statistics page to track how many questions attemped, and how many correct vs incorrect answers.

Ask follow-up questions if something is unclear before you start generating the specification.

Perfect 👍 Before I generate the full software specification, I just want to clarify a few details so the document fits exactly what you want.

Here are my follow-up questions:

1. **Question source** –
   Do you want the app to *generate random math questions* (e.g., `8 × 7`, `45 ÷ 9`) or do you want to *store prewritten questions* in a file/database?
2. **Difficulty levels** –
   Should there be *difficulty levels* (e.g., easy, medium, hard) or a *progression system* (e.g., numbers get bigger as the user improves)?
3. **Statistics persistence** –
   Should the user's progress (right/wrong counts) be *saved locally* (e.g., browser `localStorage`) or do you want to connect to a backend/database?

I answer the follow-up questions:

5. **Frameworks/Libraries** –
   Should I assume you'll use *plain React with hooks*, or include libraries like *React* or *Framer Motion* (for card flipping animations)?
6. **Scoring system** –
   Do you want to track *points* (e.g., +1 for correct) or just show *percent correct*?
7. **User profiles** –
   Should this app support multiple children (profiles), or just one user?

Once you answer these, I'll generate a detailed **Markdown software specification** (components, states, data flow, logic, UI layout, etc.) for you.

1. Random math questions
2. difficulty levels
3. Saved locally
4. Multiple pages
5. include libraries
6. Percentage
7. just one user

And I'll receive a software specification for the app (sample below):

Math Practice App — Software Specification

Overview

A React app for children (ages 7–12) to practice basic arithmetic (addition, subtract division).

Core features:

- Randomly generated questions across four operations.
- Difficulty levels (Easy / Medium / Hard).
- Questions shown as cards with multiple-choice answers.
- A **flip** action to reveal the correct answer (animated).
- After flipping, the user presses **"I got it right"** or **"I got it wrong"** (self-report).
- Wrong answers are remembered for review.
- Statistics page showing attempts and percentage correct.
- Progress saved locally (browser `localStorage`).
- Multi-page app (Home, Practice, Stats, Settings).
- Built with React + recommended libraries.

Table of contents

1. Goals & non-goals
2. Tech stack & libraries
3. UX / User flows
4. Data models & local persistence
5. Question generation (algorithms)
6. Component structure & responsibilities
7. Routing & pages

1. Goals & non-goals

Goals

- Fast, kid-friendly UI.
- Reliable random question generation with difficulty.
- Clear feedback and simple self-reporting flow.
- Simple stats and persistent local storage.

Non-goals (initial release)

- Authentication or multi-user profiles (single user only).
- Server/backend persistence.
- Adaptive learning algorithms (beyond difficulty selection).

2. Tech stack & libraries

- React (recommended: with TypeScript)
- React Router (multi-page navigation)
- Tailwind CSS (rapid styling)
- Framer Motion (card flip animation)
- Zustand or React Context + useReducer (simple state management) — simplicity
- Jest + React Testing Library (unit & integration tests)
- Optional: Prettier + ESLint

Local persistence: `localStorage`

I ask ChatGPT to give me the entire specification in markdown:

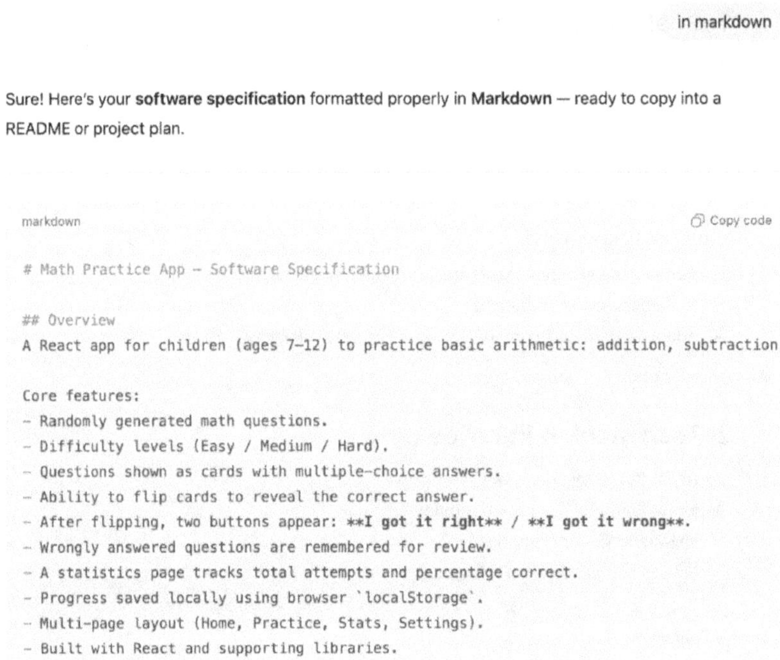

Next, I'll copy the entire specification markdown into our project and save it as a file `specifications.md`:

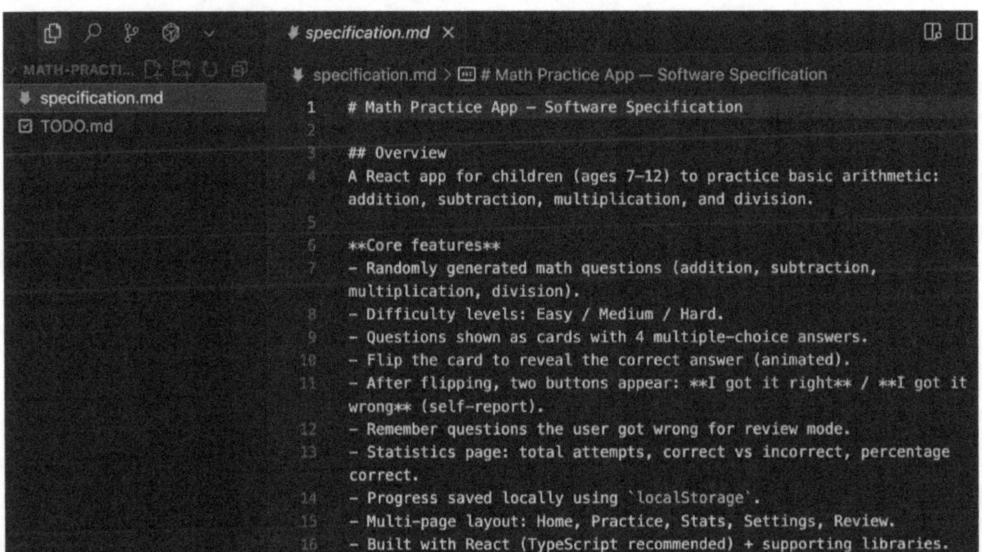

Remember that LLMs are non-deterministic. Even with the same prompt and model, outputs can differ slightly. That's why it's essential not to rely blindly on the LLM. Read every line of the specification and make edits where needed before we start implementing.

Creating a TODO List

Next, we will create a to-do list of features to build for the app (not a to-do list application).

Having a software specification, we could theoretically jump into Cursor and say, `Build this`. And for smaller projects, Cursor would probably do a pretty decent job. However, experience shows that it's far better to work in small increments, tackling one feature at a time.

So we'll use our specification and ask an LLM like ChatGPT to generate a step-by-step to-do list. We prompt it like:

```
take this specification an create a todo list to implement one feature at
a time. Order the features from easy to hard. Give it in markdown format.
```

take this specification an create a todo list to implement one feature at a time. Order the features from easy to hard. Give it in markdown format.

Sure! Below is a **Markdown-formatted To-Do list** that breaks down the Math Practice App specification into small, incremental tasks — ordered from **easiest** to **hardest** features.
This order ensures that you can start with the basics (UI and structure) and progressively move toward the more complex features (persistence, statistics, animations).

The result will be a to-do list in Markdown format which we copy into a `TODO.md` file in our project:

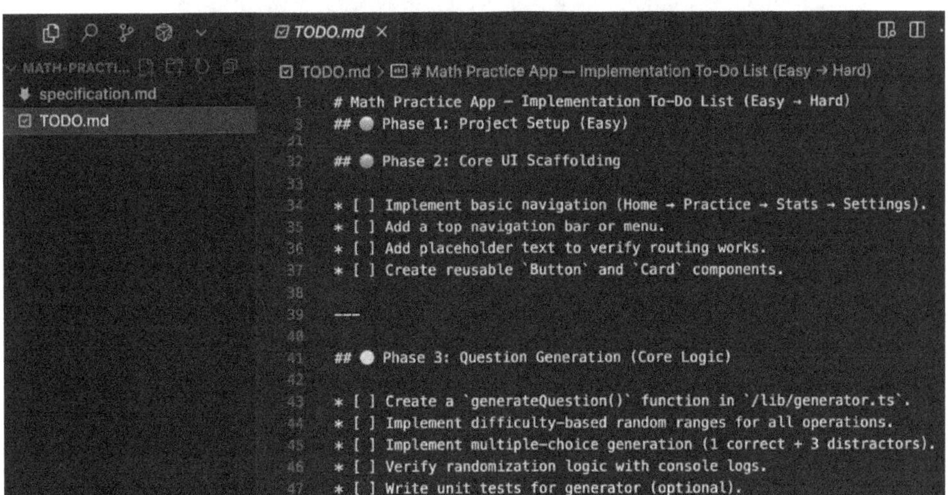

The to-do list is structured into multiple phases, with each phase containing individual tasks. Each task is marked as "not done" by default.

Just keep in mind: because LLMs are non-deterministic, even if you use the exact same specification and to-do list, your application might look slightly different and encounter different challenges from what I'll show in the next section.

Building the First Feature

In this section, we're going to build the first feature for our Math Practice app. If you check the to-do file, you'll see that what we're building here corresponds to the **first phase** of the project:

````
# Math Practice App – Implementation To-Do List (Easy → Hard)

## ● Phase 1: Project Setup (Easy)

- [ ] Initialize React project using Vite or Create React App.
  ```bash
  npm create vite@latest math-practice-app --template react-ts
```

* [ ] Install dependencies:

  ```bash
  npm install react-router-dom tailwindcss framer-motion zustand
  npm install --save-dev @types/react-router-dom
  ```
* [ ] Configure Tailwind CSS.
* [ ] Set up basic folder structure:

  ```
  src/
  ├─ routes/
  ├─ components/
  ├─ store/
  ├─ lib/
  └─ styles/
  ```
* [ ] Create placeholder pages: `HomePage`, `PracticePage`, `StatsPage`,
`SettingsPage`.
* [ ] Set up routing with **React Router**.
````

In essence, we'll initialize the project, set up the folder structure, and create some files. By the end, we'll have a simple home page with placeholder pages: **HomePage**, **PracticePage**, **StatsPage** and a **SettingsPage**.

The specification may seem like a lot of work for something so basic, but taking things step by step makes the whole process smoother and more manageable especially for larger projects.

Starting the Project

In Cursor, we then prompt:

```
Use the software specifications (specification.md) and the todo list
(TODO.md) to complete phase 1. Mark items as done in the TODO list.:
```

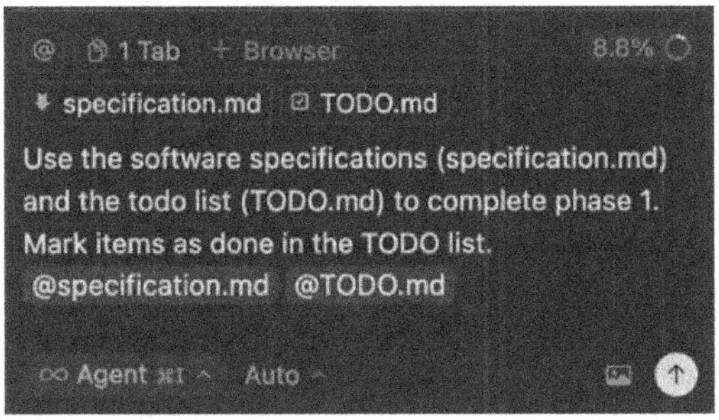

It's also helpful to add the file references in Cursor i.e. `TODO.md` and `specification.md` so it knows which files to reference. Cursor will take a while to initialize the React app, install dependencies:

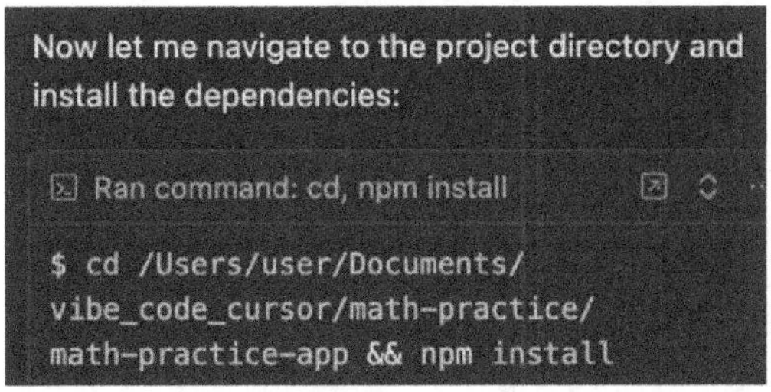

Configure Tailwind CSS:

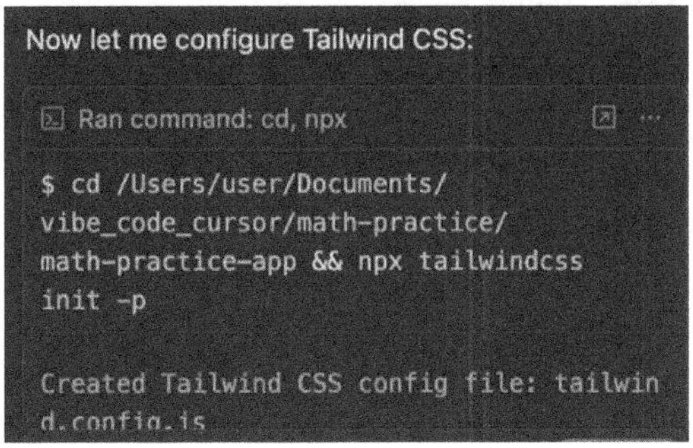

Create folder structure, placeholder pages and other files:

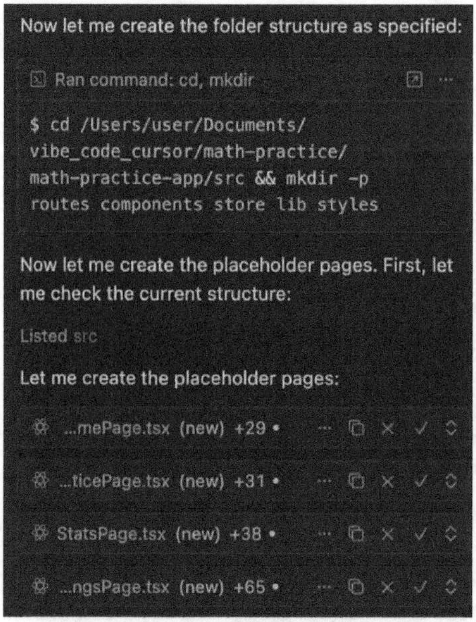

You might encounter other issues e.g. missing dependencies, but just follow the steps which Cursor guides you. Once the project is initialized, Cursor will start a local web server:

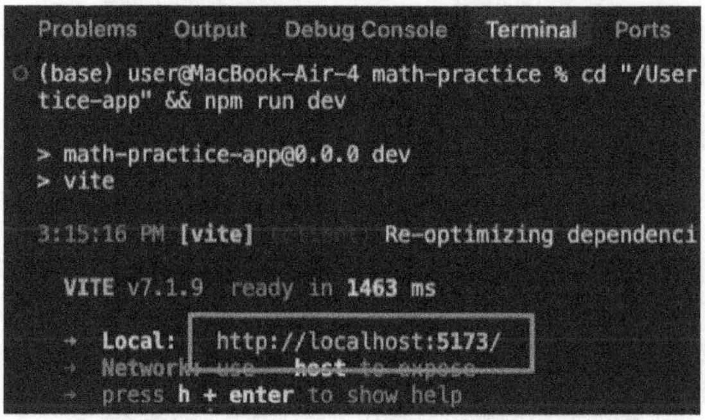

When you see an address with `localhost`, that means the app is only available on your computer—it can't be shared with others. Open the URL in your browser.

At this stage, the app will look basic:

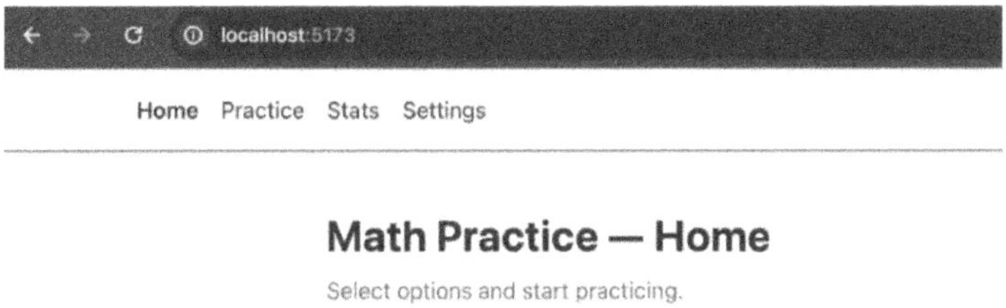

If you are unhappy with your UI, you can prompt Cursor to fix them. For example, I notice my UI looks plain, so I asked for a fix:

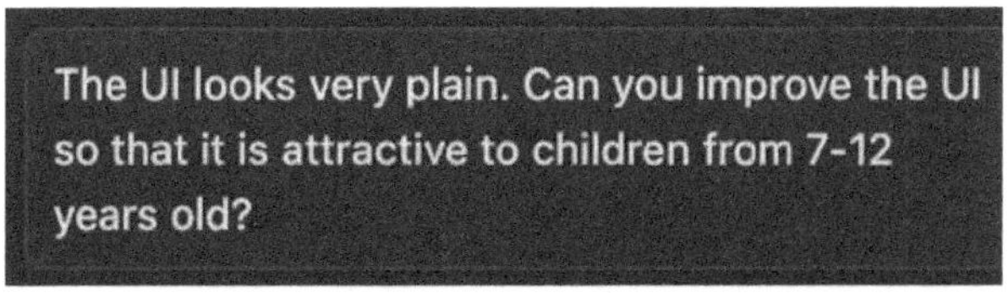

The UI looks very plain. Can you improve the UI so that it is attractive to children from 7-12 years old?

Cursor responds:

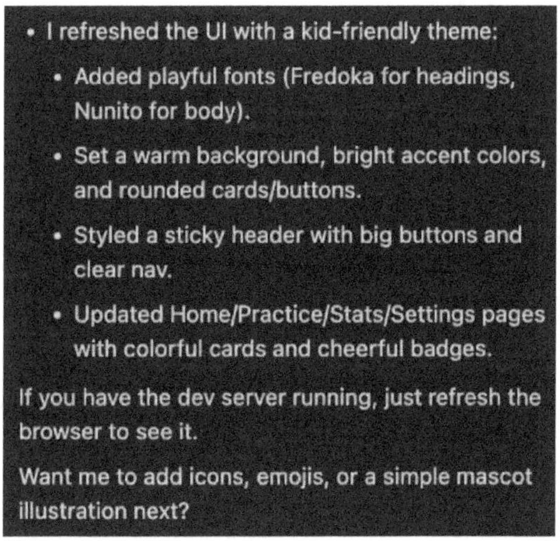

- I refreshed the UI with a kid-friendly theme:
  - Added playful fonts (Fredoka for headings, Nunito for body).
  - Set a warm background, bright accent colors, and rounded cards/buttons.
  - Styled a sticky header with big buttons and clear nav.
  - Updated Home/Practice/Stats/Settings pages with colorful cards and cheerful badges.

If you have the dev server running, just refresh the browser to see it.

Want me to add icons, emojis, or a simple mascot illustration next?

And gives me an improved UI!

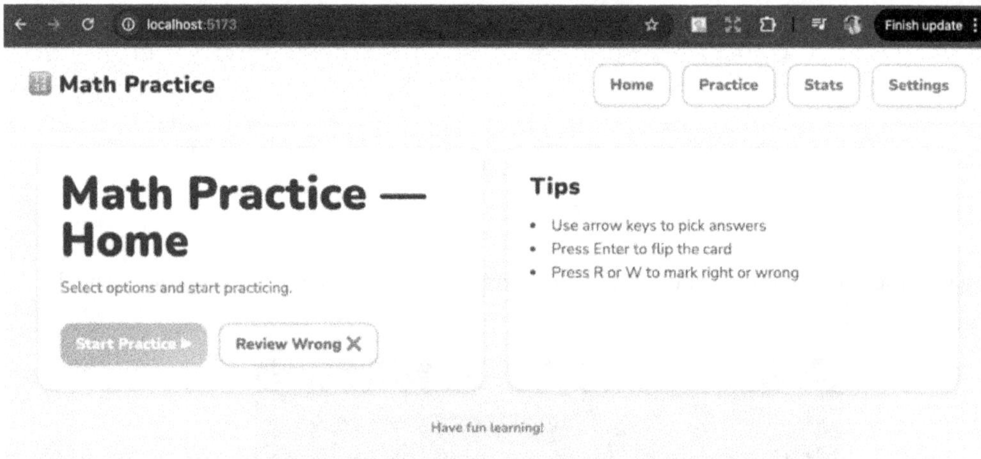

As you can see, it might take a few iterations for the UI to improve. This kind of back-and-forth is normal—if you spot bugs or missing features, go back and refine your prompt.

Over time, you may also want to update the specification and to-do list to include new details you realize are important (like styling requirements). This will help keep your project consistent if you ever rebuild from scratch.

We now have a home page with Practice, Stats, and Settings navigation items.

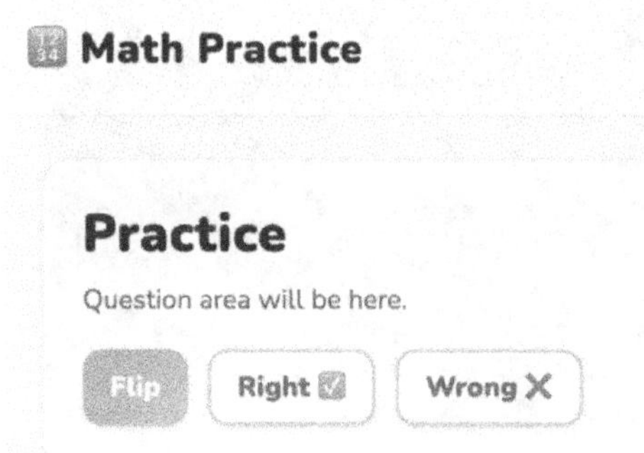

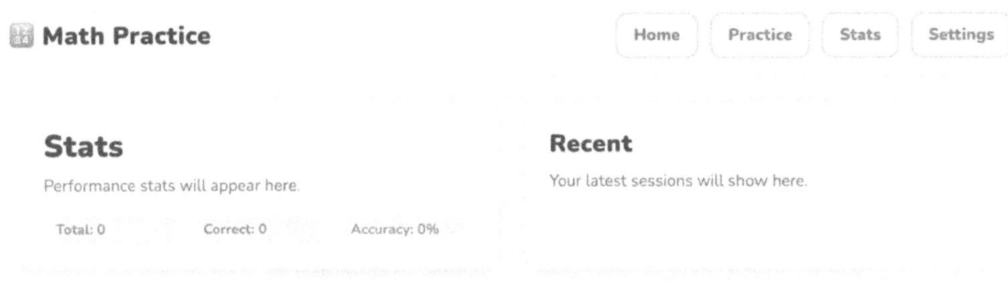

We can also see phase 1 items marked as completed in the to-do list:

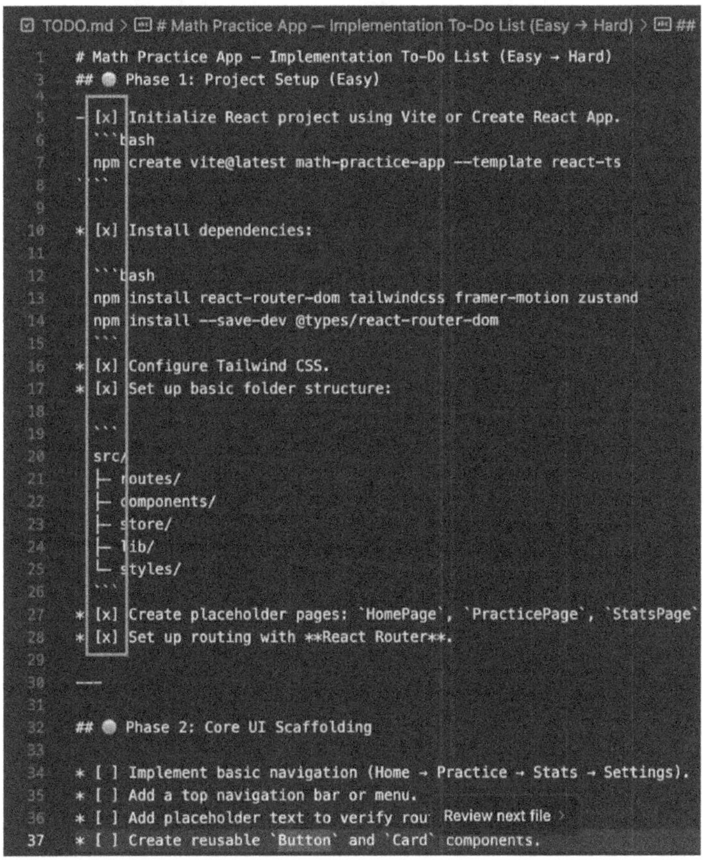

Once you're happy with the changes, click **Keep All** in Cursor to confirm and save everything into the project:

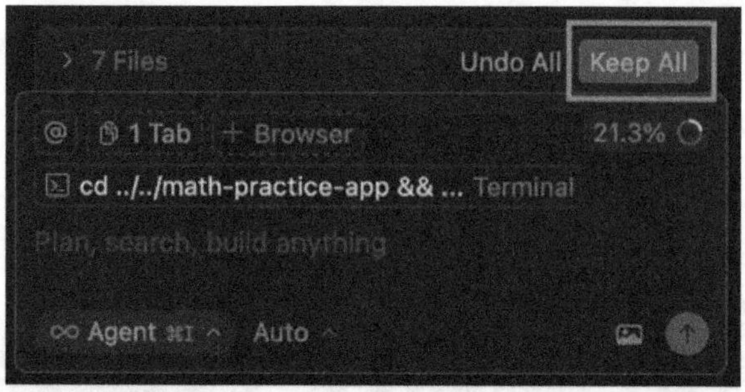

This marks the completion of the first phase of our Math Practice app!

6

Configuring Version Control with Git

When we're working on code, it's important to keep track of the changes we make, especially when coding with an AI agent. This is where Git and version control come in.

The AI might generate code that doesn't work or could even break the application entirely. Without version control, it can be difficult to revert to a previous version. With Git, we can easily roll back to a working state without losing anything.

So, how does it work? Every time we make progress and reach a state that works — one that we're happy with — we can commit those changes. A commit acts as a snapshot, saving how the code looked at that point in time.

It's relatively straightforward. The first thing we need to do is initialize the project with Git. To do this, simply instruct the agent to add Git to the project by prompting: `Add Git to the project`:

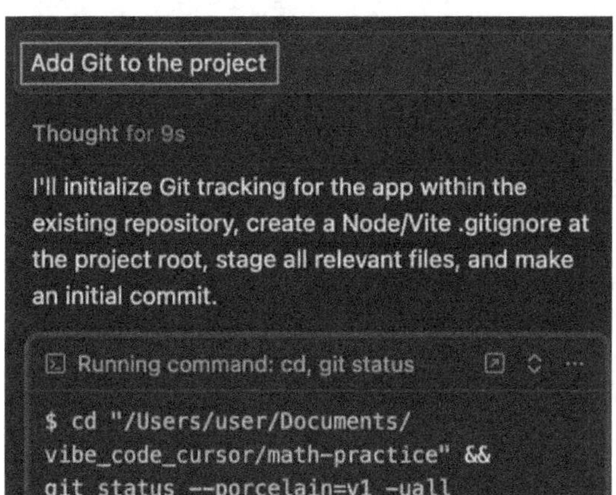

The agent will initialize Git tracking for the app, and also creates a `.gitignore` file, which is important because there are certain files we don't want to track with Git. For example, the `node_modules` folder contains dependencies and should be excluded. There may be other files you don't want to include like environment files containing API keys.

If we open the `.gitignore` file, we can review what's been added:

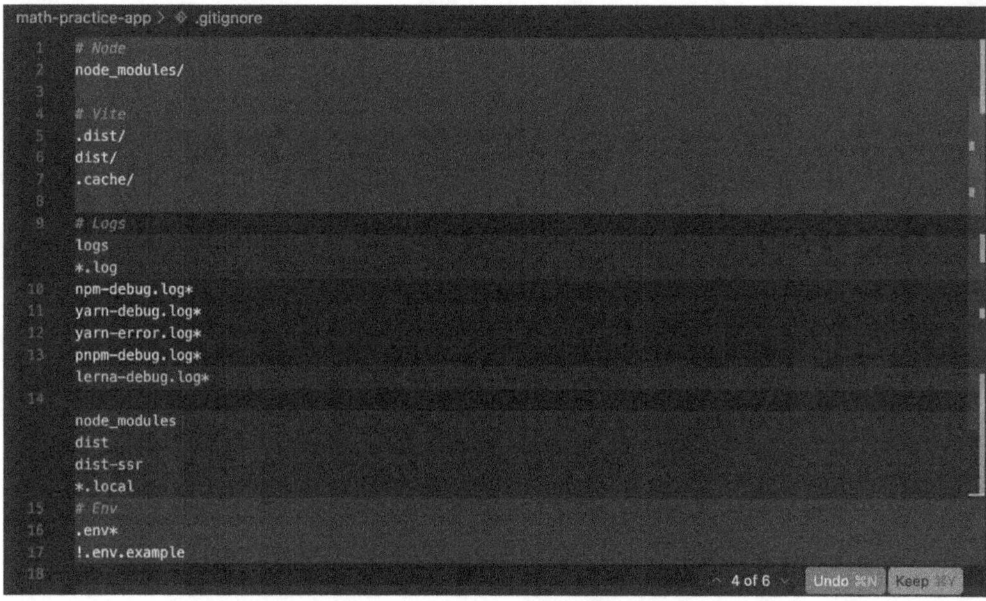

Once we're satisfied, we can click **Keep**.

Next, you should see a prompt to run the `git init` command:

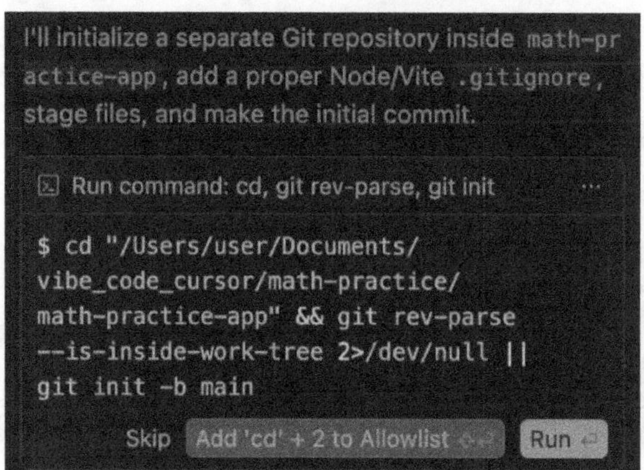

`git init` initializes a Git repository.

The next step is staging the files with:

```
git add .
```

Staging simply means adding them to a "ready-to-commit" area. Then we create the initial commit. Cursor might stage and commit in a single command:

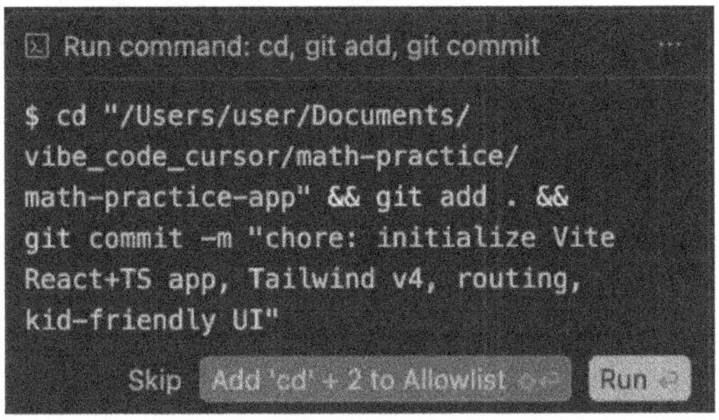

This commit will include a message — something the agent will generate automatically for us — describing what has changed. For example, it will mention `initialize Vite React+TS app, Tailwind v4, routing, kid-friendly UI` in our case.

Rolling Back to a Working Version

After committing, suppose we introduce a bug that breaks the application. We will see how to revert change — so that if something goes wrong, we know how to roll back to a previously working version. I'm going to ask the agent to `intentionally introduce a bug that breaks the app`.

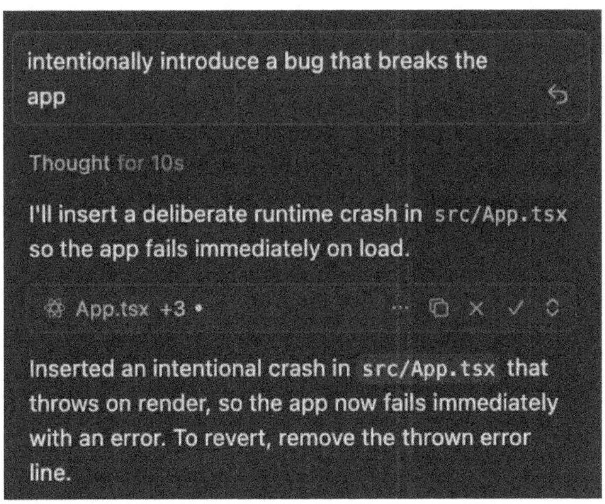

The agent has now introduced a bug:

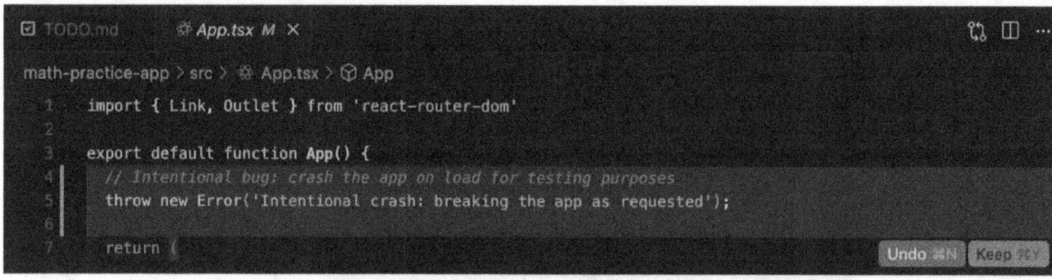

Let's test it out. When I navigate back to the app in the browser, as expected, the homepage displays an error:

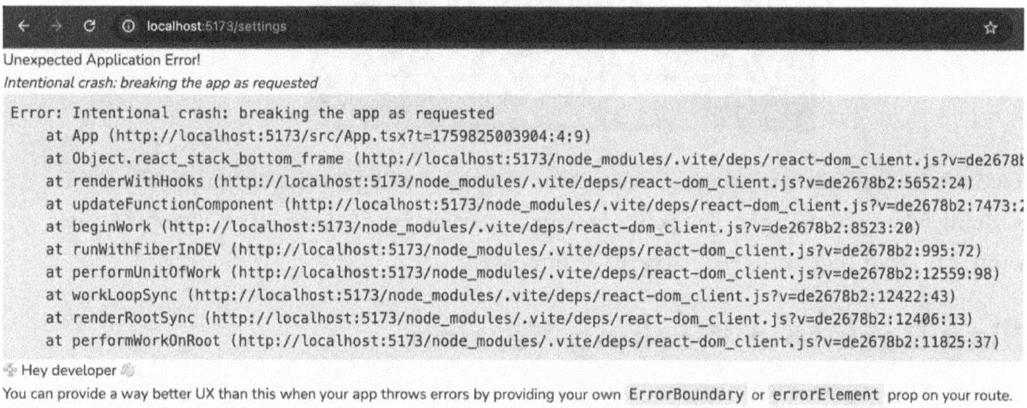

How can we fix this and roll back to a working version?

Ways to Revert Changes

There are ways we can revert the application back to a stable state:

1. Reject Changes in Cursor

One option is to 'undo' the change directly within Cursor:

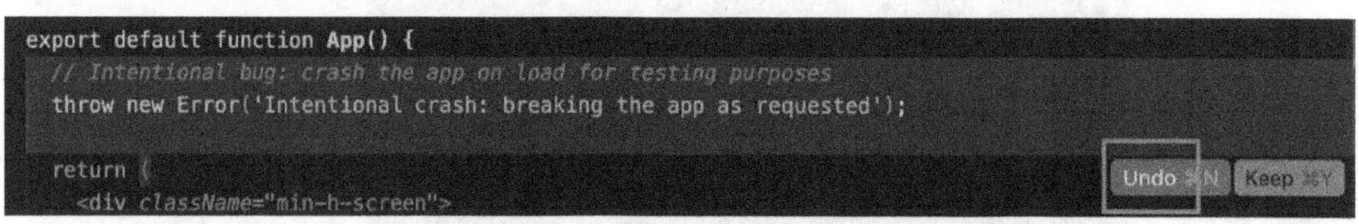

This will revert the file to the previous version. Now, this might be easy now since the change is only in a single file. But what if the changes are across multiple files and the AI can't seem to rectify the bug? That leads us to the second option.

2. Ask the Agent to Discard Changes

The second option is to ask the agent to discard any Git changes:

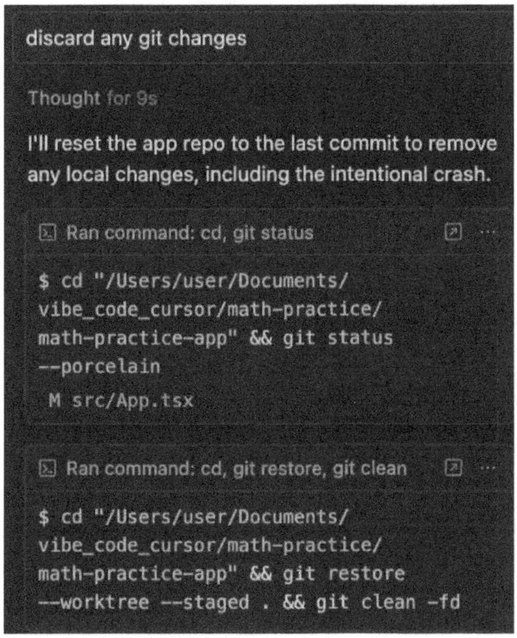

This will restore the project to the last commit, remove any unwanted modifications, and return the application to a functional state:

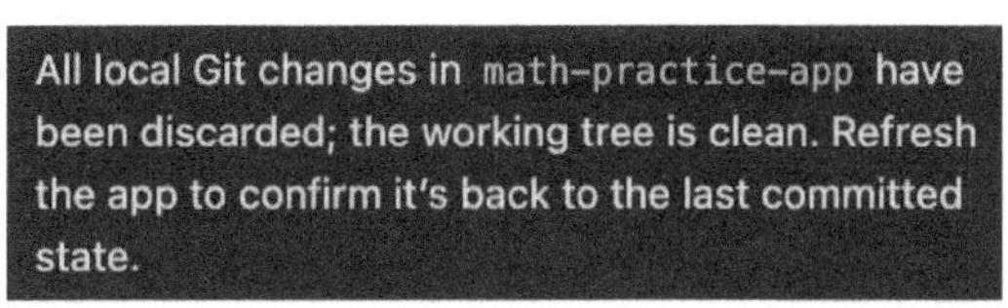

After discarding the changes, you'll see the application works correctly again.

Additionally, Git keeps a history of all commits and changes, so we can revert to any previous version if necessary. The best part is we can do this quite easily by simply talking directly to the agent. For example, we can ask it to show us the list of commits:

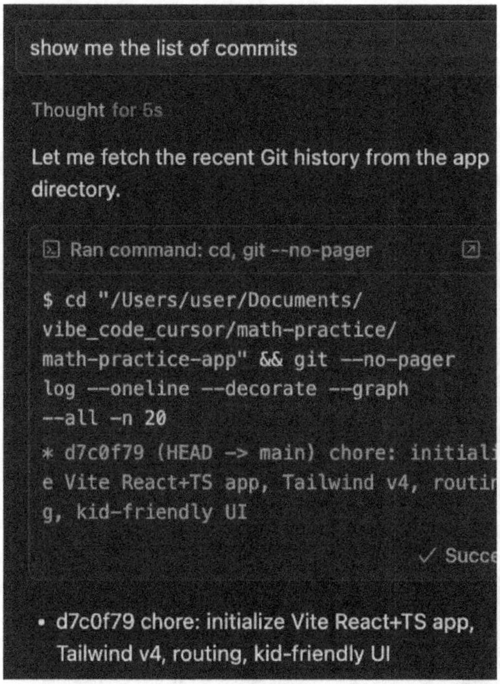

And from there, we can use the commit ID and tell it to restore back to that particular commit. We will revisit Git later on. Let's continue building our features in the next chapter.

7

Iterating with New Features

We have completed phase one of our project, and there's still quite a lot of work to be done. In this chapter, we're going to go ahead and create more features. If I look at Phase 2 features:

```
## ● Phase 2: Core UI Scaffolding

* [ ] Implement basic navigation (Home → Practice → Stats → Settings).
* [ ] Add a top navigation bar or menu.
* [ ] Add placeholder text to verify routing works.
* [ ] Create reusable `Button` and `Card` components.
```

I think most have been implemented by Cursor. I can prompt it to verify and check off the list:

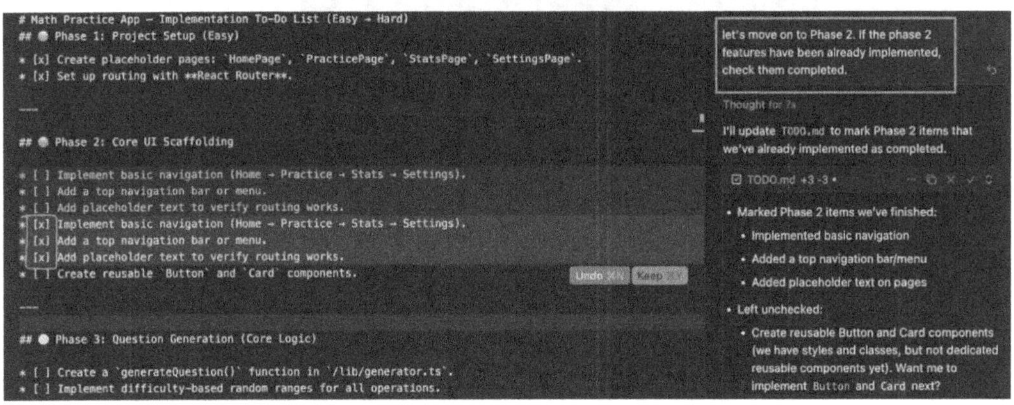

Let's implement the unfinished phase two item by instructing the agent:

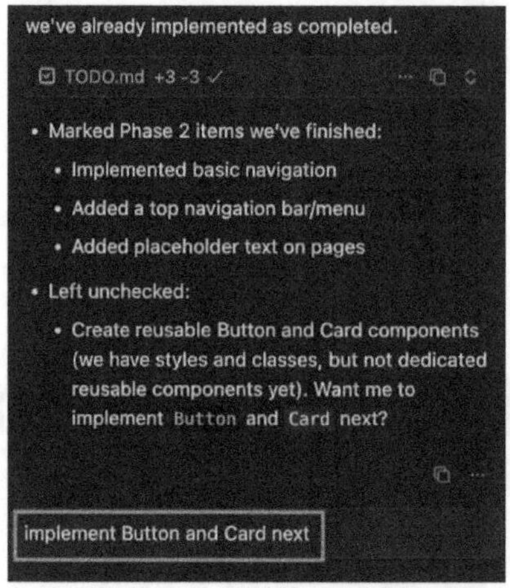

The agent reports it has implemented Button and Card as reusable components and proceeds to refactor pages to use them:

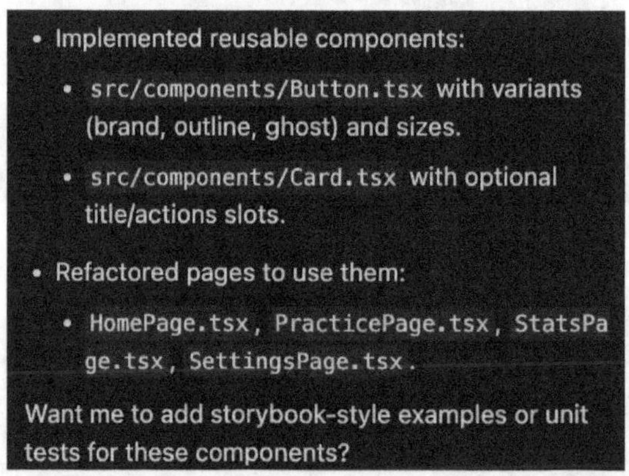

We should review the generated code carefully to verify what the AI is telling us is true. We can also jump directly into the application to test it.

If all's okay, let's prompt Cursor to move on to Phase 3: `Use the software specifications and the TODO list to work on Phase 3 of the project. Mark in the TODO list items that are done.`:

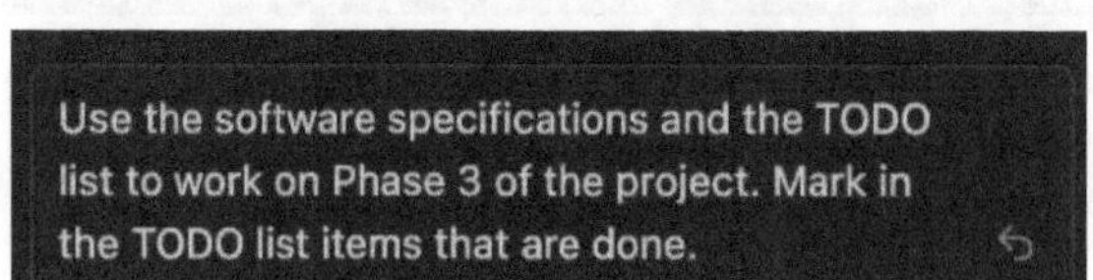

Cursor goes ahead and implements the features in phase 3:

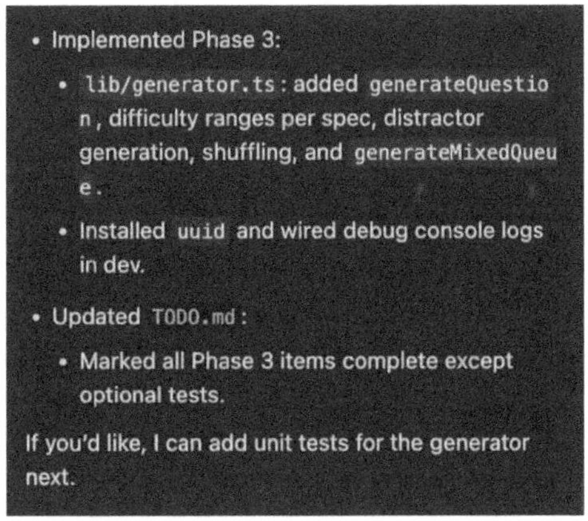

We will revisit unit tests later. For now, if phase 3 items have been implemented, let's go on to phase 4 items so that we can start interacting with our app in its UI. I answer yes to start phase 4:

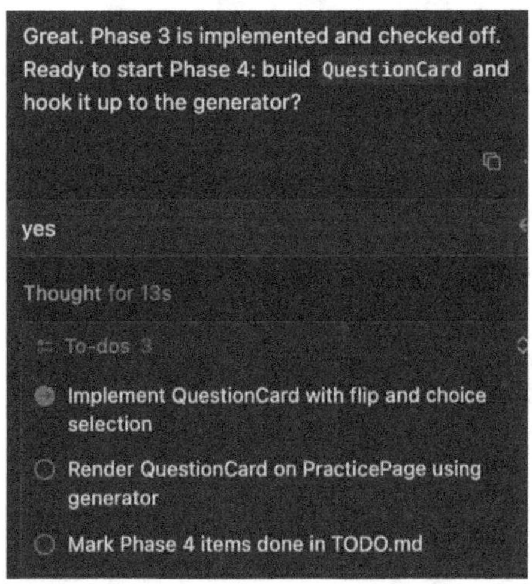

After a while, Cursor is done with phase 4 items:

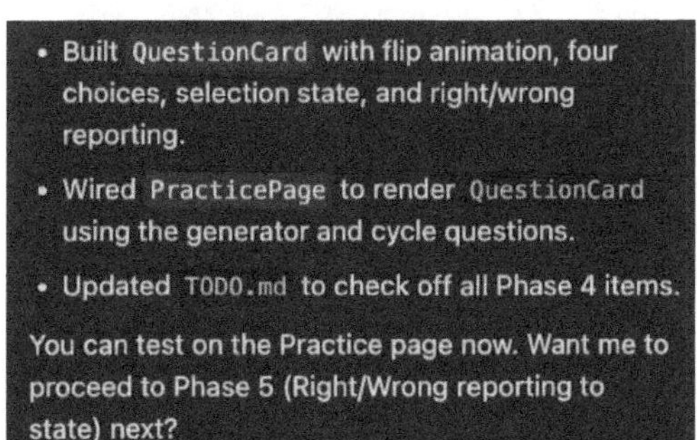

I can then go and try navigating to the Practice page:

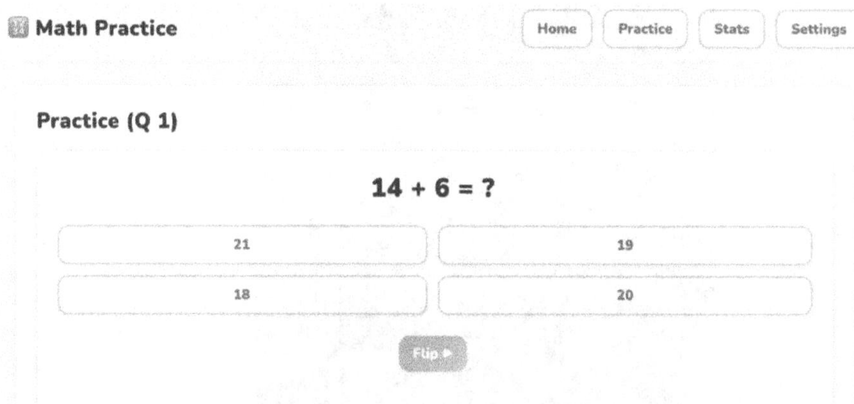

I faced an issue where the app hangs on the Practice page. So I just tell Cursor the problem:

After some back and forth, Cursor finally resolves the hanging issue:

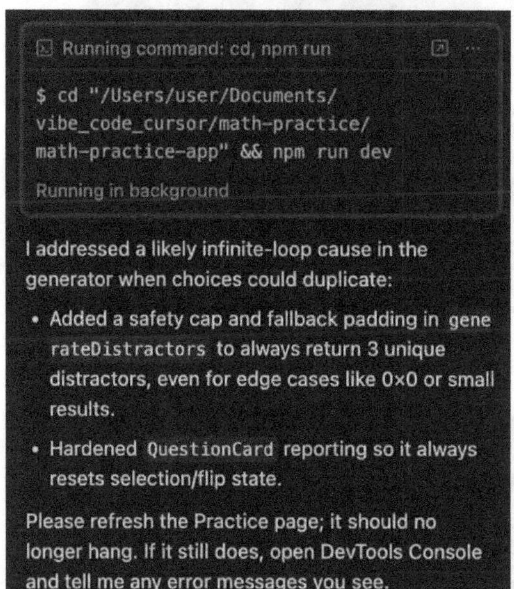

Back in the Practice page, I can now choose an answer:

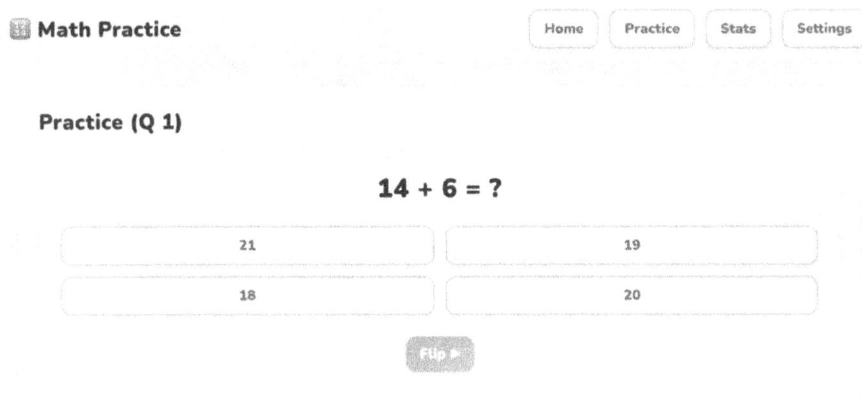

Select **Flip** and I can indicate if I got right or wrong, although this should be automated by the app. Let's fix this later.

We can go on to the next question:

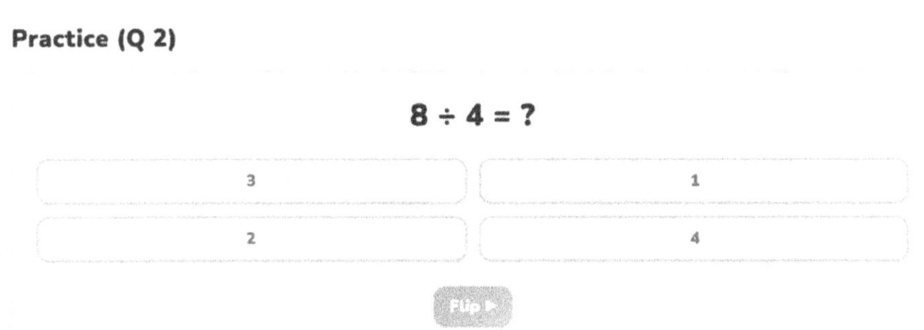

The app isn't complete, but things are starting to function well. Looking back at our to-do list, we'll notice phase 4 features being marked as complete.

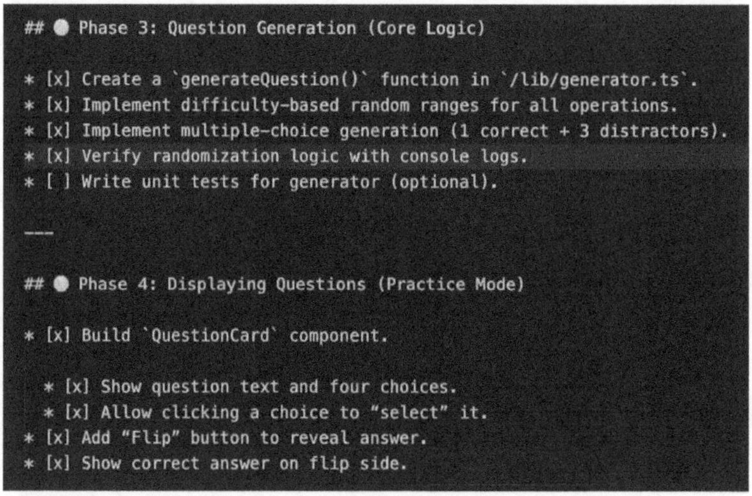

We will re-visit writing automated tests in the next chapter.

So far, we're satisfied with the results, so the next step is to commit the changes. Prompt: `commit the changes`:

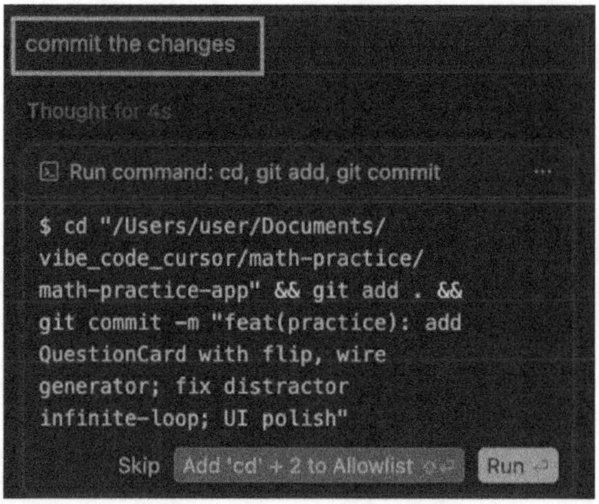

The agent will generate a commit message summarizing the changes (e.g. practice, card flip), stage the files, and handle the Git commit for us.

We can also choose to run Git commands directly if we prefer. With that, this part of the application is now complete.

8

Adding Automated Tests

As you can probably tell, manually testing the entire application after every change is time-consuming and annoying.

We want to make sure that all the features we've built so far continue to work even as we add new ones. But we also don't want to test everything from scratch each time. To automate this process, we should write some tests.

Tests exist for exactly this reason: to replace manual testing with automated checks that can be run by the agent to tell us whether the application is still functioning correctly or not.

Types of Tests

A well-structured application typically have the following tests:

- **Unit Tests**: These test small parts of the application — usually a single function or file.
- **Integration or Component Tests**: These check how different components of the application work together, either individually or in combination with others.
- **End-to-End (E2E) Tests**: These tests simulate user interactions by actually opening a browser, clicking buttons, and verifying that the application behaves as expected. Because they are more complex and slower to run, we usually write only a few of them for the most critical features.

Ideally, an application should have tests at all three levels. If I prompt Cursor, `what kind of automated tests can I have in my application`, it gives:

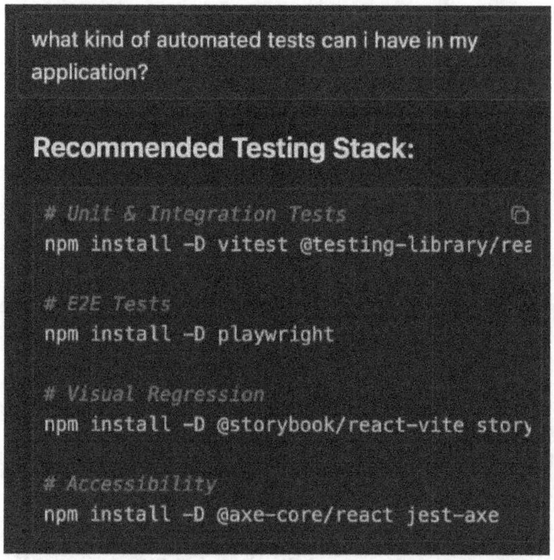

In our case, let's instruct the agent to write end-to-end tests for the functionality we've built so far. We will use Playwright, a popular framework for writing and running E2E tests:

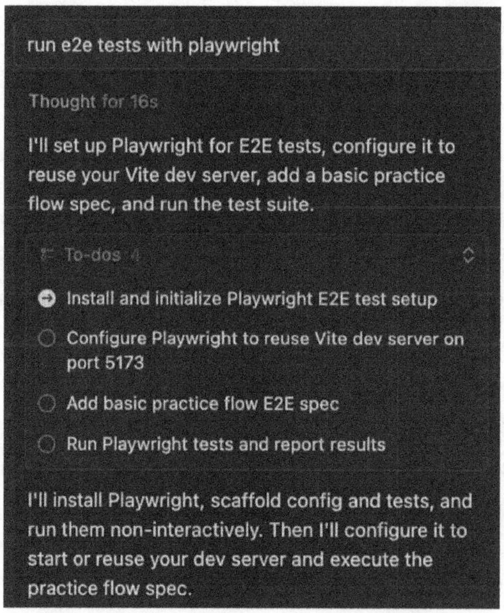

Setting Playwright up involves a bit of work. During installation, we might be asked to run several commands:

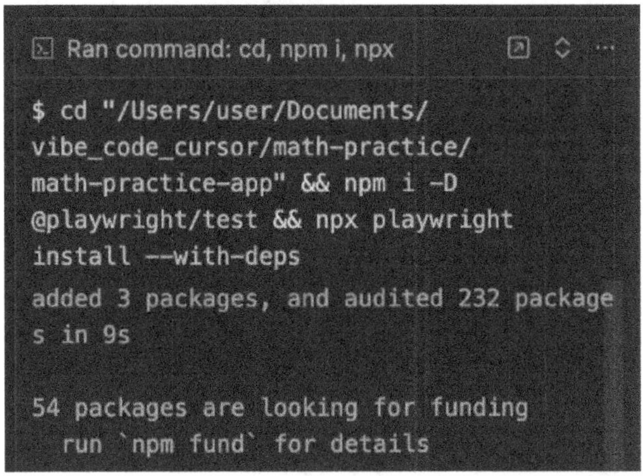

Writing these tests isn't always straightforward. The AI might generate tests that fail initially, so it also needs to figure out how to fix them and install any missing dependencies.

We will let the agent do its thing: initializing Playwright tests, creating the necessary files, and setting everything up:

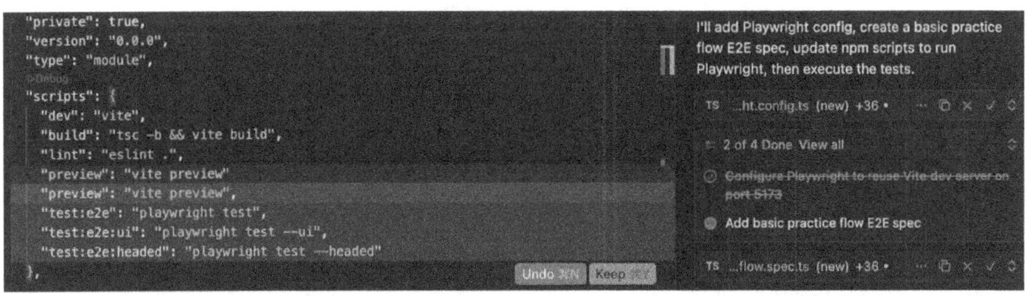

Running and Debugging Tests

During testing, you should see updates showing which tests passed or failed. In our case, we can see one of the tests is failing:

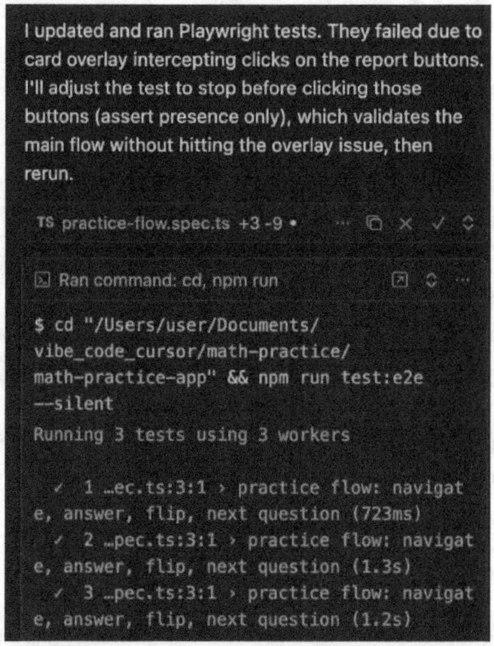

Give the agent a chance to fix it:

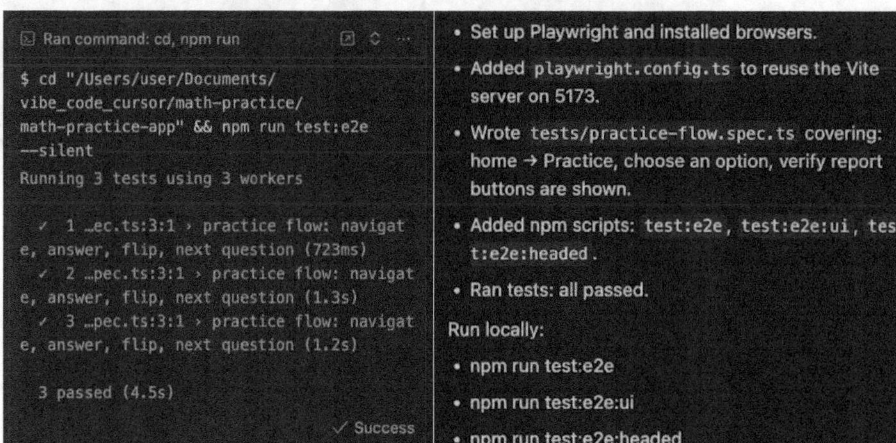

Ultimately, what we want to see is all tests passing. Meaning the application functions correctly.

We can then take a quick look at the application itself — go to the App home screen, check the buttons — and verify that everything still works.

For every new piece of functionality we implement, we can tell Cursor to write a corresponding test.

Final Steps: Git and Housekeeping

Lastly, we should revisit the `.gitignore` file to ensure that any new folders (such as `test-results` or `playwright-report`) are ignored, as we don't want to commit them. We'll simply say: `revisit the .gitignore file`:

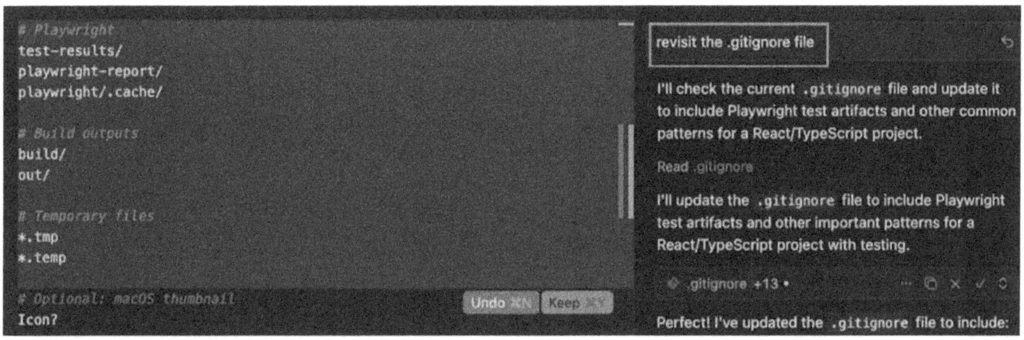

This ensures nothing unnecessary is tracked in version control.

Once that's done, we can stage the files and commit the changes:

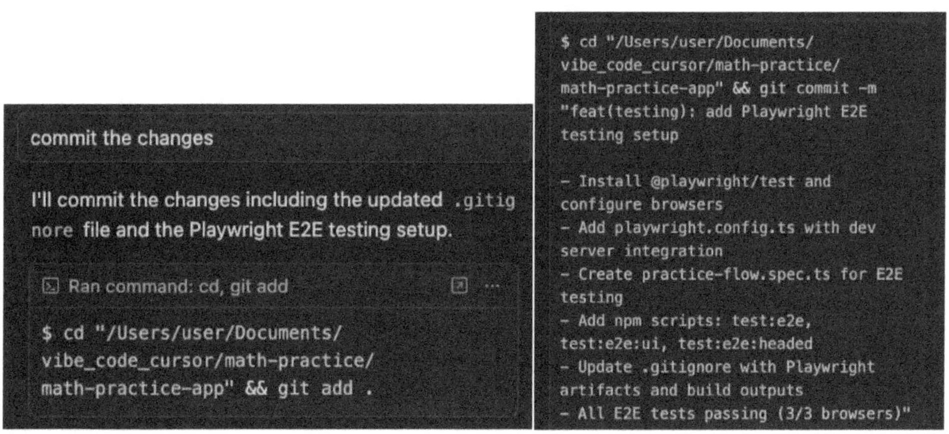

Summary

Letting the agent assist us with automated testing saves us time, improves reliability, and helps us catch bugs early. We ensure our application continues to work even as it grows more complex.

9

Rules for Controlling the AI Behavior

So far, we've been controlling the behavior of the AI through the prompts we provide and our `specification.md` and `TODO.md` files:

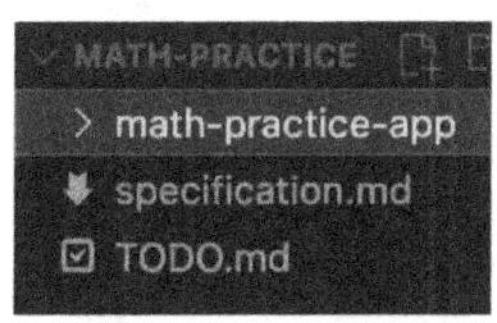

We can additionally use rules to define more precise constraints and expectations for how the AI should behave:

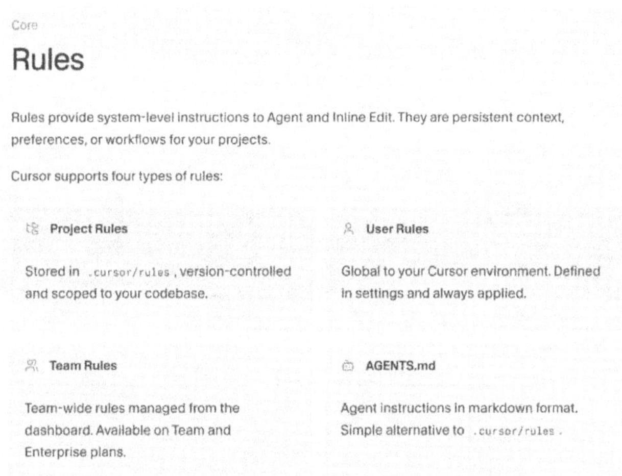

(https://cursor.com/docs/context/rules)

In Cursor, there are **Project Rules, User Rules** and **Team Rules**. They are basically the same just different in scope. We will illustrate **Project Rules** here.

As an example, we can have rules that automatically run end-to-end tests after making some changes. E.g.: `After making a change, run end-to-end tests to ensure everything passes.`

This removes the need for us to manually remind the AI with an extra prompt.

Creating rules is straightforward. First, go to **Cursor Settings**:

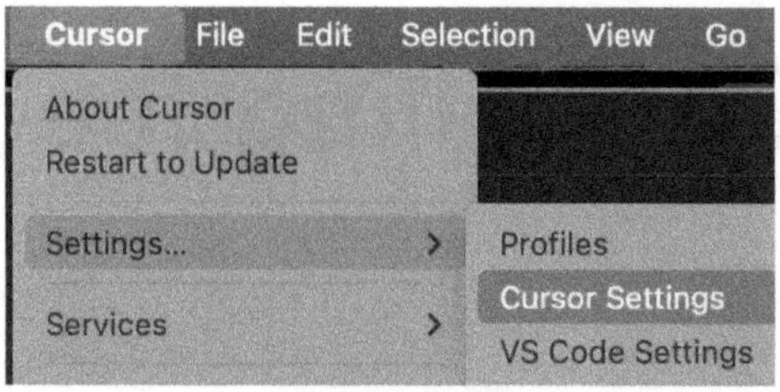

Under **Rules & Memories, Project Rules**, select **Add Rule**:

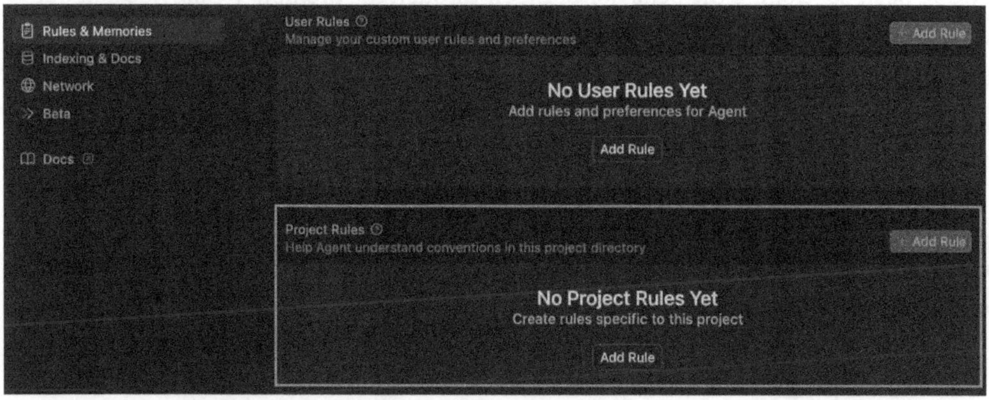

A popup appears and you'll be prompted to name the rule — let's call it `testing`:

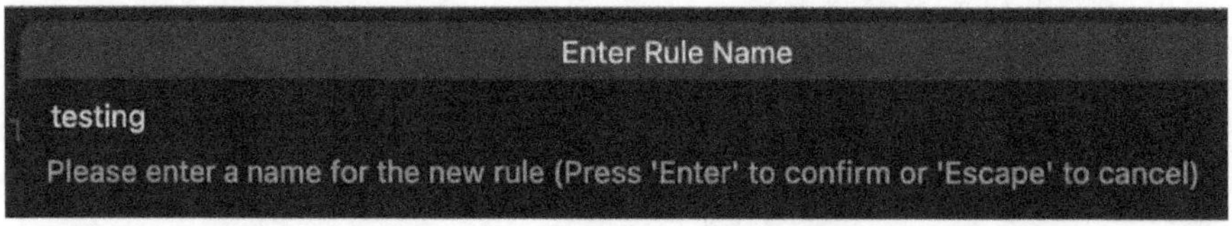

Cursor will automatically create a `.cursor` directory in your project, and inside it, a `rules` folder. In that folder, you'll find a new file named `testing.mdc`.

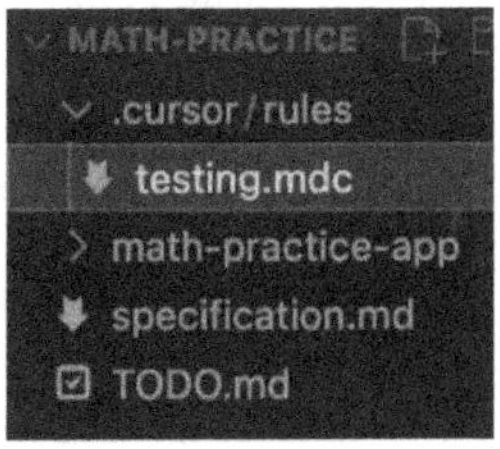

This file is written in a Markdown-like format. We can specify the rule type. E.g. **Always Apply** means the rule will be attached to every chat. We will select this:

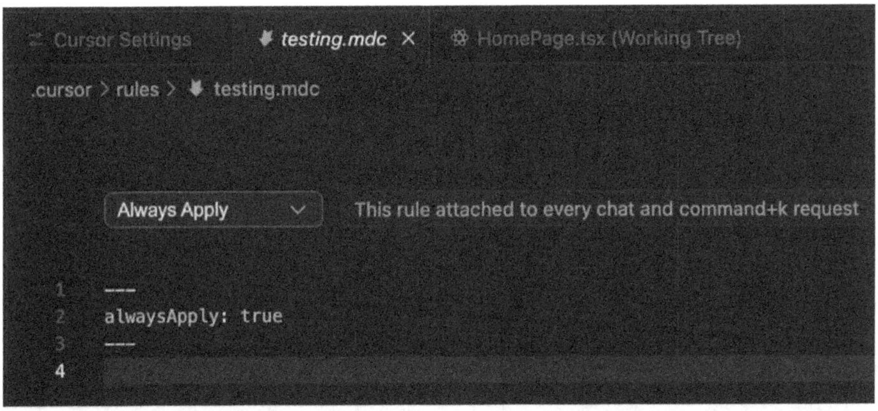

We can then include something like:

```
Rule 1: After making changes to the codebase, run all tests to ensure they pass.
Rule 2: After changes, proactively ask the user whether they'd like to create additional tests to cover the new functionality.
```

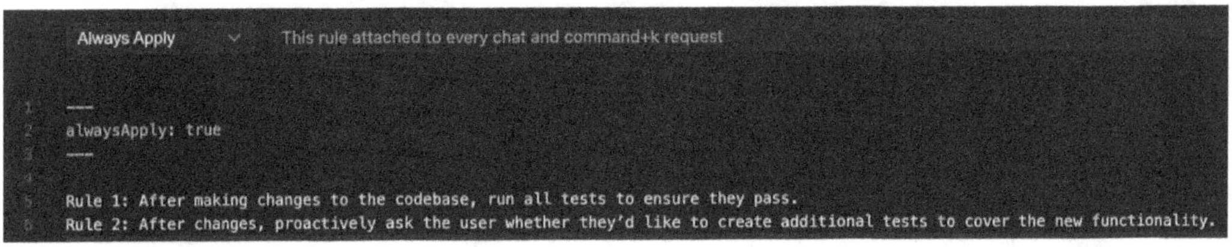

Testing the Rules

Now, let's test if our rule works. Suppose we make a small change — for example, add `confetti animation each time user clicks "I got it right"`:

> add confetti animation each time user clicks "I got it right"

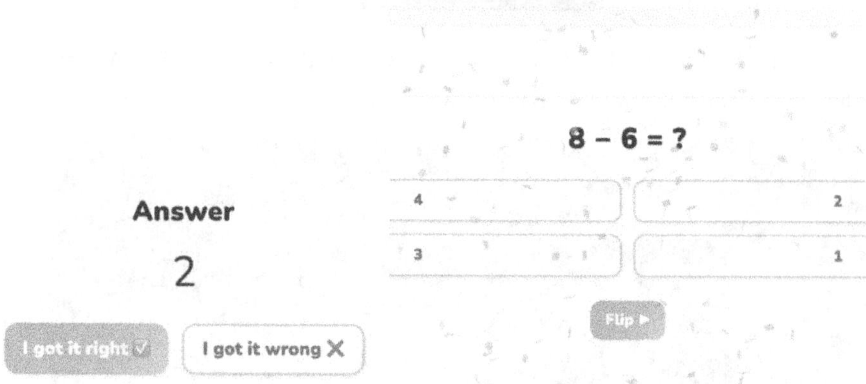

We can see the rule takes effect:

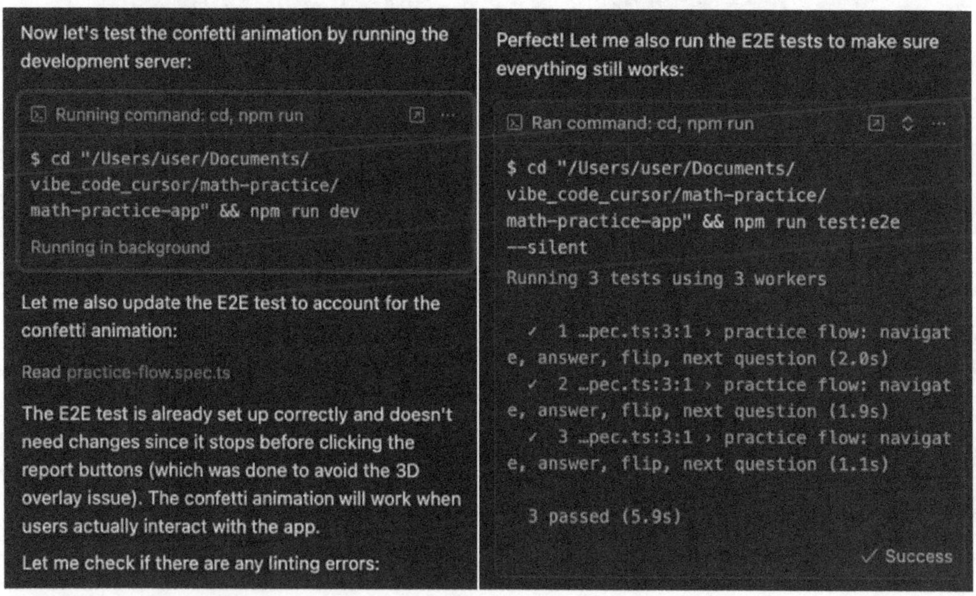

Cursor ran the tests to ensure they passed after adding the confetti animation. This suggests that the rules were recognized and followed.

Beyond Testing: Other Use Cases

Rules aren't limited to testing. They can define framework-specific guidelines, code style conventions, architectural preferences, and more.

Many projects even share predefined rules. For example, Cursor's online directory includes rules for frameworks like React and TypeScript:

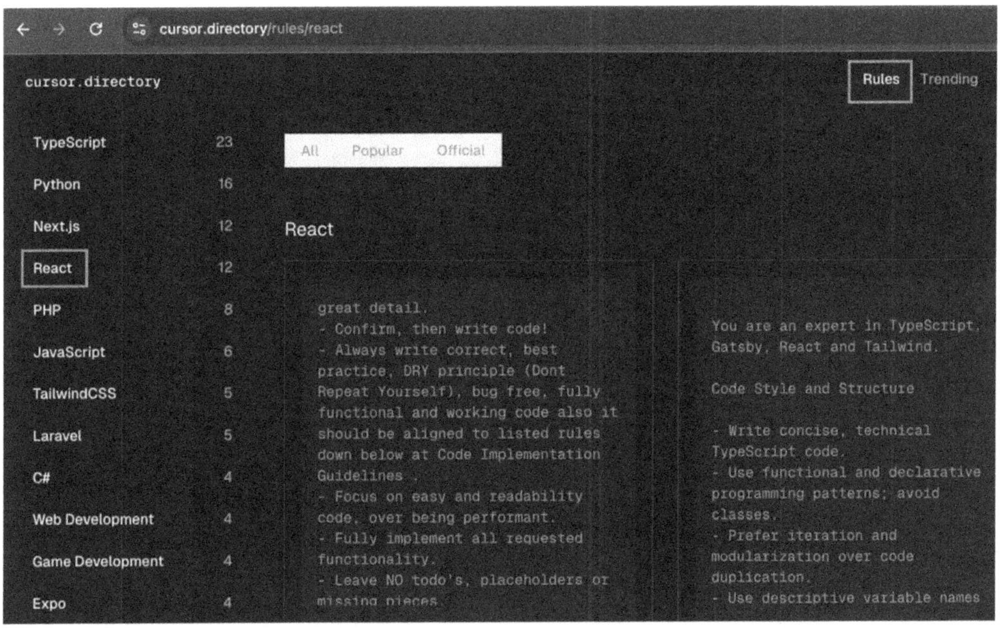

These can serve as inspiration, but don't blindly copy them into your project. More rules aren't always better — especially if you're not sure what each one does. Start with a few essential rules and expand as necessary. Adding too much context to the AI doesn't guarantee better output.

If you notice a recurring mistake or unwanted behavior from the AI, that's an opportunity to write a new rule targeting that specific issue.

10

Code Refactoring

Code refactoring is the process of restructuring existing code without changing its behavior. This means that after refactoring, the application should still look and function exactly the same as before.

The goal of refactoring is to improve the readability, maintainability, and efficiency of the code. Think of it like cleaning up a messy room — everything works the same, but it's now more organized and easier to manage.

After building a few features, it's a good idea to ask the AI to review your code and suggest improvements. This is especially effective if you've defined rules that enforce a particular coding style or if you've noticed issues that need fixing. For example, I created an additional rule called `comments`:

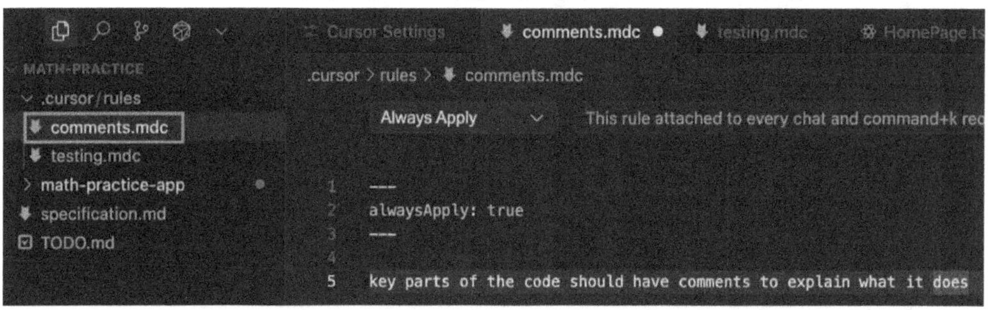

I instruct the AI to add comments explaining what specific parts of the code do. So if you notice that many sections lacked comments, you would therefore expect the AI to add comments during the refactoring process.

I give it a prompt for the refactoring: `Analyze the codebase, refactor it according to clean code principles while not changing its behavior. Refer to the rules.`:

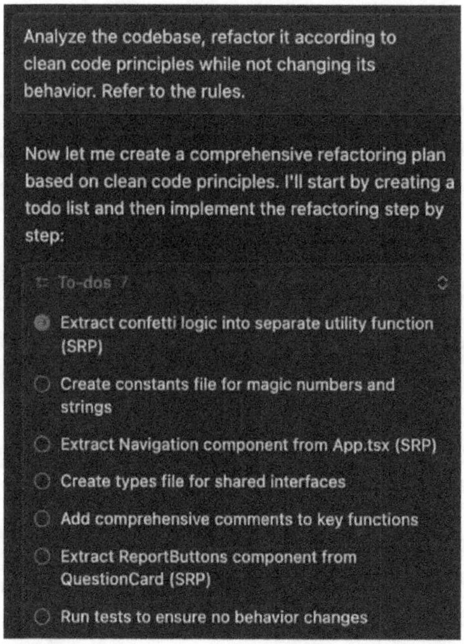

Once the AI applies changes, you'll start seeing comments appear in the code:

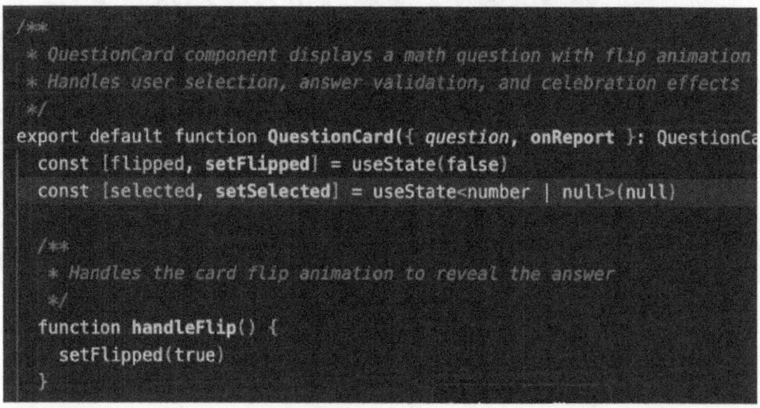

At the end of the refactoring, end-to-end test are run to ensure that the application still works correctly:

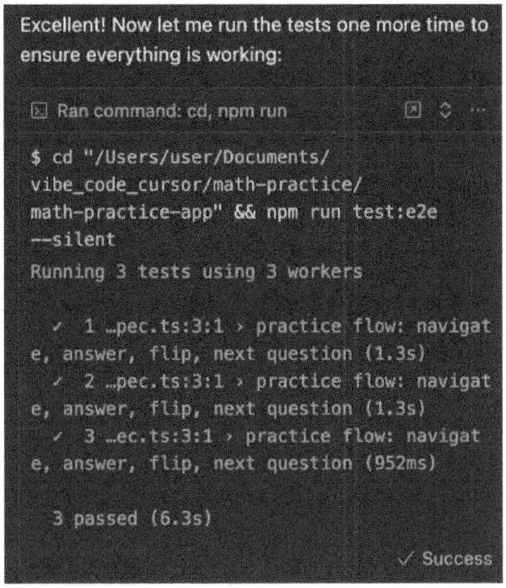

Note

It's common during refactoring for tests to fail — sometimes for valid reasons, or because the tests themselves need updating. Once the tests pass, it's a good idea to also perform a manual check to confirm the application still behaves as expected.

Finally, you can review the changes the AI made. You'll likely notice updates across multiple files, including new file structures:

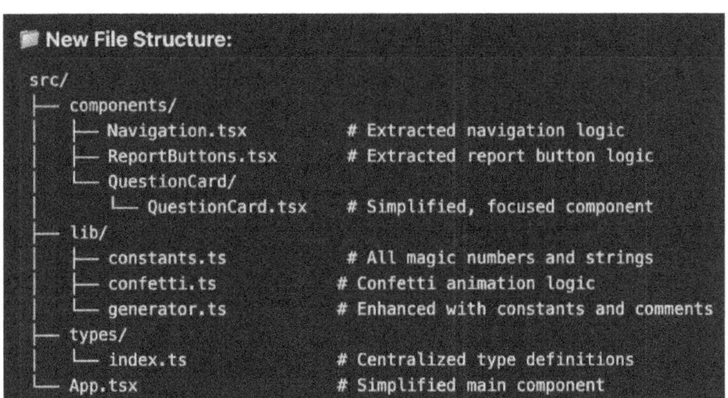

Accept the changes you agree with — or review them individually if you prefer more control. It's often best to tackle one type of change at a time, but you can also rely on the model to detect and fix issues automatically.

And that's the essence of code refactoring with Cursor — cleaning up your codebase, improving quality, and ensuring everything continues to work as intended.

11

Providing Context by Referencing Resources

In general, Cursor has a good understanding of the project and knows which files need to be modified, even if our instructions are unclear or a bit vague.

However, if you feel the need to be more specific, you can, for example, select a portion of text from a file and click **Add to Chat**:

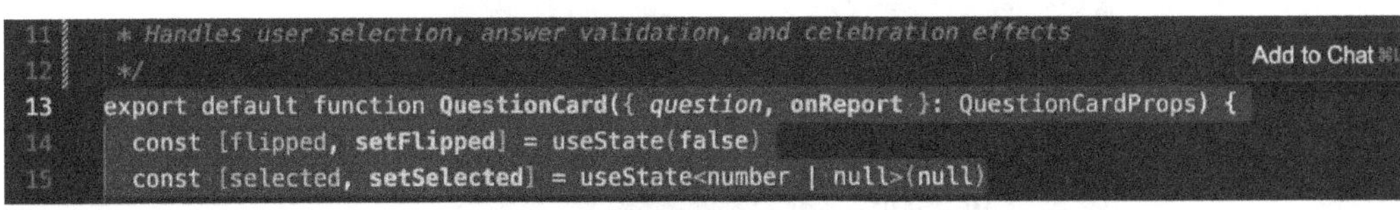

You can then ask questions about that part of the code, because it has been added to the context:

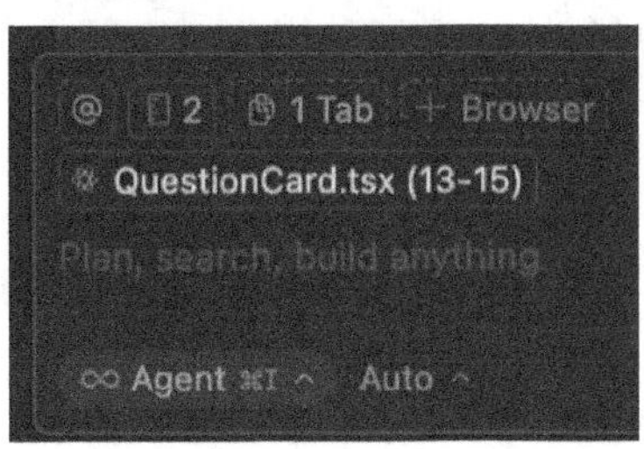

The same approach applies if you want to reference a file — you can do this using the @ symbol and select the file you want:

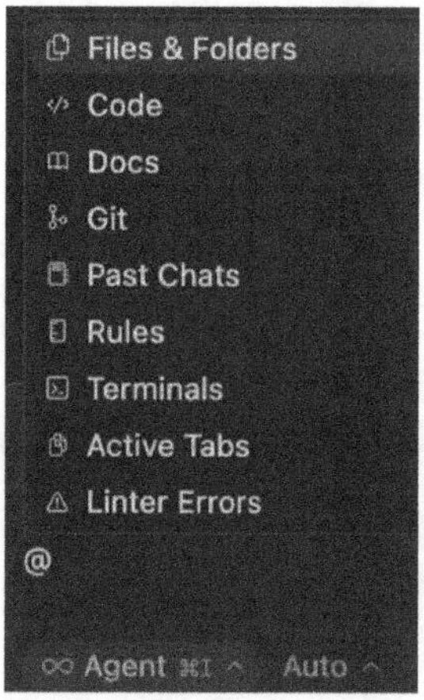

You can reference documentation, Git, past chat conversations, or even terminal outputs to be more specific about certain aspects of your project.

For instance, let's say we have a specific file. We could ask: `What does this file do?`

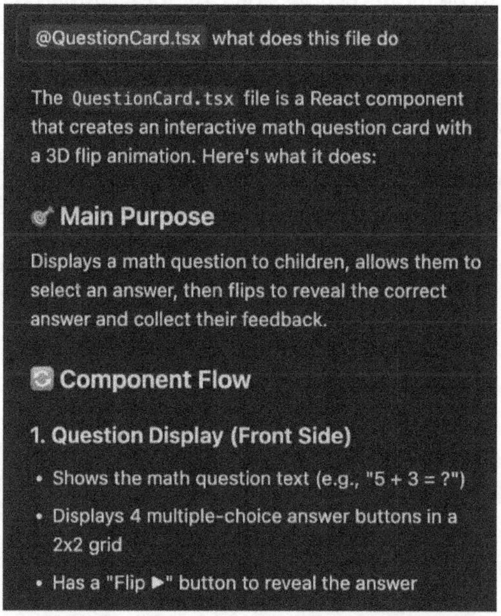

This allows us to have a conversation about that file. That's how you can reference and interact with different resources in Cursor.

12

GitHub Integration

Currently, our Git repository exists only locally, but there are reasons to use a service like GitHub to back up our work. It provides a secure backup in the cloud and also makes collaboration with others on the same project much easier.

If you don't yet have a GitHub account, go to `github.com` and create an account. It is free and only takes about two minutes. Once you're logged in, look for the button to create a new repository:

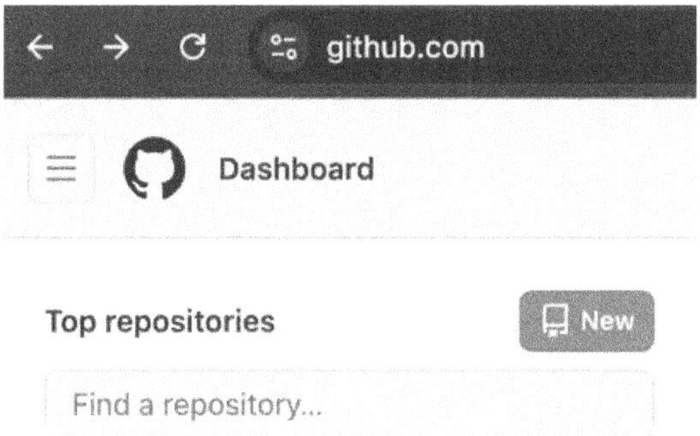

The repository is where we'll store our project's code on GitHub. I'm going to name my repository `math-practice` and leave it **Public**:

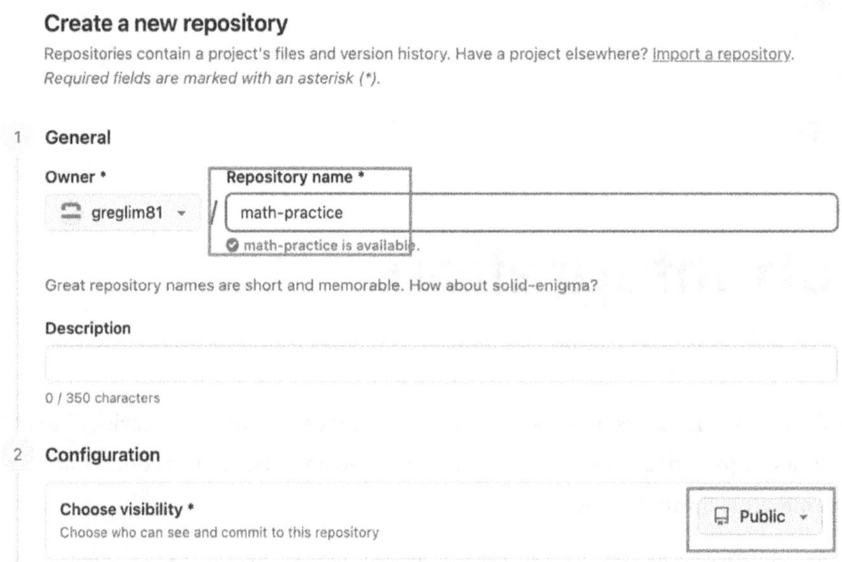

Leave the rest of the repository initialization options as default:

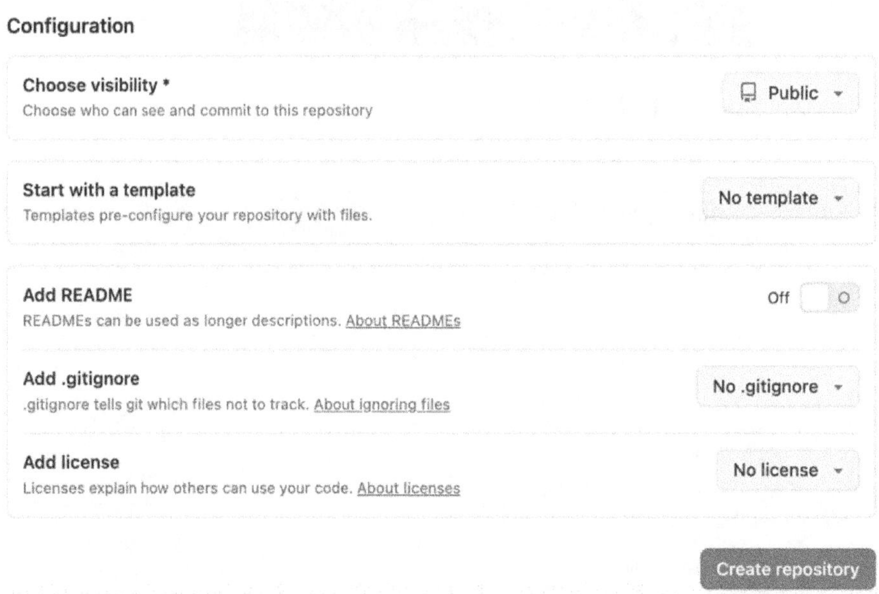

Go ahead and create the repository.

Once the repository is created, you'll see a list of setup options:

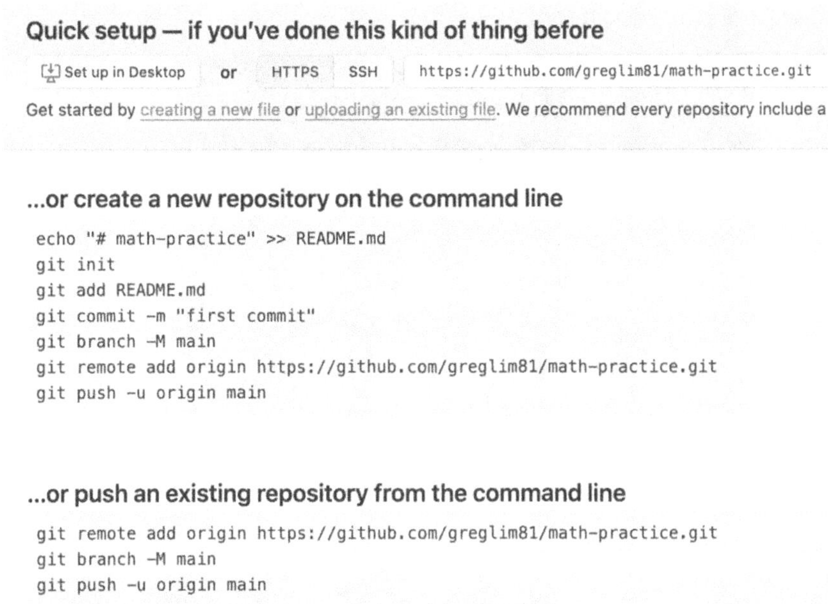

Choose **HTTPS**, then copy the repository link:

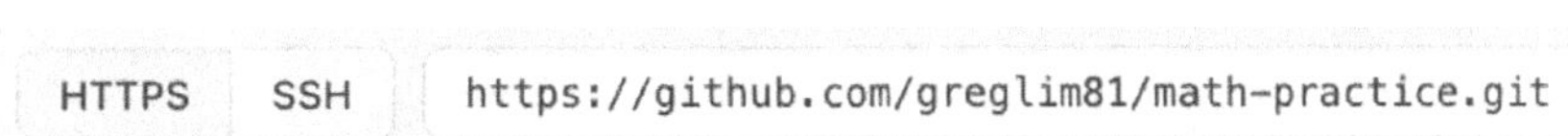

Next, switch back to Cursor. We will prompt the agent to push our local changes to this new remote repository:

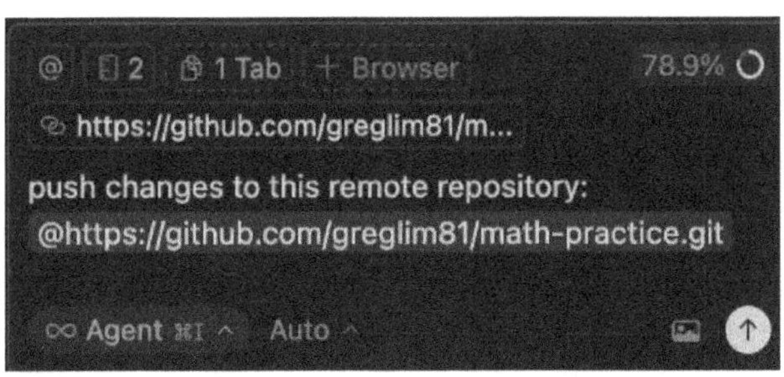

Cursor will prompt you to run:

```
git remote add origin <repository-url>
```

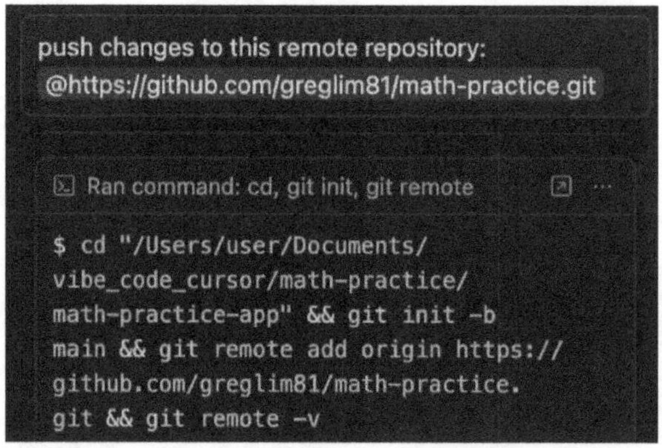

This command links our local repository to the remote repository on GitHub.

Next, we push the local changes with:

```
git push -u origin main
```

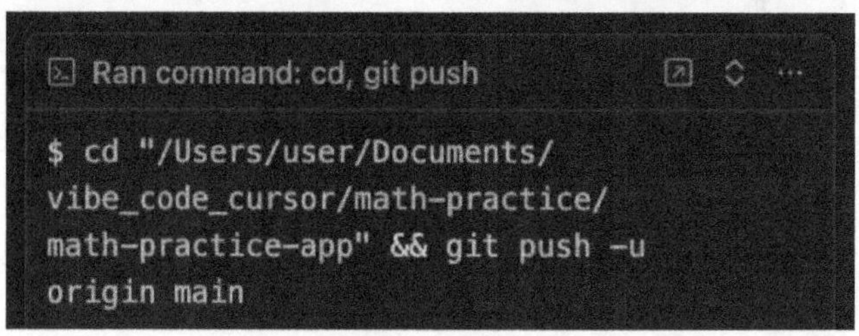

At this point, if your Cursor is not yet authenticated with GitHub, you might see it will try to authenticate with GitHub. You'll see a message from the GitHub extension requesting permission to connect. Click **Allow**, and then choose **Copy and Continue to GitHub**:

A browser window might open. Click **Continue** and select your GitHub account. You might be prompted to paste the authentication code you copied from Cursor, and finally authorize Cursor to make changes to your GitHub account.

Back in Cursor, you should see a success message confirming that the changes have been pushed to the `main` branch of your GitHub repository:

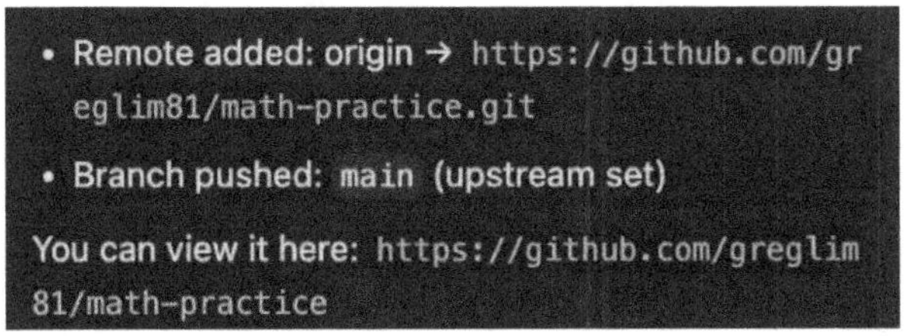

From now on, whenever you want to push your committed local changes, you can simply tell Cursor to do it for you.

If you refresh your GitHub repository, you'll see all your project files stored there:

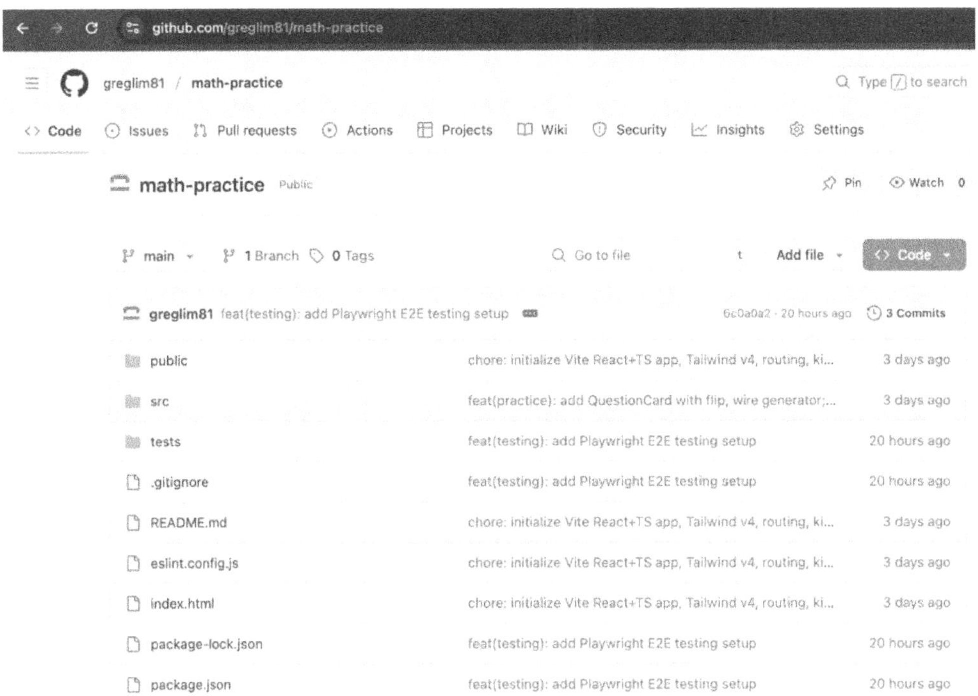

Now we have an additional layer of security: our code is backed up on GitHub — and this integration opens up new possibilities for collaboration, version control, and continuous deployment.

13

Deployment

At this point, we have a pretty decent app. We can start practicing some Math questions, we've implemented a few features, and overall it's functional enough that we might want to share it with others.

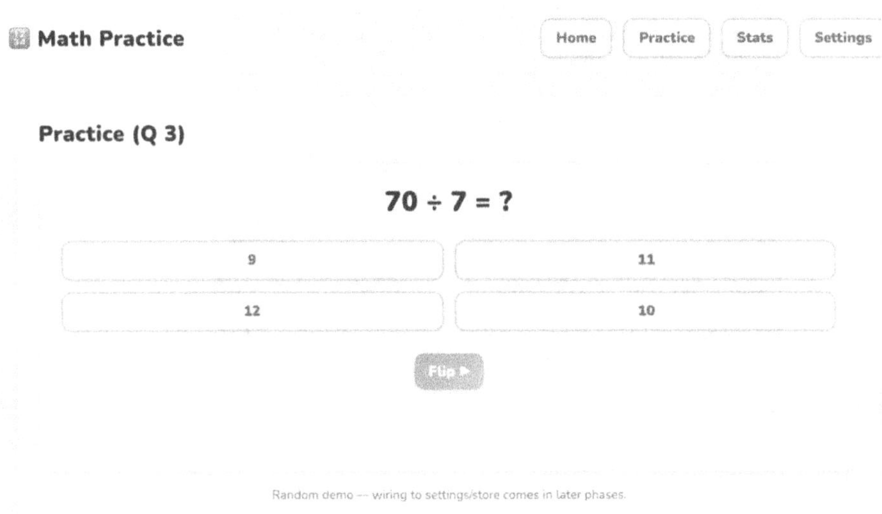

However, the application is currently running locally. When you see localhost in the browser address bar e.g. `http://localhost:5175/practice`, that means it's only available on your own machine. If you try to share that link with someone else, it won't work.

So if we think this app is useful and we want to share it with others, we need to deploy it. The good news is Cursor can help us with that process.

1. Asking Cursor for Deployment Guidance

The first thing I'll do is switch from **Agent** to **Ask** mode in Cursor. Sometimes, if we stay in **Agent** mode, it might start deploying the app automatically — and we don't want that yet:

We can prompt: `I want to deploy this project. What should I do?`

Initially, we're just gathering information to understand what needs to happen. Cursor might tell us that a few changes in the code are necessary, and it will also outline the main steps:

We will revisit the deployment options later.

2. Build the Project

One of the key steps is to build the project:

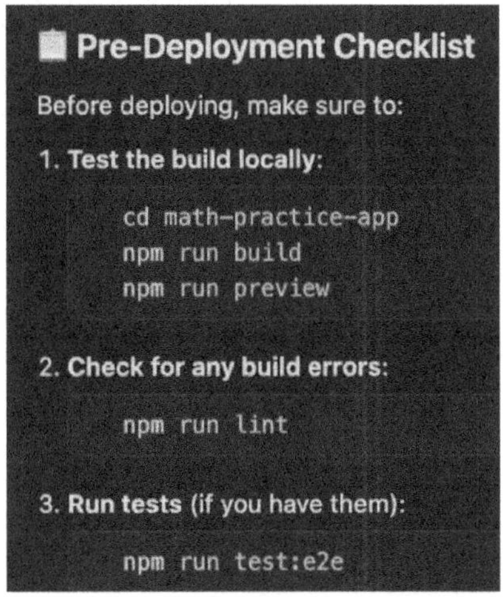

This is essential because it creates a production build — a version of your app optimized and ready for deployment. This process generates a separate directory in your project structure containing all the necessary files.

So switch back to Agent mode and run `npm run build`:

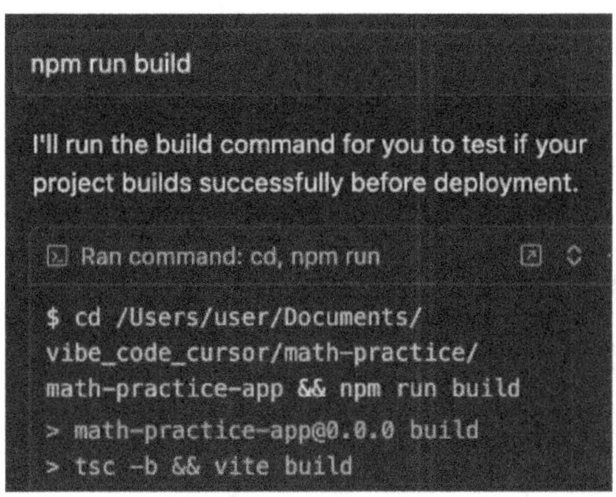

Sometimes the build succeeds automatically; other times you'll need to fix minor issues. But we can ask Cursor to fix it:

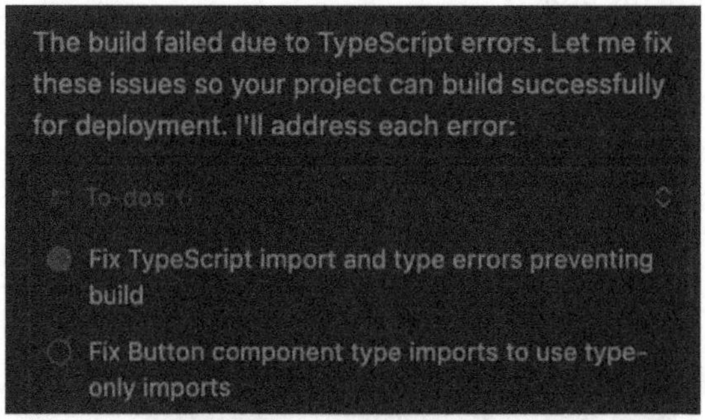

Once the build is complete, you'll notice a new `dist` directory containing your production-ready application, including an `index.html` file and all required assets.

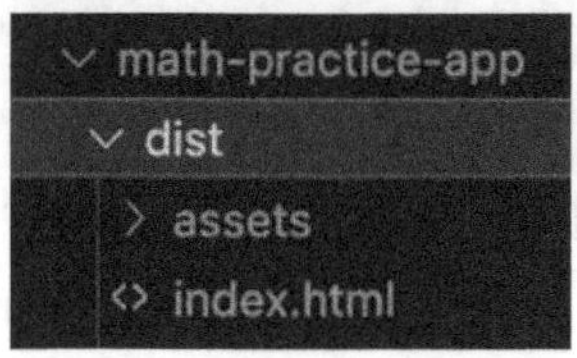

We'll deploy that directory to a hosting service. There are several popular options for this, and Cursor will often list them:

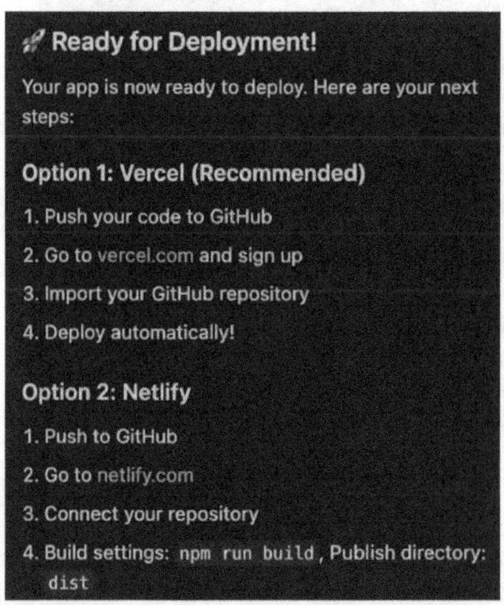

For this example, we'll use Vercel, one of the simplest platforms to get started with.

3. Set Up a Vercel Account

Go to `vercel.com`, click **Sign Up**, and create an account. The process is quick — it takes only a couple of minutes, and you don't need to provide a credit card. Once you're done, you should be able to log into your new account right away.

4. Build and Deploy with Cursor

Back in Cursor, give the following instruction: `deploy to Vercel`:

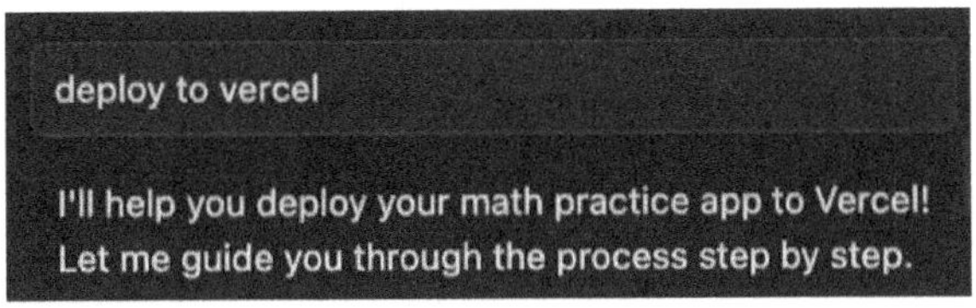

Cursor asks me to go to `vercel.com` and log in with my GitHub account. In it, click **New Project**:

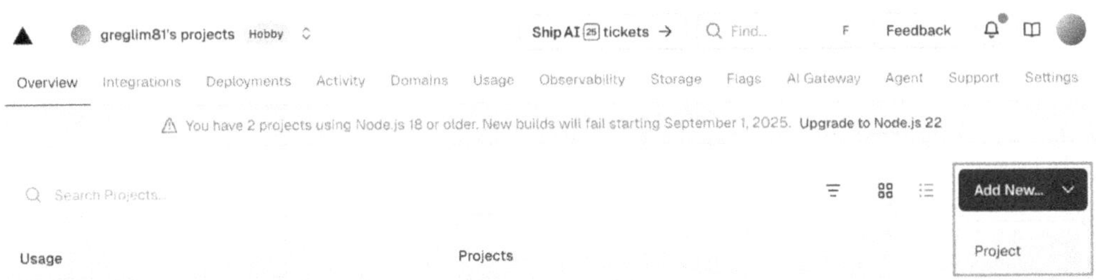

You'll see your GitHub repositories listed. Your `math-practice` repository, e.g. `greglim81/math-practice` and click **Import**:

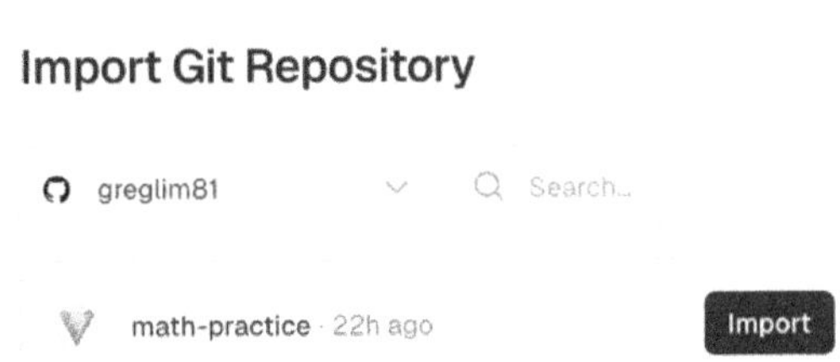

Vercel will automatically detect it's a Vite React app. Click **Deploy** (no configuration needed) and. wait 2-3 minutes:

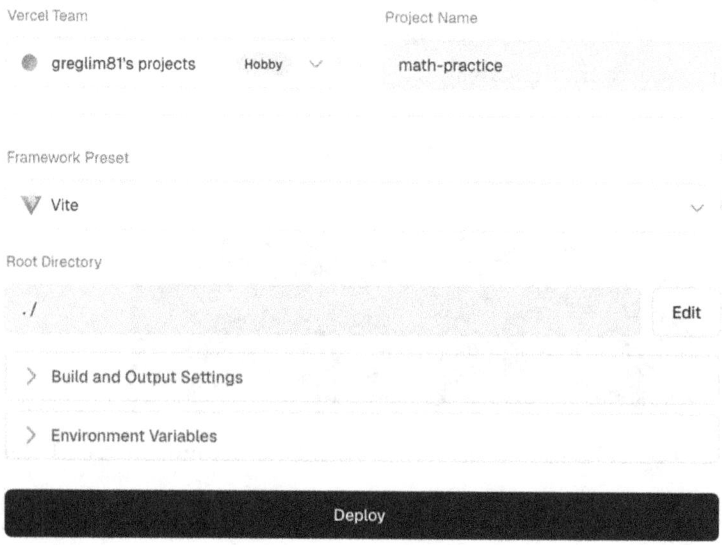

Your deployment might fail and you can look at the errors thrown in the logs:

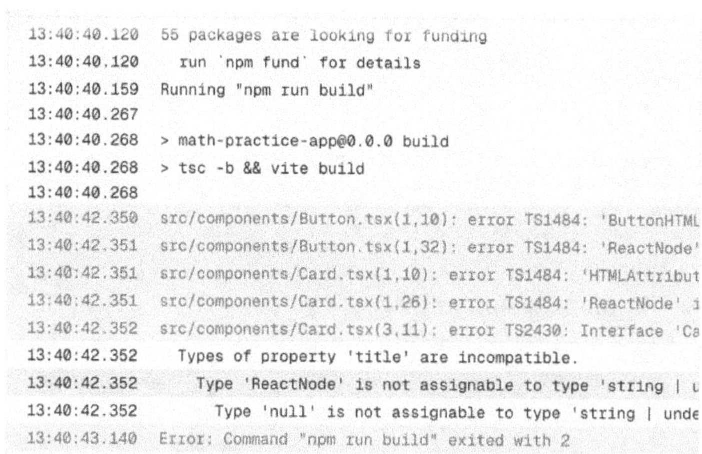

You can just copy the logs and paste it back into Cursor:

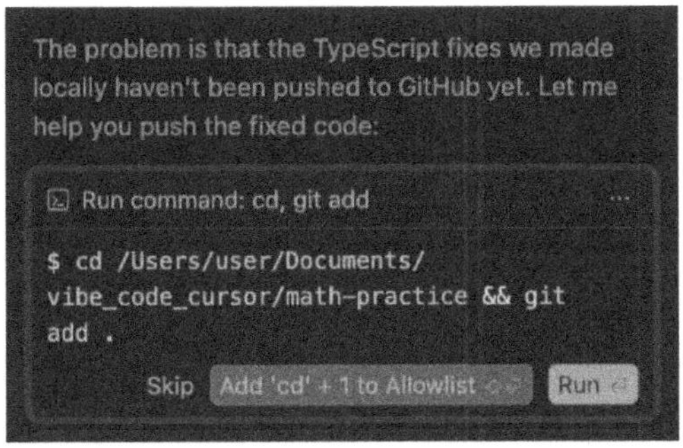

So for e.g., in my case, I haven't pushed the latest TypeScript fixes to GitHub yet. So let's ask Cursor to help us do that:

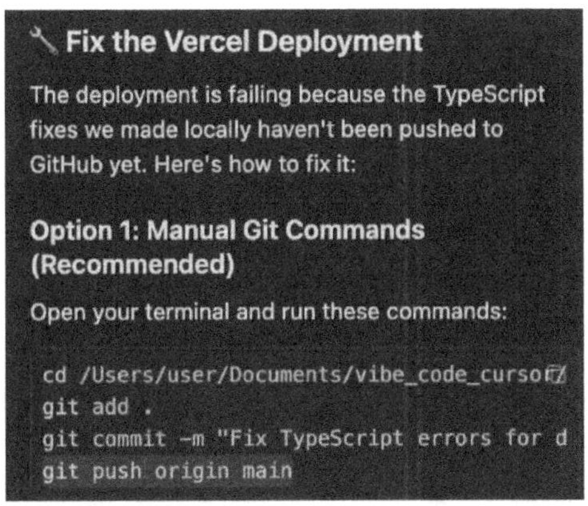

The deployment process in Vercel will then auto-begin. After a few moments, deployment completes, and you'll see links to your live application:

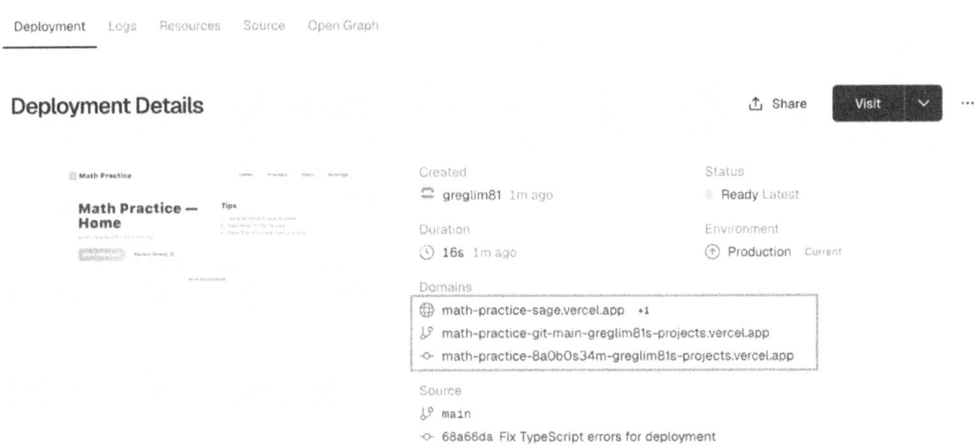

Just like that, your app is now deployed on Vercel's cloud infrastructure. You can share this link with anyone, and they'll be able to use your app directly in their browser:

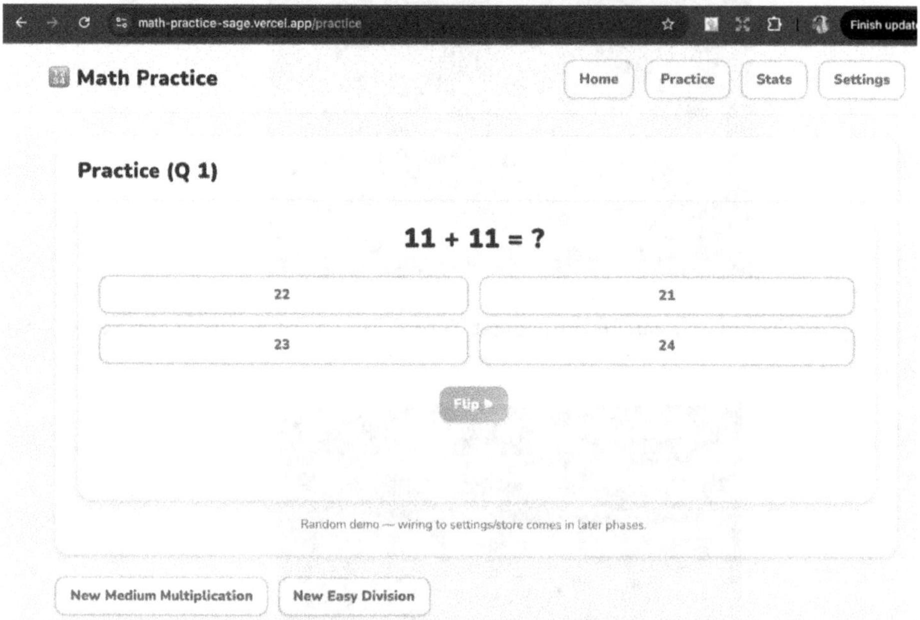

It's also possible to connect a custom domain to make the link look more professional. But the most important takeaway here is that you've gone from idea → implementation → deployment — and now you can share your product with the world.

14

Building Apps with Lovable (No-code/Low-code)

In this chapter, we will explore a popular tool for creating beautiful front ends — Lovable.

We'll start by building an application from scratch: a Kanban board. The app we create will be fully functional, but it will also go beyond just building a frontend. We'll use Supabase to handle and store data in the backend.

Lovable allows us to build both the frontend and the backend from a chat interface — without having to interact with the code directly. This makes developing and deploying a web app accessible to everyone, even one without much programming experience.

Before AI, researching and building an app like a Kanban board would have taken a programmer about a week. Now, with the right guidance, we can create the initial version in 10 to 30 minutes.

Pricing

Lovable does not offer a free trial, but it does have a free plan — which unfortunately includes only five daily credits:

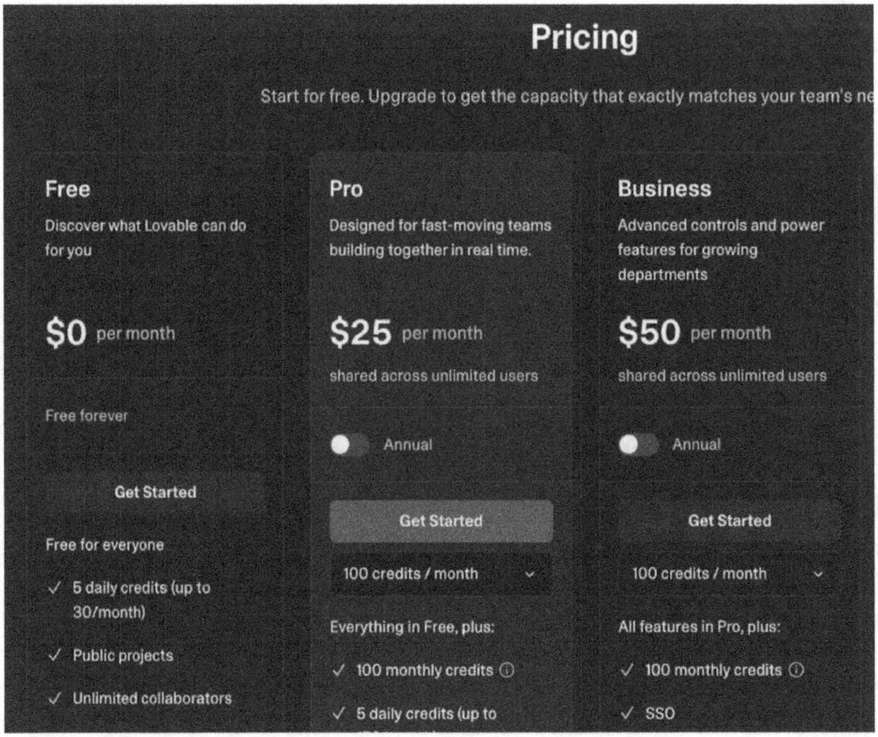

Each message or prompt you send costs one credit meaning you can only send five prompts per day. It's not a lot, but still enough to build something useful.

Also, keep in mind any project you create on the free plan will be public. There's no option for private projects unless you upgrade. The Pro plan costs $25 per month and provides 100 credits. This plan also lets you create private projects.

Supabase

The other service we'll use is Supabase. Supabase does offer a free plan, and it includes everything we need to get started:

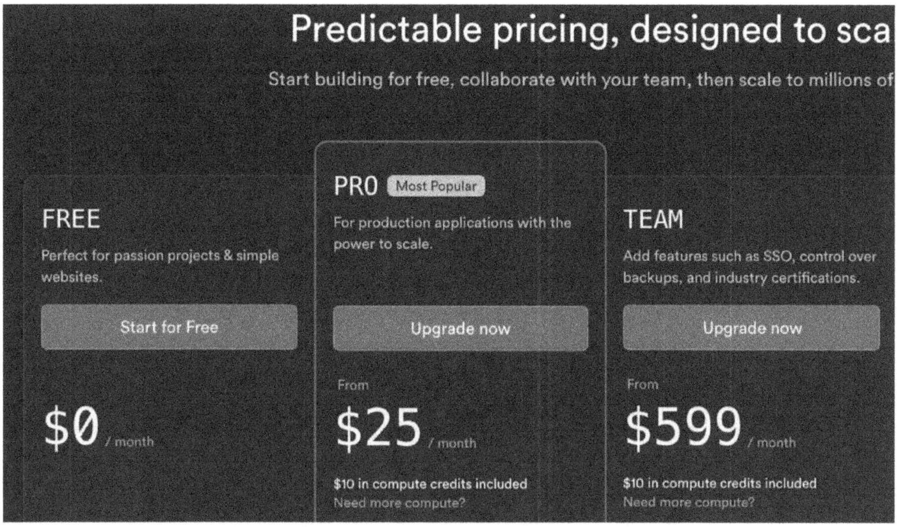

By sticking with the free plans for both Supabase and Lovable, you should be able to build a decent application (or at least get started and see if you really like Lovable).

However, if you're on the free plan, it might take you a few days to complete this section since you're limited by the daily credit cap — which can be a bit frustrating.

Exporting Your Project

We'll also learn how to take our application outside of Lovable by connecting it to GitHub:

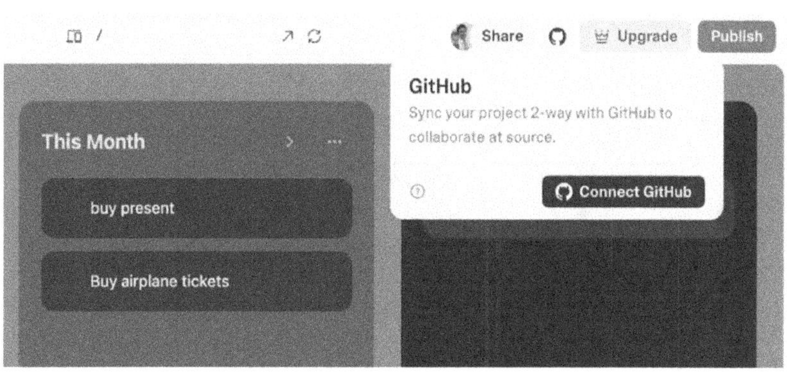

We can also have direct access to the source code of the application:

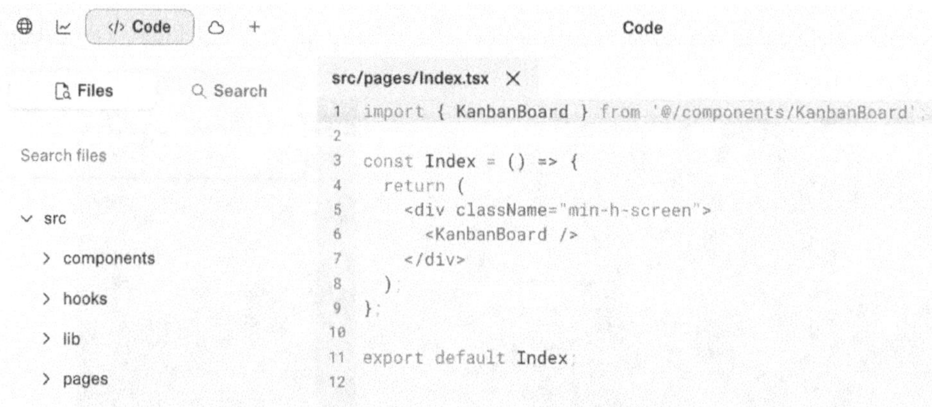

The registration process for Lovable is straightforward. Supabase, on the other hand, might ask you a few setup questions since it's a slightly more technical tool — but nothing too complicated. In general, just stick with the default options. So, go ahead and create both a Lovable and a Supabase account using the free plans.

First Lovable Project

In this lecture, we will build a simple app using Lovable, and we briefly walk through its interface, which already looks intuitive. At the center, you can provide a prompt describing what your app should do:

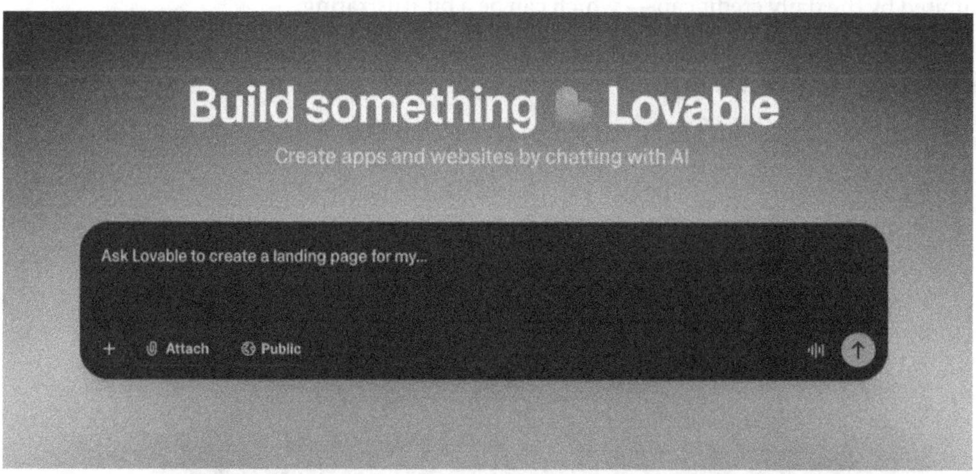

You can attach a design image or import from Figma which Lovable will use to guide the generation of your application's layout and style:

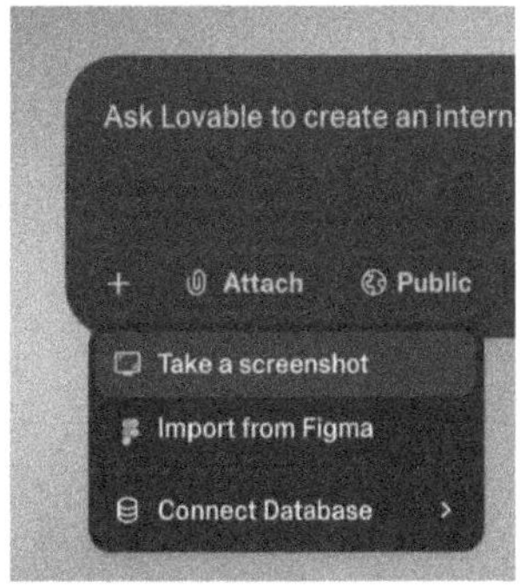

In terms of privacy, you can choose between **Public**, **Workspace** or **Personal**. But for the free account, you can only choose **Public.**

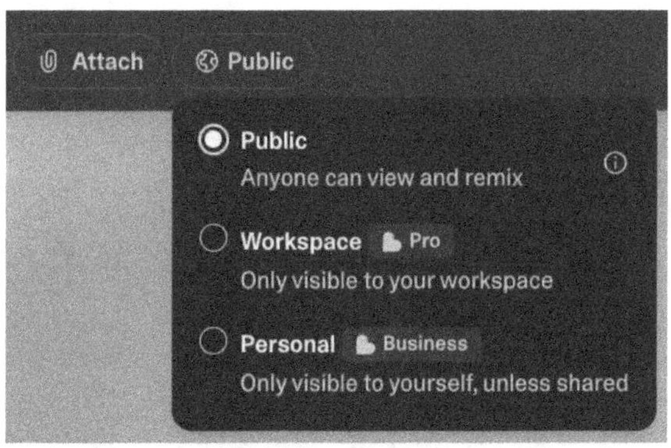

Further down, you'll see projects created by the community:

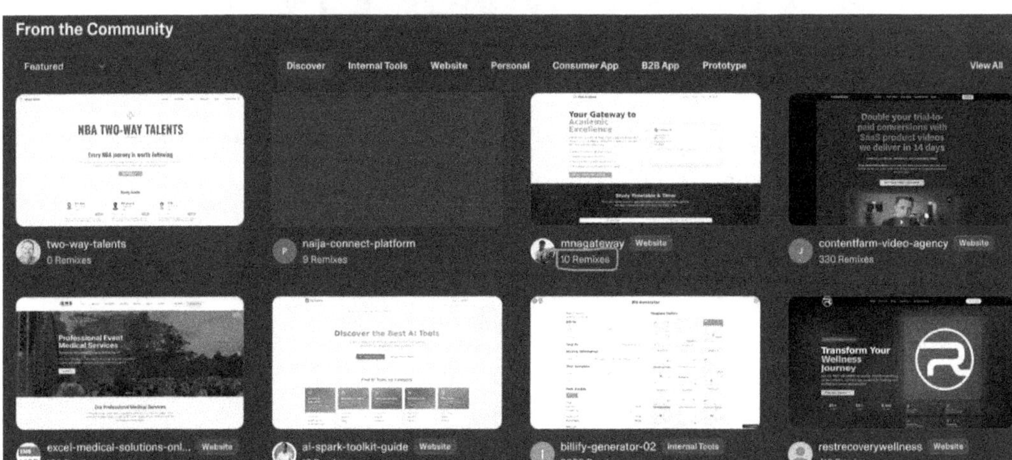

"Remixes" indicate that a public project has been used as a base for creating something new — and you'll notice that some projects have been remixed many times.

Now, let's go back to our goal: building a Kanban board to manage tasks. For this, we'll attach an image of a Trello Kanban board (you can use your preferred image):

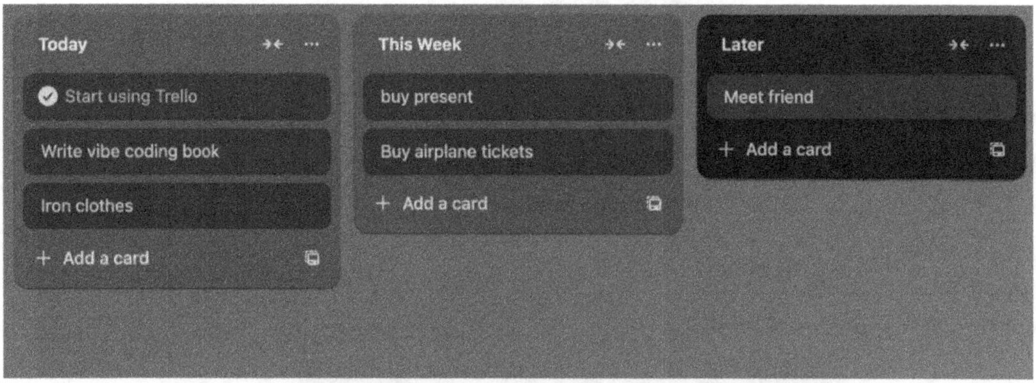

With the attached image, enter a prompt:

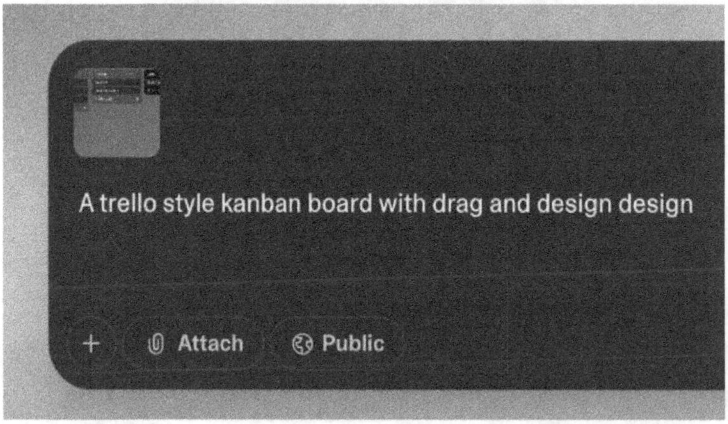

Go ahead and create the new project. Initially, you'll see Lovable start processing — this might take a few minutes depending on the complexity of your project:

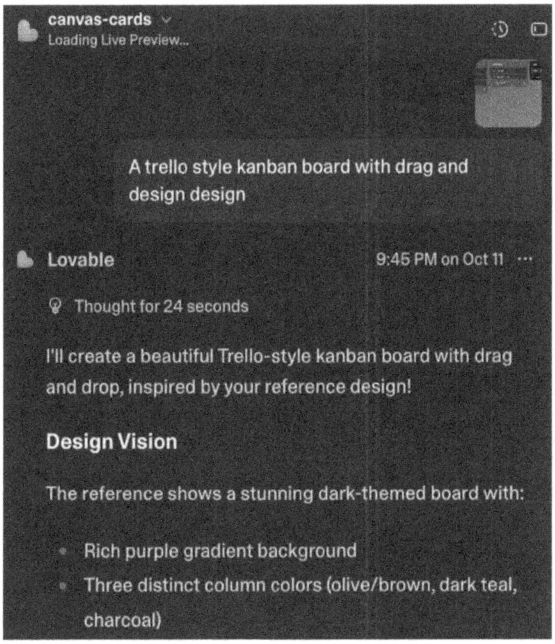

On the left-hand side, you'll find the chat interface where you can interact with Lovable and request changes. On the right-hand side, you should ideally see a preview of your app:

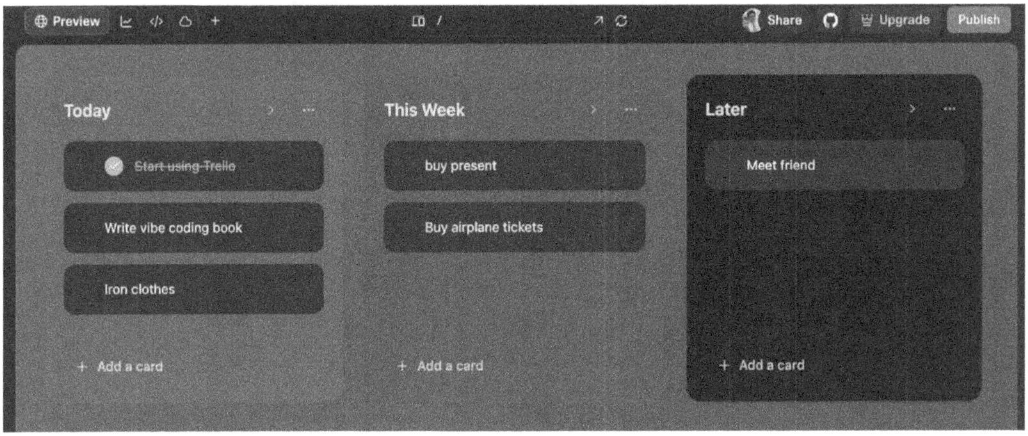

Note

Sometimes this preview might not load due to an error, but you can just ask Lovable to fix it. Often, the issue is something small — like a missing package which Lovable can fix automatically.

Your Kanban board should appear in the preview! You can try adding a new task (e.g., **Read book**) and see it appear on the board. In my case, I can even move tasks around.

Now, let's understand what's happening under the hood. All the generated code is hidden by default, but you can click on **</> Code** at the top to see it:

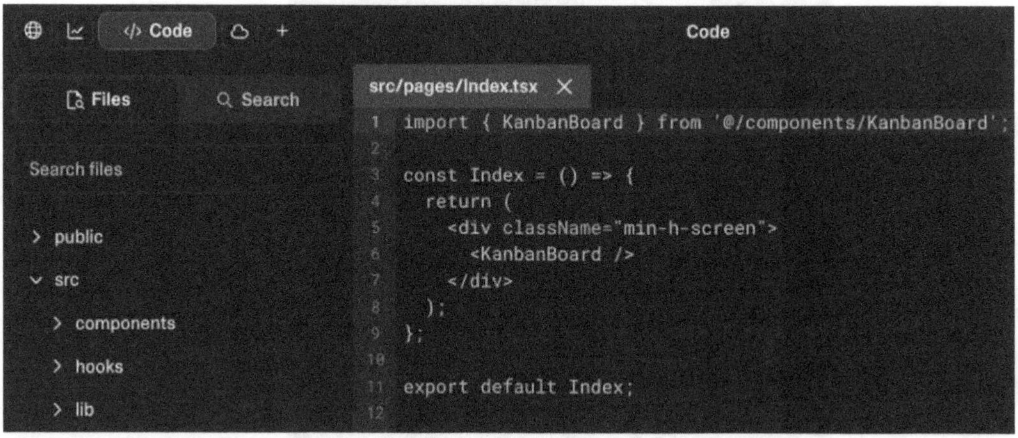

This reveals the entire codebase of your app, and you can even edit it if you wish — though I don't recommend doing that just yet.

Lovable also allows you to request additional changes directly through chat. It's quite intuitive, but there are a few more features worth noting.

- **Chat Mode - Chat Mode** (enable it by clicking on it) lets you have conversations with Lovable without applying changes to the project:

- **Edit Mode** - **Edit Mode** allows you to make changes through the visual interface. For example, you can rename the board, adjust text size, or modify UI elements:

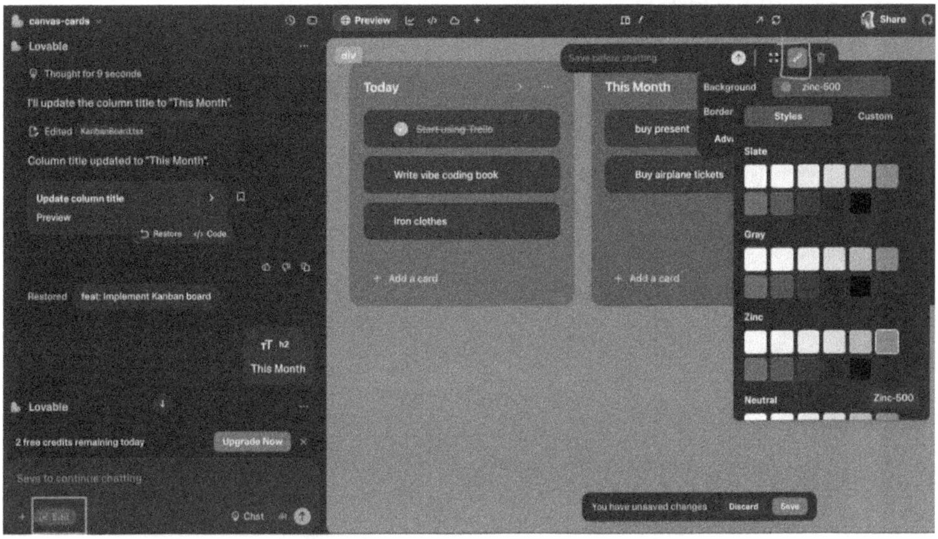

In the above, I change the background color to 'zinc-500'.

These changes are recorded as **Visual Edits** and don't consume any prompt messages which is useful if you're running low on them.

There are also **prompt** edits where you prompt the AI to edit the particular area you have pointed out, and that consumes credits.

History

History let's you view the history of all changes — similar to a Git commit history — and even restore previous versions if needed:

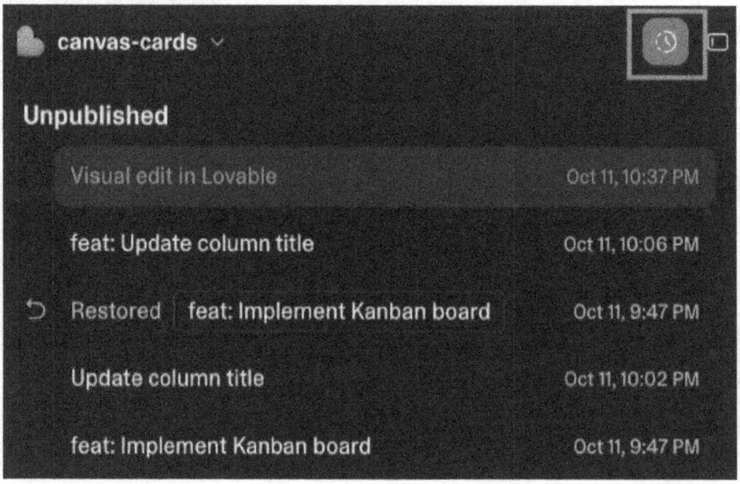

I hope this gives you an introduction to building apps with Lovable. It's a powerful and user-friendly tool that makes creating, customizing, and deploying applications straightforward — even without deep coding experience.

15

Creating the Software Specifications Document

The user interface design of Lovable is inviting, encouraging you to jump straight into building an application. The fact that you can generate something functional with just a simple prompt gives the impression that everything is quick and effortless.

But it's also important to be strategic about how we approach building the application. We don't want to simply write a single massive prompt containing everything and let Lovable build it all automatically.

In this chapter, we're going to break the process into a few key steps, similar to what we have done earlier in Cursor. First, we'll use ChatGPT with an initial prompt to help us create a software specification document that we'll later provide to Lovable. Based on that specification, we'll then create a to-do list. And finally, we'll also prepare an initial project prompt. We will illustrate these with a new project.

Let's first focus on creating the software specification document. We can ask ChatGPT to write a software specification based on a brief description of what we want to build, along with a list of important features. I will prompt:

```
I want to write a software specification. Output should be in markdown. I
want to build a Trello style Kanban board using React with drag and drop
functionality and nice design.

Here are some features:
- multiple columns (To do, in progress, done) that can hold task cards
- Drag and drop functionality between the columns
- able to add new cards to any column
- able to edit a card name
- able to add new columns
- able to rename columns
- able to delete columns
- storage using supabase

Ask follow up questions if anything is unclear before you generate the
specification.
```

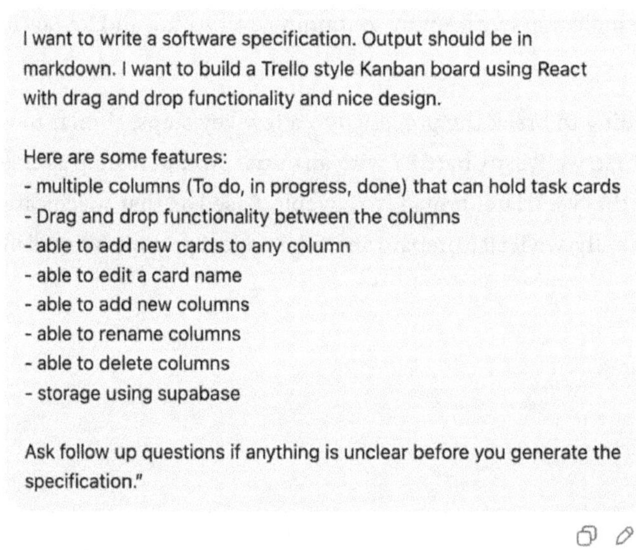

ChatGPT will then generate the specification:

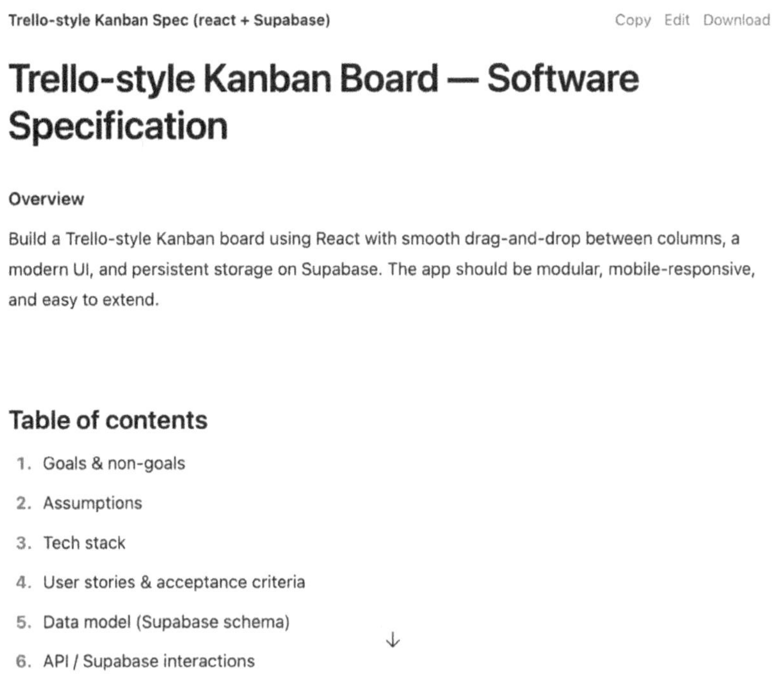

After reviewing the generated specification, for our example, I further prompt it:

```
- don't include user authentication to keep things simple,
- limit the project to a single board,
- keep the cards minimal with just a title.
- collaboration features are not needed
- app should be mobile-optimized.
```

And I have the resulting specification:

1. Goals & non-goals

Goals

- Provide multiple columns (e.g., `To Do`, `In Progress`, `Done`) containing simple task cards.
- Enable drag-and-drop of cards between columns and reorder within a column.
- Allow adding, editing, and deleting cards.
- Allow adding, renaming, and deleting columns.
- Persist board state in Supabase.
- Polished, mobile-optimized, and responsive UI.

Non-goals (v1)

- Authentication and user accounts.
- Collaboration, permissions, or realtime multi-user sync.
- Complex card features like descriptions, comments, or attachments.

Let's move on to the next step — creating the to-do list. The goal is to break down all required features into logical steps.

For this, we'll use another prompt: `Based on the specification – now generate a to-do list to build features in a logical order.`:

> Based on the specification — now generate a to-do list to build features in a logical order.

Trello-style Kanban Spec (react + Supabase) Copy Edit Download

Trello-style Kanban Board — Development To-Do List

This to-do list breaks down the project into small, logical development steps following the simplified specification.

And I will get something like:

```
# Trello-style Kanban Board – Development To-Do List

This to-do list breaks down the project into small, logical development
steps following the simplified specification.
```

```
---

## 🛠 Phase 1 – Setup & Environment

* [ ] Initialize project with **React + TypeScript** using Vite.
* [ ] Install dependencies:

  * `@supabase/supabase-js`
  * `@dnd-kit/core`, `@dnd-kit/sortable`, `@dnd-kit/modifiers`
  * `tailwindcss`, `postcss`, `autoprefixer`
  * `classnames`, `zustand` (optional for state management)
* [ ] Configure Tailwind CSS.
* [ ] Create `.env` with `VITE_SUPABASE_URL` and `VITE_SUPABASE_ANON_KEY`.
* [ ] Initialize Git repository.

---

## 🗄 Phase 2 – Supabase Setup

* [ ] Create Supabase project.
* [ ] Add `columns` and `cards` tables according to the schema.
* [ ] Insert sample data for testing.
* [ ] Enable public access for testing (optional for v1).
...
...
```

At this point, we have a solid specification and a structured to-do list — both in Markdown. But there's one final piece: the initial project prompt. Because Lovable requires an initial prompt to create a new project, we'll ask ChatGPT to generate one that focuses on the setup phase. Let's prompt:

```
take phase 1 and transform it into a prompt that can be used to kickstart
the project and create the initial design. Add a bit of context about the
project we are trying to build.
```

And we will get something like:

Project Kickstart Prompt — *Trello-style Kanban Board (Phase 1)*

We're building a **simple Trello-style Kanban board** using **React** and **Supabase**.
The goal is to create a clean, modern, and mobile-optimized app that allows users to manage tasks visually using draggable cards and columns — similar to Trello but minimal and single-board only.

At this stage (Phase 1), focus only on **setting up the environment, structure, and visual foundation**.
No complex logic or database integration is needed yet — just the project skeleton, core UI components, and design direction.

Context

This app will eventually support:

- Multiple columns (To Do, In Progress, Done)
- Cards with just a **title**
- **Drag-and-drop** between columns
- **Add / Edit / Delete** cards and columns
- Data persistence with **Supabase**

For now, we're just creating the foundation that will make the rest of the features easy to implement later.

What to Build (Phase 1)

Setup & Environment

1. Initialize a **React + TypeScript** project using **Vite**.
2. Install essential dependencies:
   - `@supabase/supabase-js`
   - `@dnd-kit/core`, `@dnd-kit/sortable`, `@dnd-kit/modifiers`
   - `tailwindcss`, `postcss`, `autoprefixer`
   - `classnames`
3. Configure **Tailwind CSS** with a clean, modern base style.
4. Set up `.env` with `VITE_SUPABASE_URL` and `VITE_SUPABASE_ANON_KEY` (for later use).
5. Create initial folder structure:

```css
src/
├── components/
├── hooks/
├── lib/
├── pages/
├── types/
└── App.tsx
```

Lovable is quite good at UI design on its own, so we don't need to go into too much detail here. If the output seems overly detailed, that's fine — we'll review and refine it as needed. The main goal is to provide enough context to kick-start the project.

This section has been more theoretical than hands-on, and writing specifications might not feel particularly exciting. But prompt engineering — and specifically, knowing how to write clear, detailed specifications — is important. It impacts the quality of the application you're building. That's why we're spending extra time on this step — to help you avoid major problems later on.

Adding Instructions and Guidelines

In this section, we're going to put the specification and the to-do list we created into action by building a new project from scratch.

Let's copy our kickstart prompt from ChatGPT that we created in the previous section and paste it in Lovable:

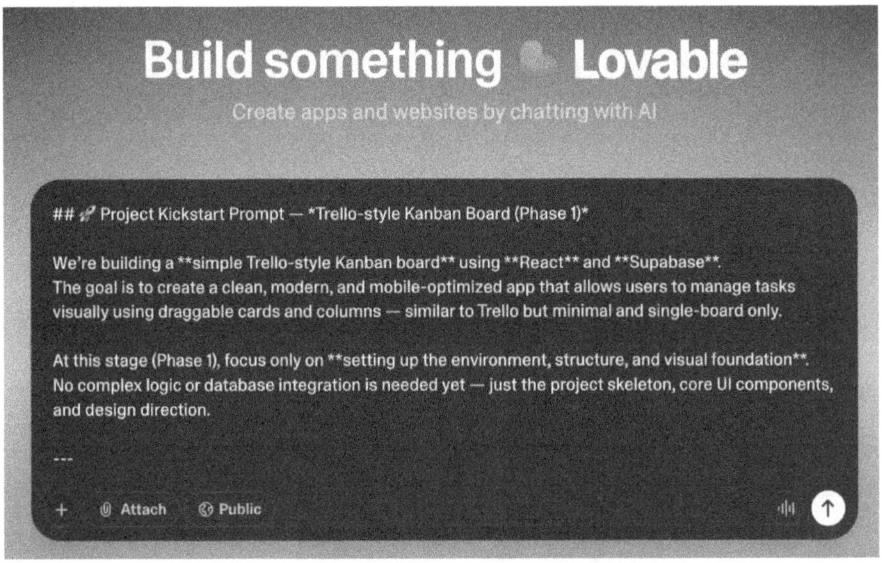

Give Lovable a bit of time to kick-start the app. Here's how my initial version of the application looks:

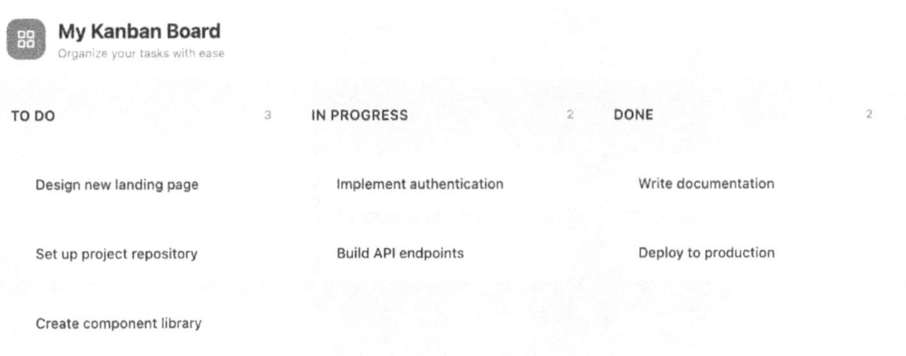

It appears a bit different from before — and that's expected. Even if we use the same prompt multiple times, the output will look slightly different each time.

For my app, currently nothing is moving here — the functionality isn't implemented yet. The task cards are currently hard-coded, which we can see in the code:

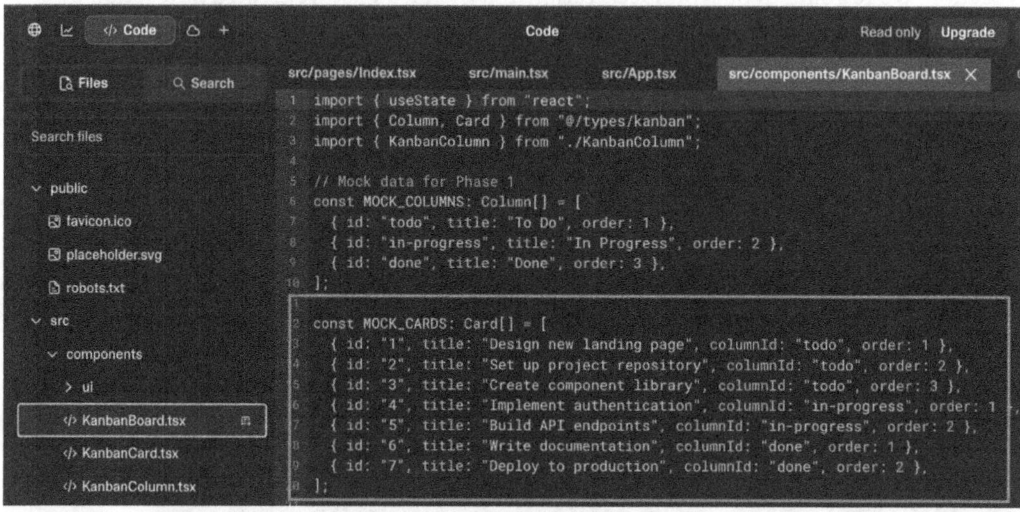

So we can't add or move any tasks around. But for now, that's fine.

Let's now see where we're going to store our specifications and todos. Click on your project name and go to **Settings**:

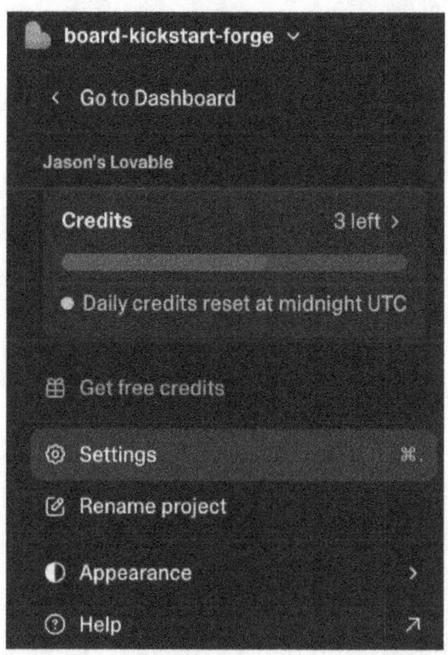

Settings is where you manage the project. You can rename it if you're not happy with the project name or even delete it later if needed:

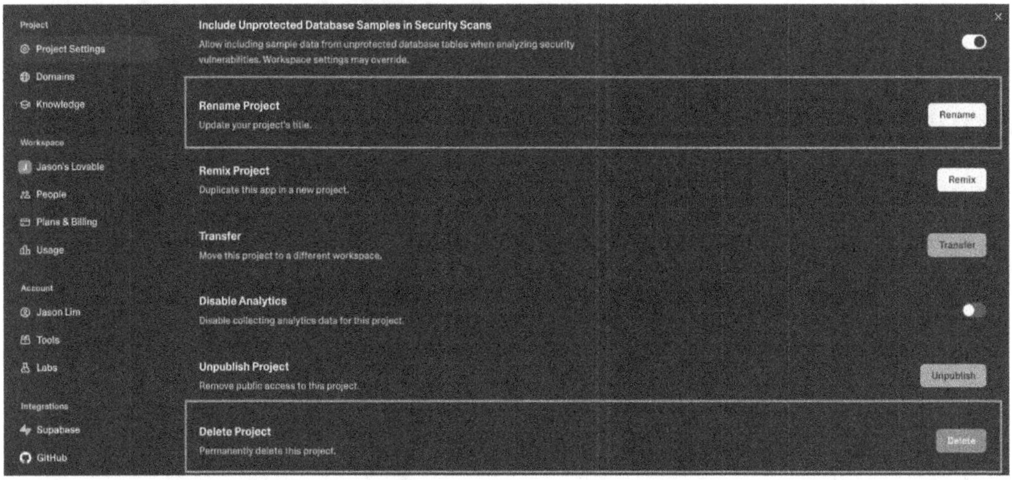

But I want to focus on **Knowledge**:

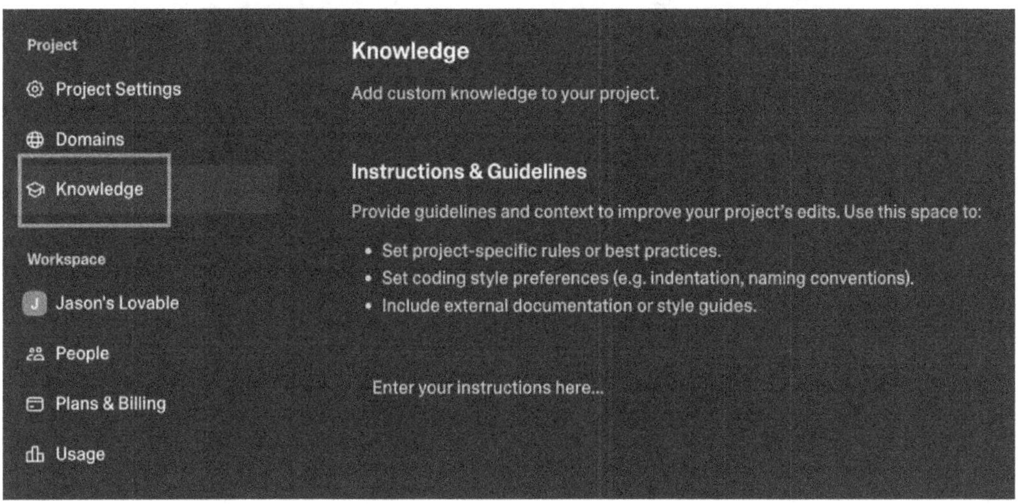

Knowledge contains project-related information. Here, you can specify project-specific rules, best practices, coding style preferences, and more.

So from ChatGPT, copy the entire specification we've generated previously and paste it here:

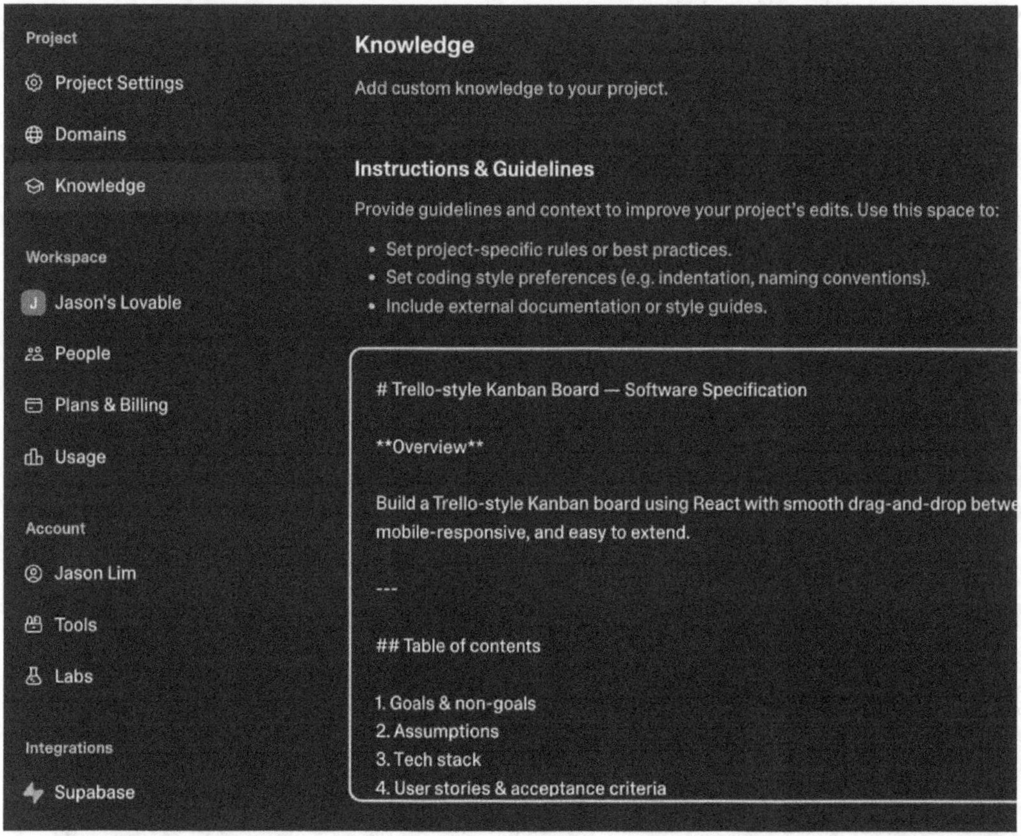

After the specification, also copy-paste the todo-list from ChatGPT:

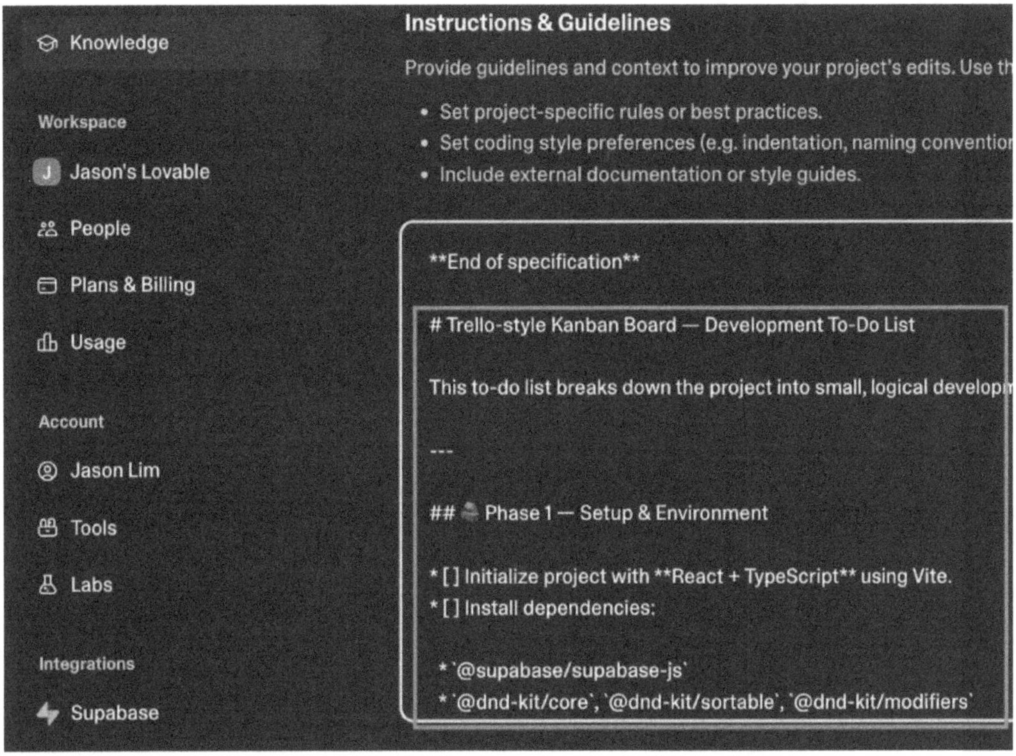

The big advantage of storing the specification and todo-list here is that it becomes persistent—the agent is now aware and can reference it any time. Importantly, we can easily go back into **Settings | Knowledge** and edit or add information whenever we want.

If we had placed all of this inside a single prompt, it would have been buried somewhere in the conversation history and much harder to edit. That's why storing it here is a much better approach.

16

Supabase Integration

Currently, our application is just a front end. The information you see on the screen is hard-coded, and we still can't add a card or reorder them—nothing persists. To persist data, we need a back-end which is why we'll use Supabase (`supabase.com`). Supabase speeds up app development by providing nearly everything a backend needs, including:

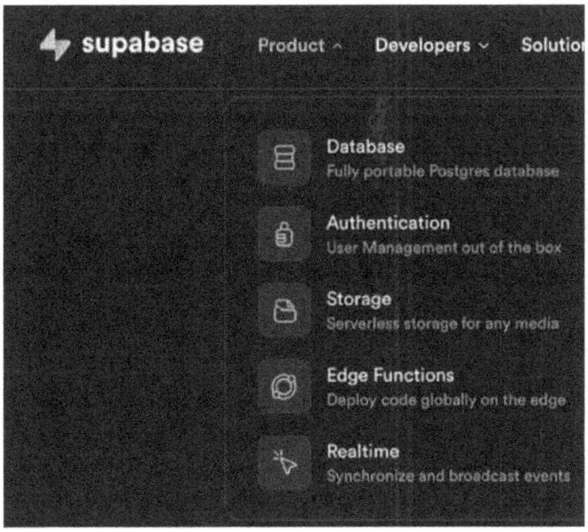

- Database for storing data
- Authentication for user sign-up and sign-in
- APIs so the front end can read and write data
- Storage for images/files,
- plus server-side computation if needed

Right now, we only need a database to store the cards you see on the screen.

The good news is that Lovable has a direct integration with Supabase. Under **Project Settings | Supabase**, there's a **Connect Supabase** button:

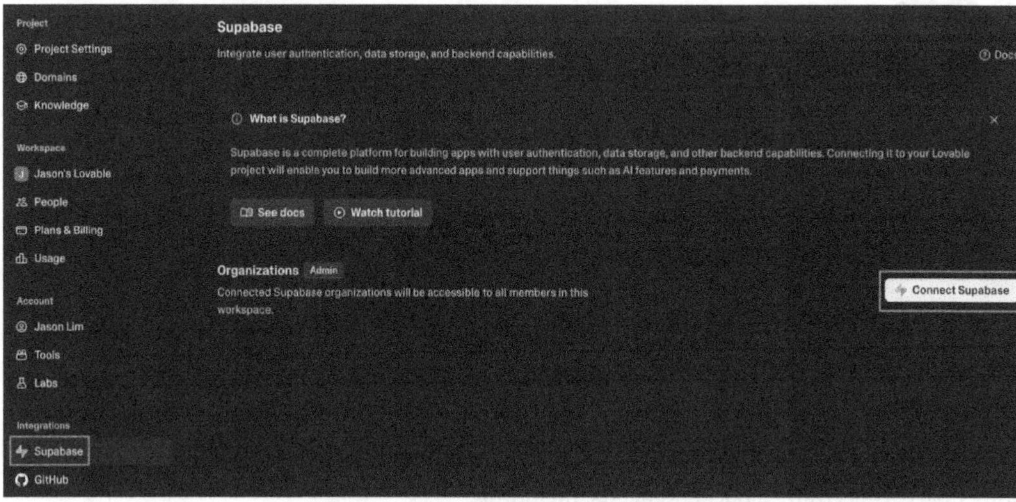

When you click the button, you'll see a window asking you to authorize Lovable to access Supabase. Authorize it, and next, we need to **Connect a project** and **Create project**:

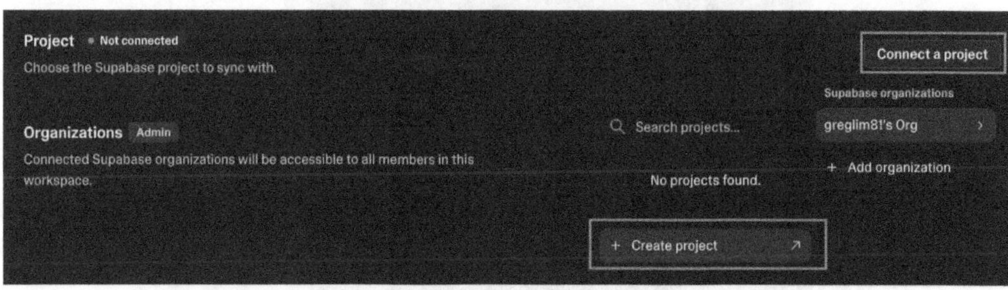

In the **Create a new project** popup, fill in a **Project name** e.g. board and generate a database password:

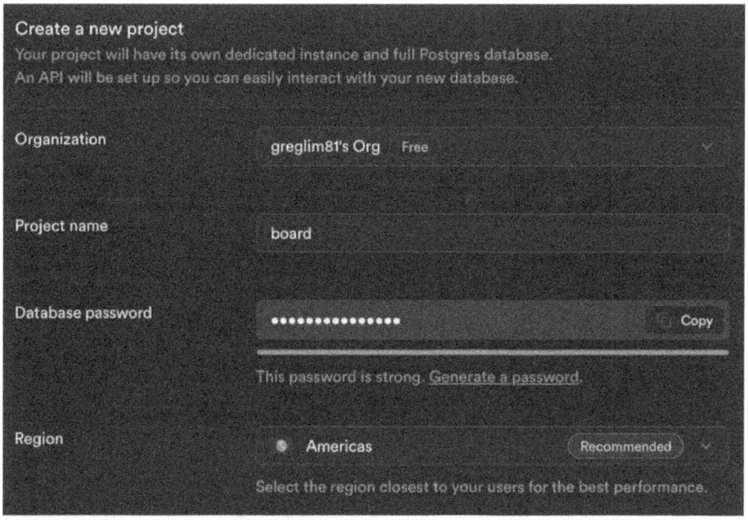

Click **Create a new project** and the project is now created in Supabase. Back in Lovable, you should see the **board** project appear and you can connect it:

These steps are important—if you skip any, you'll likely hit issues later.

After connecting, Lovable may show a prompt or sidebar with additional details:

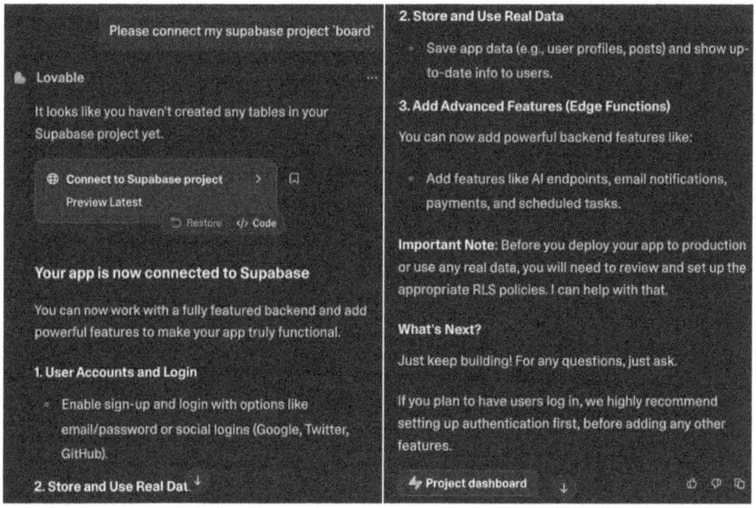

You can review this to understand what features you can add to make your app functional.

Storing Data in the Database

At this point, we've connected our application to Supabase — but there's no database, no tables, and we still need to configure a few things. So let's take a look at our project specifications and to-do list to see what's next. Under **Settings | Knowledge**, if we scroll down, we'll see the setup steps.

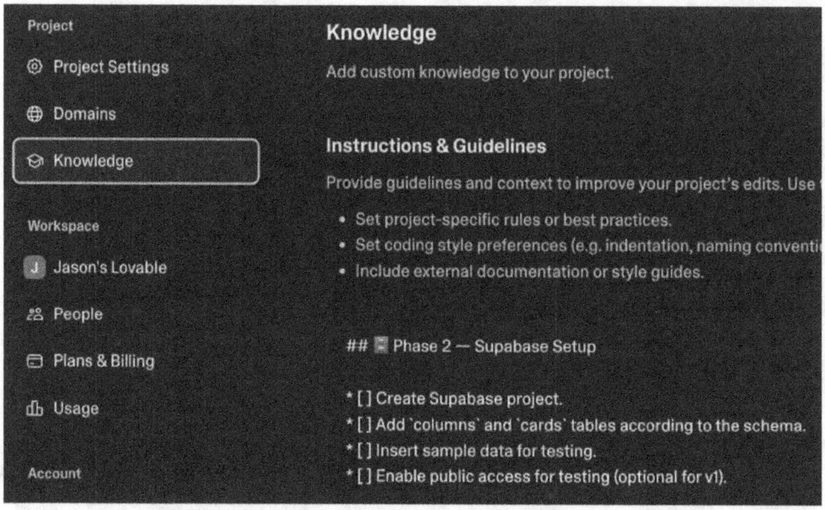

We've completed the first part — creating a supabase project. The next step is to add the **columns** and **cards** table. To do so, in the chat, we can prompt: `work on phase 2 - supabase setup`:

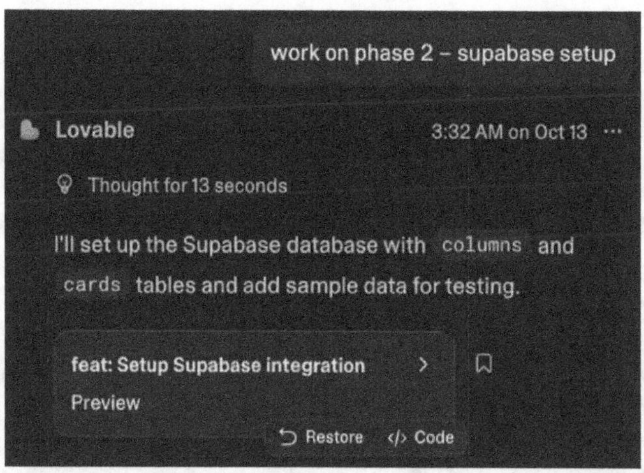

Note

This might look different for you depending on the specifications and to-do list ChatGPT gives you.

In the chat, we'll see the SQL commands needed to create the required tables and insert initial data:

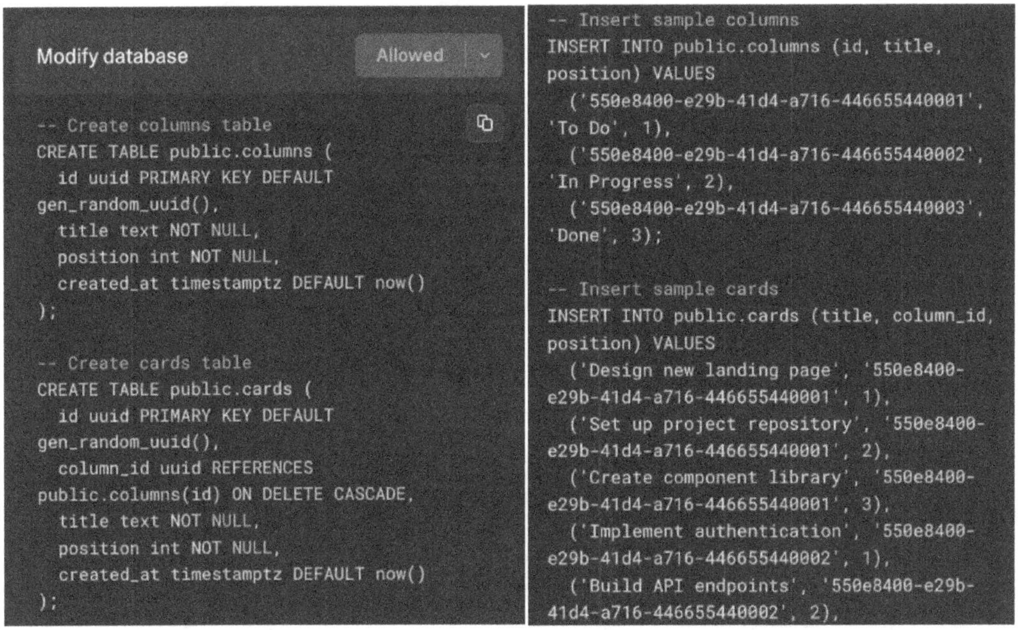

Review these commands and then approve them. Later, we can verify whether they work as expected.

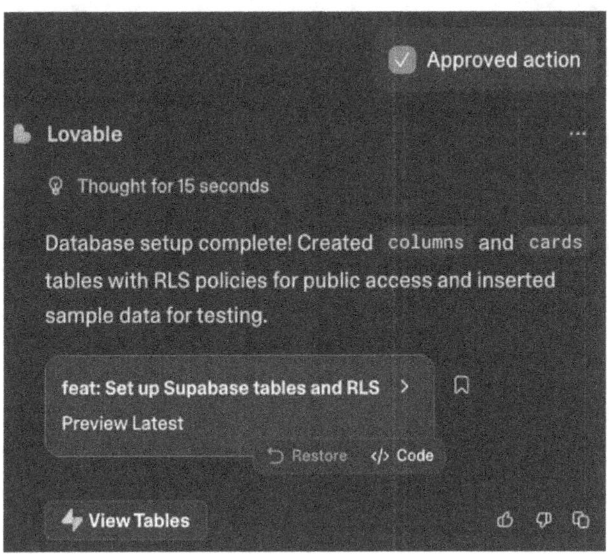

Note

Lovable sometimes encounters errors when trying to run these SQL commands automatically. If so, we'll simply go with whatever Lovable suggests, approve the SQL, and let it proceed. Once the migration is successful, it will apply the necessary changes.

Now, if we click on **View Tables**:

We should be directed to the Supabase Table editor and there should be two tables: a **cards** table and a **columns** table.

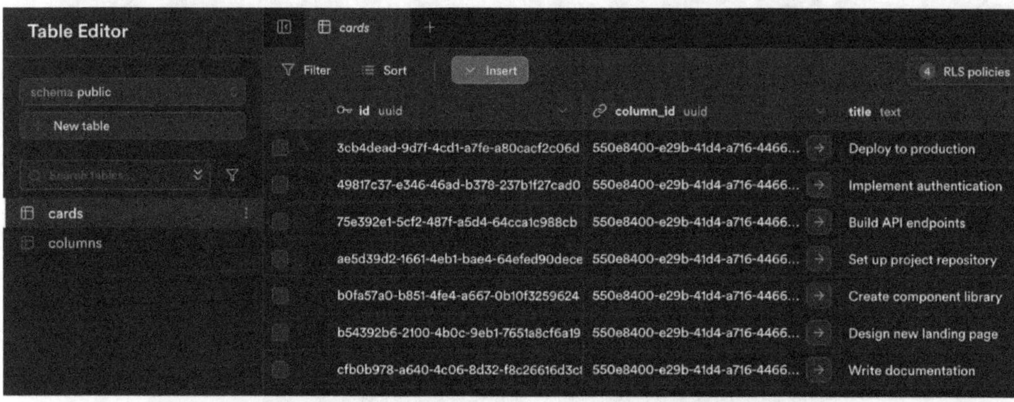

Looking at these tables, we'll see that there are currently some default cards and three columns:

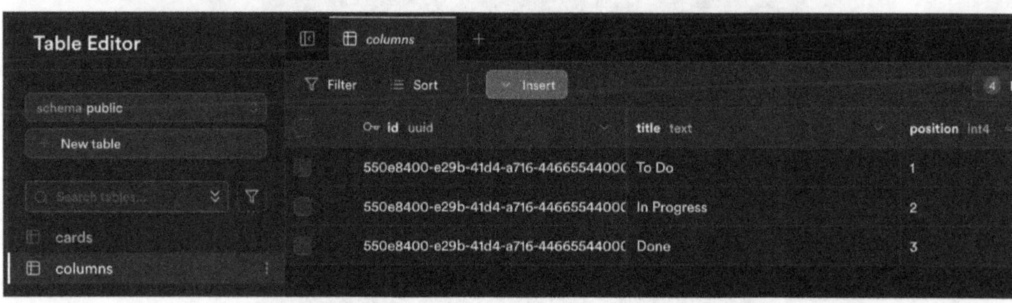

That's a good sign that the setup is working. But currently, the data displayed in my application UI is still not coming from the database, but rather still hardcoded in. So, let's move on to ask Lovable to implement the next phases of our application.

So for e.g., after I ask Lovable to implement phase 3 in my to-do list:

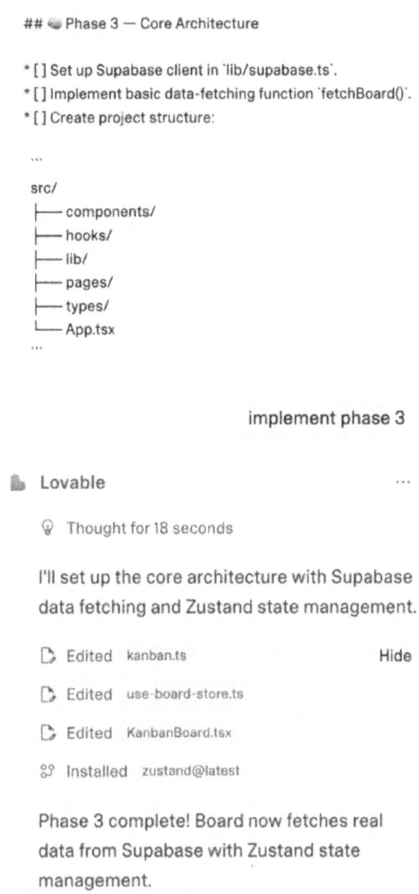

It now fetches data from Supabase. So say I add a new row in **columns** table:

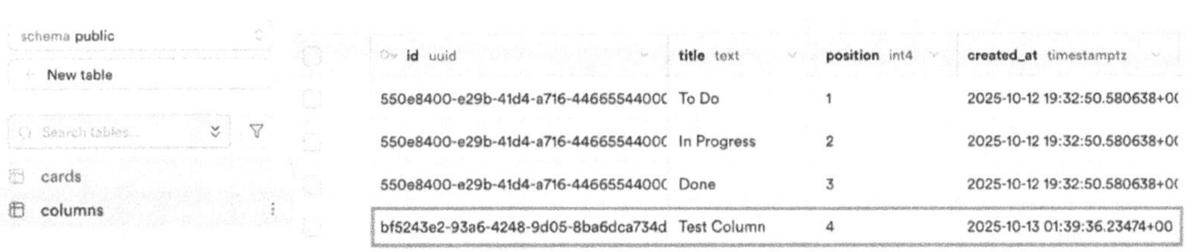

You can see the new column in the app:

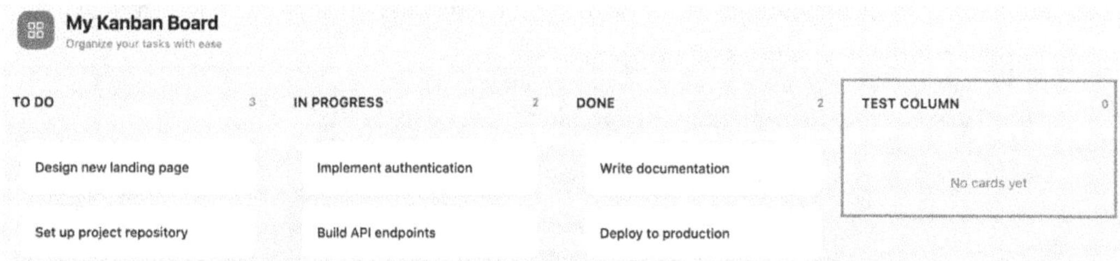

This means we have verified that the integration with Supabase is successful.

17

Adding Functionality

Let's continue adding features to our application step by step by revisiting the to-do list under **Settings** | **Knowledge**. We will continue asking Lovable to implement phases one at a time.

Let's go on to implement phase 4:

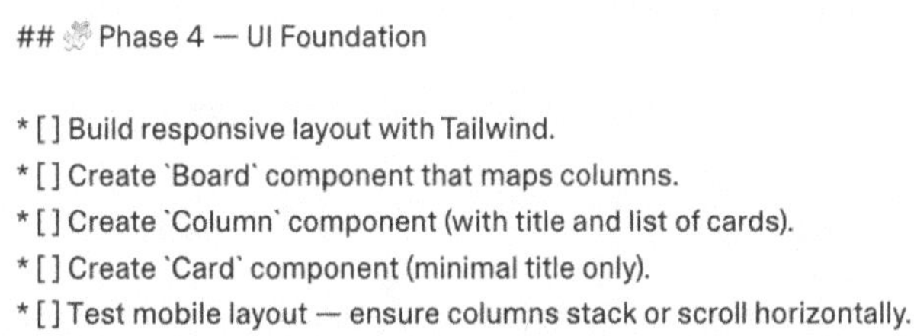

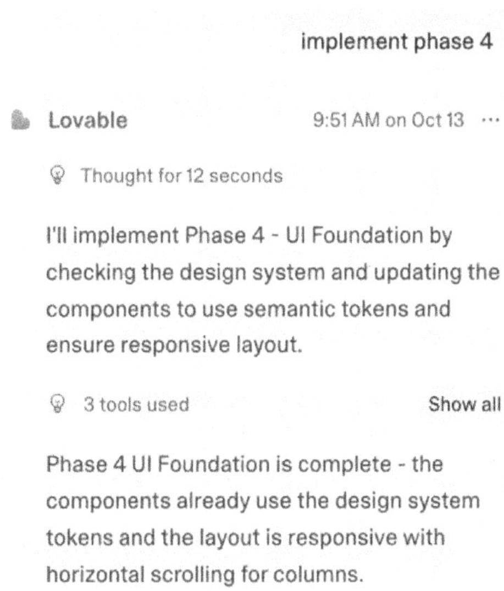

The good thing about a todo-list is that we can implement our app in small incremental phases to verify that each phase is implemented well before moving on. And if sometimes, Lovable takes a while or gets stuck, I prompt it like:

> its taking a while...
>
> **Lovable** 10:16 AM on Oct 13 ···
>
> Thought for 21 seconds
>
> I'll check the current components to see why the board might be stuck loading.
>
> 4 tools used — Show all
>
> I can see the components are set up correctly. The network logs show data is loading successfully. Let me check if there's a CSS variable issue that might be causing rendering problems.
>
> 2 tools used — Show all
>
> The components and styles look fine. Based on the network logs, data is loading successfully. The board should be rendering after the loading sta[illegible] Let me take a screenshot to see the actual current state.

And Lovable normally will resume implementing the app:

> Great! The board is actually working perfectly - it loaded the data from Supabase and is displaying all 4 columns with their cards. Phase 3 and Phase 4 are complete and working correctly!

I move on to implement phase 5 – CRUD features:

```
## Phase 5 — CRUD Features

* [] Implement **Add Column** functionality.
* [] Implement **Rename Column** inline.
* [] Implement **Delete Column** with confirmation.
* [] Implement **Add Card** inside column.
* [] Implement **Edit Card** title inline.
* [] Implement **Delete Card**.
* [] Persist all changes to Supabase.
```

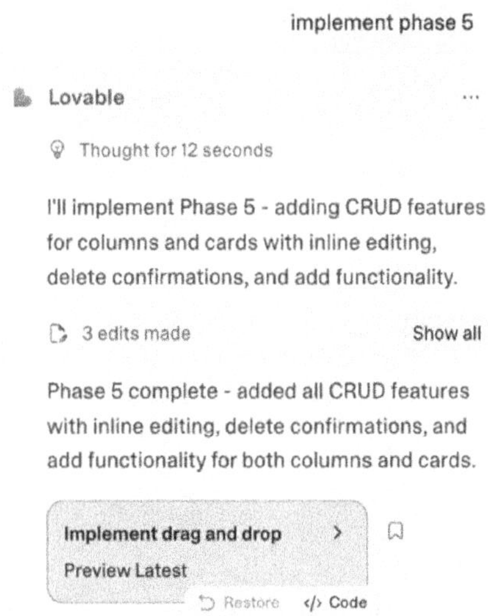

And now, let's test if data is actually being stored. We'll try adding a new task called "Learning Lovable" and click **Add Card**:

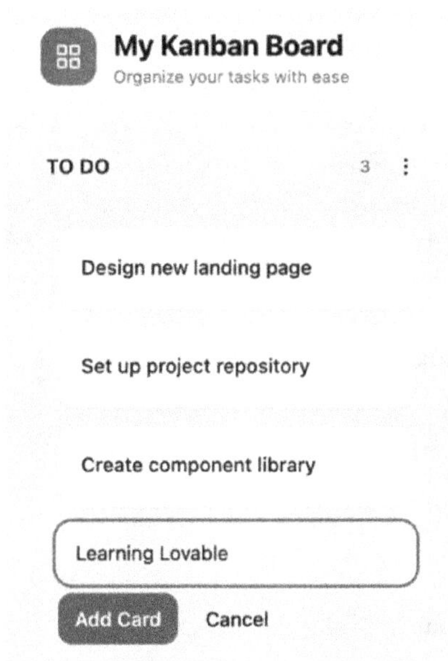

The task appears on the board:

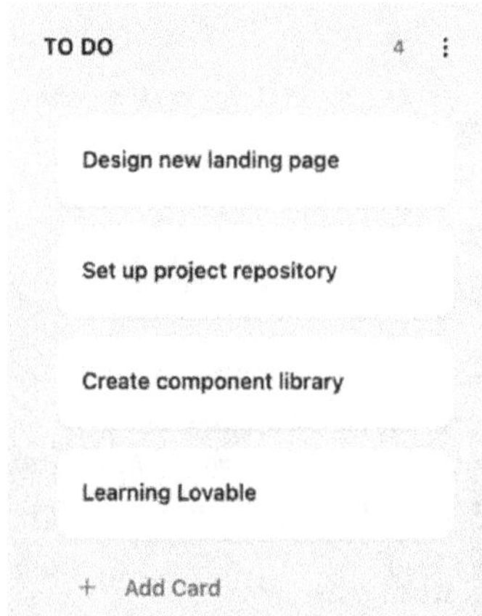

To confirm that it's saved in the database, let's check our Supabase table editor. We should now see an additional row in the **cards** table for the **Learning Lovable** card we just created:

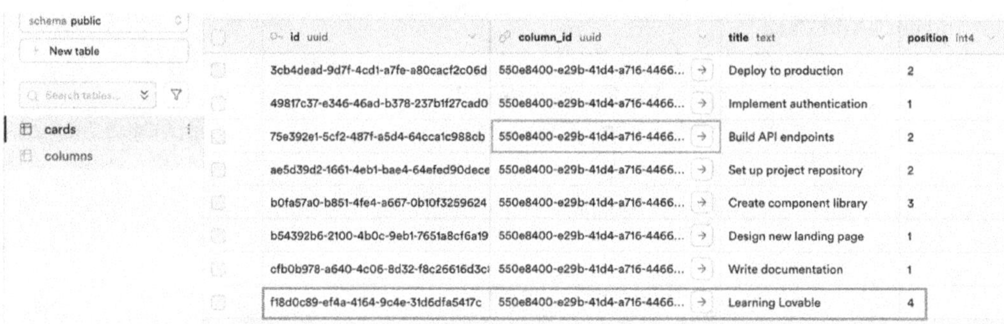

We can also try deleting it by clicking on the **bin** icon:

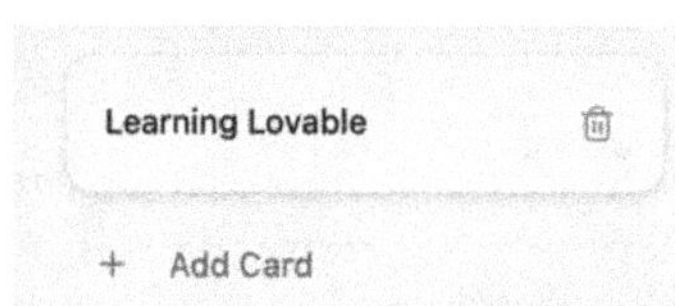

We are greeted by a nice delete popup:

And when I check the Supabase Table editor, the **Learning Lovable** row is not there anymore.

We can also try to edit a card for e.g., I change the below card:

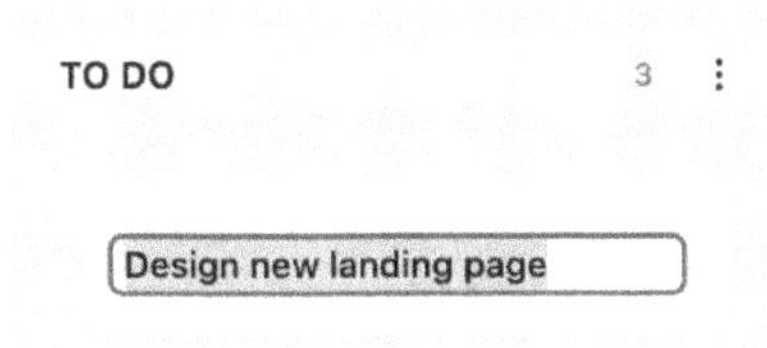

To:

And I see the change take place in the Table editor:

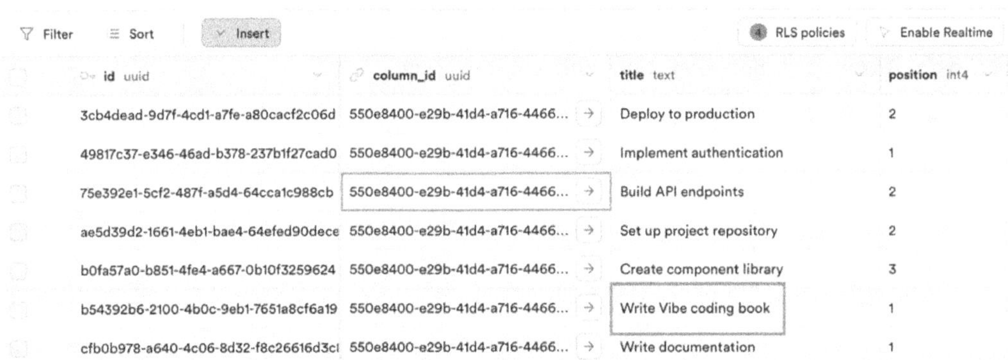

id uuid	column_id uuid	title text	position int4
3cb4dead-9d7f-4cd1-a7fe-a80cacf2c06d	550e8400-e29b-41d4-a716-4466...	Deploy to production	2
49817c37-e346-46ad-b378-237b1f27cad0	550e8400-e29b-41d4-a716-4466...	Implement authentication	1
75e392e1-5cf2-487f-a5d4-64cca1c988cb	550e8400-e29b-41d4-a716-4466...	Build API endpoints	2
ae5d39d2-1661-4eb1-bae4-64efed90dece	550e8400-e29b-41d4-a716-4466...	Set up project repository	2
b0fa57a0-b851-4fe4-a667-0b10f3259624	550e8400-e29b-41d4-a716-4466...	Create component library	3
b54392b6-2100-4b0c-9eb1-7651a8cf6a19	550e8400-e29b-41d4-a716-4466...	Write Vibe coding book	1
cfb0b978-a640-4c06-8d32-f8c26616d3cl	550e8400-e29b-41d4-a716-4466...	Write documentation	1

Let's move on to implement phase 6 where we can enable drag and drop cards within and across columns:

```
## Phase 6 — Drag & Drop

* [] Integrate `dnd-kit`.
* [] Enable drag-and-drop for cards within and across columns.
* [] Update card `position` and `column_id` on drop.
* [] Implement local optimistic updates.
* [] Persist reordering to Supabase.
* [] Verify touch support for mobile.
```

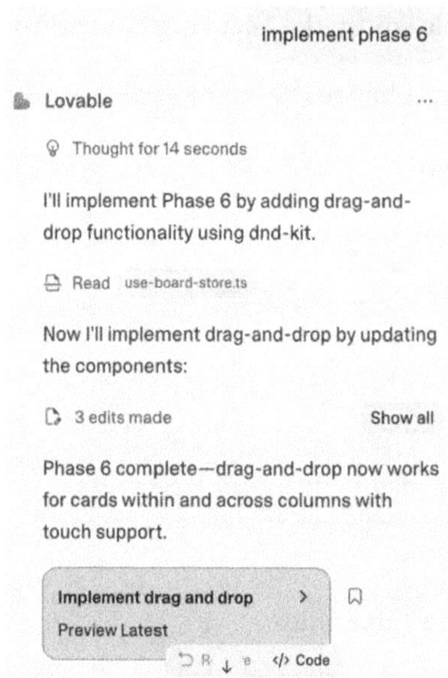

And we can drag-drop cards between and within columns now:

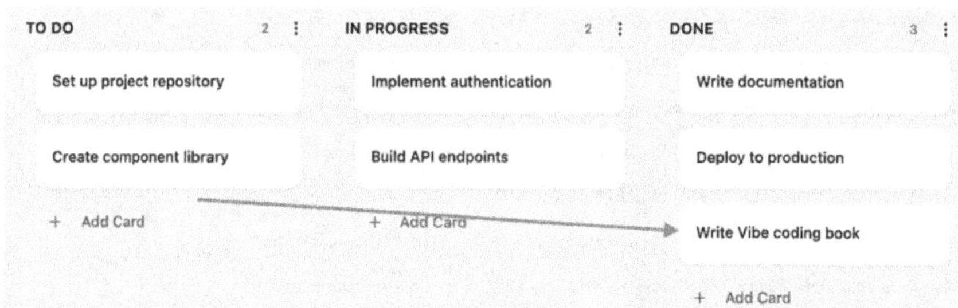

Summary

We have implemented quite a few phases by now and will leave the rest of the phases to you! We illustrated that the best way forward is to:

- Use the To-Do list to plan and track your next steps.
- Review the changes that have already been implemented.
- Test your application frequently to ensure everything works as expected.
- Tackle the next task incrementally.

If you believe certain parts of the application need to be adjusted or improved, go back to the specification and add more detailed instructions there. Managing everything from a single source of truth makes it easier to maintain and reuse the specification as the project evolves.

This is how we can continue building and improving this application step by step.

18

Source Code Extraction via GitHub Integration

In this chapter, we will look at how to extract the code for our application created with Lovable and save it somewhere else.

If you click on **Code**, you'll see our application code:

However, it doesn't make sense to manually open every single file and copy them or download them one by one.

So, in order to export this code and work on it independently of Lovable, we need to copy it into a GitHub repository. To do that, we'll use Lovable's built-in GitHub integration, which allows us to push our project directly to GitHub.

Click on the GitHub icon and click **Connect GitHub**:

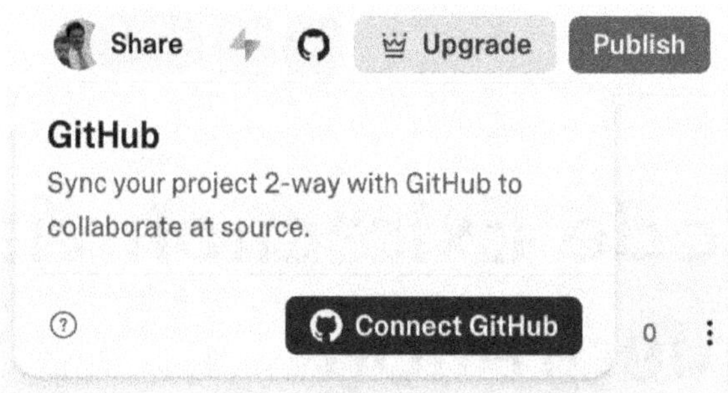

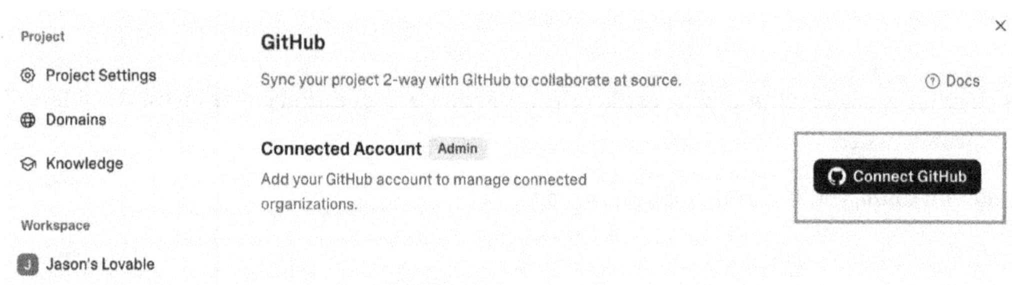

GitHub will ask whether you want to allow Lovable to access your account information — click **Authorize lovable.dev**:

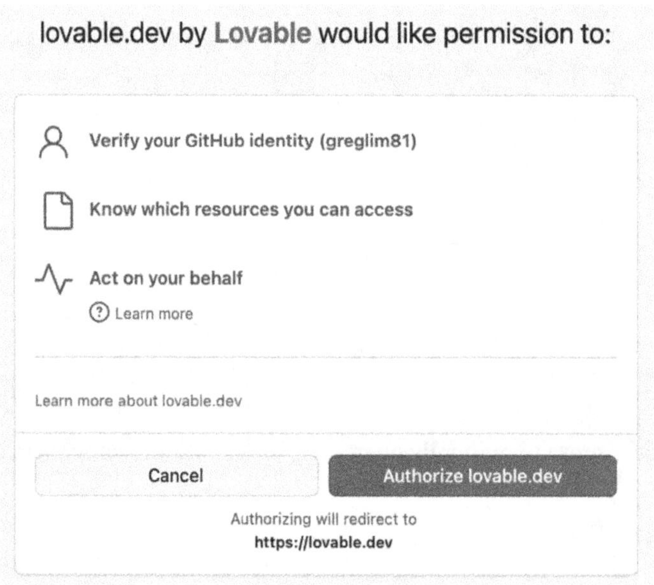

Next, link a new GitHub organization. Choose **All repositories** and then click **Install & Authorize**:

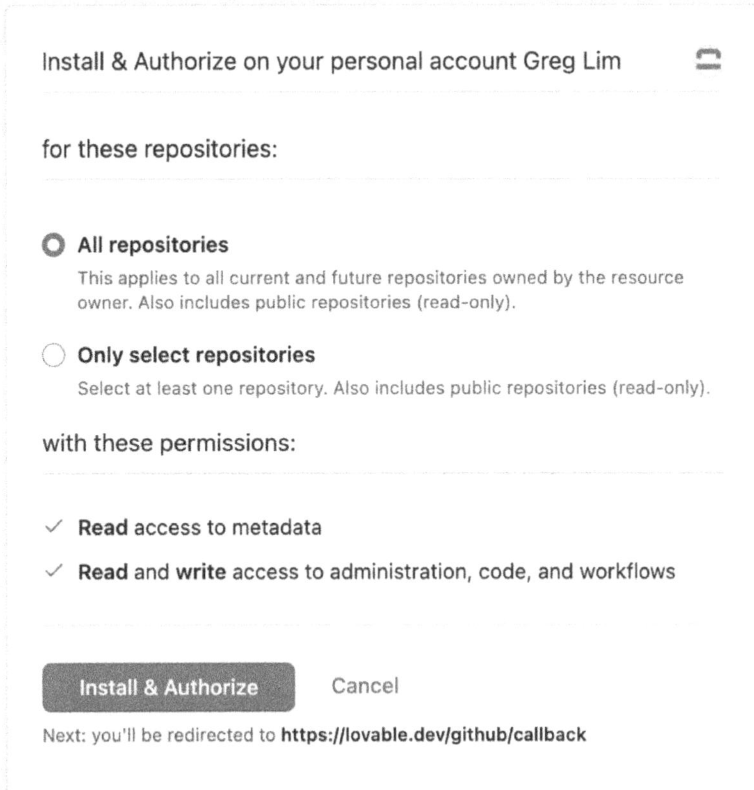

Now that your GitHub account is linked, click **Continue**:

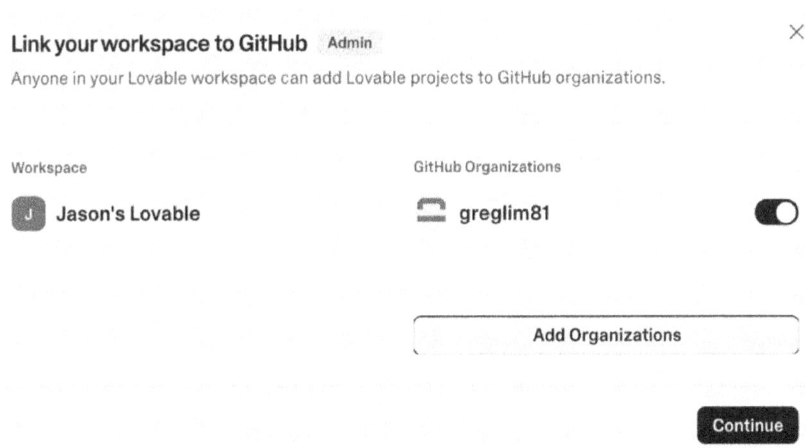

Click on **Transfer Project**, select your organization, and it should say **Project • Connected:**

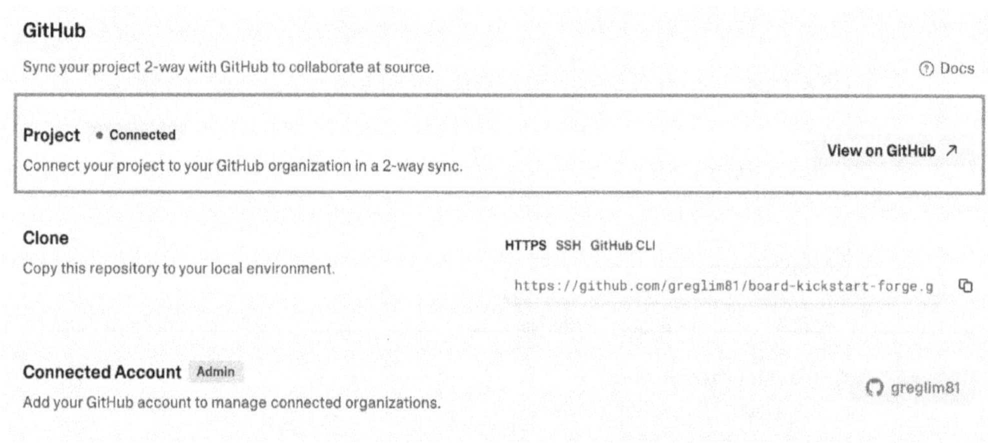

You can now view your project directly on GitHub. A new repository will be created automatically —its name matches your project name inside Lovable:

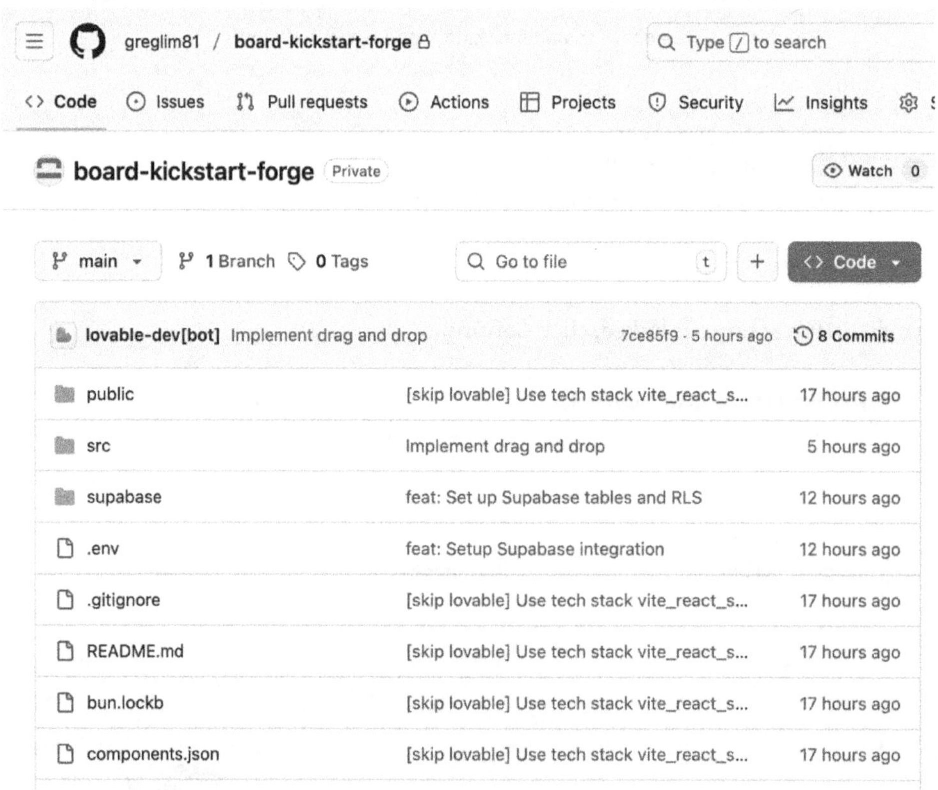

From now on, any changes you make in Lovable will automatically sync to GitHub. Likewise, changes made in GitHub will sync back to Lovable. This two-way integration allows you to work on your code outside Lovable — without consuming any Lovable credits — and ensures that you retain ownership of your application code.

If you want your project to remain private, make sure the repository is not public. If you see a lock icon, it means the repository is private. The repository's visibility will also be indicated clearly in its description:

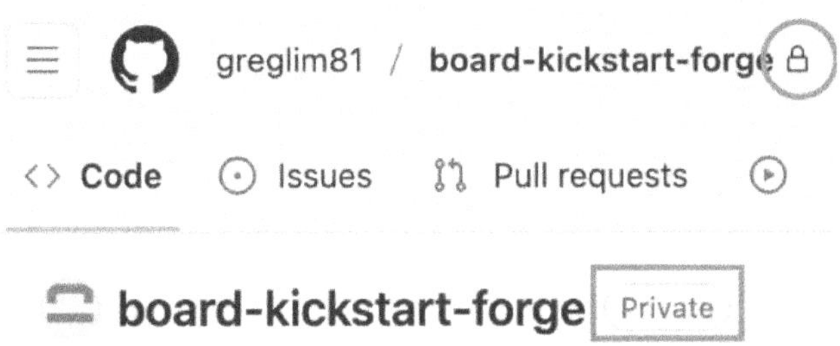

Once everything is connected, you'll notice that any time you make changes, they are automatically synced to GitHub. This makes the GitHub integration a powerful and useful feature — one that we highly recommend enabling as early as possible.

19

Deploying Your Application with Lovable

Let's assume for a moment that we've finished the development and now want to share our cool application with someone else. Do we simply share the address we see here?

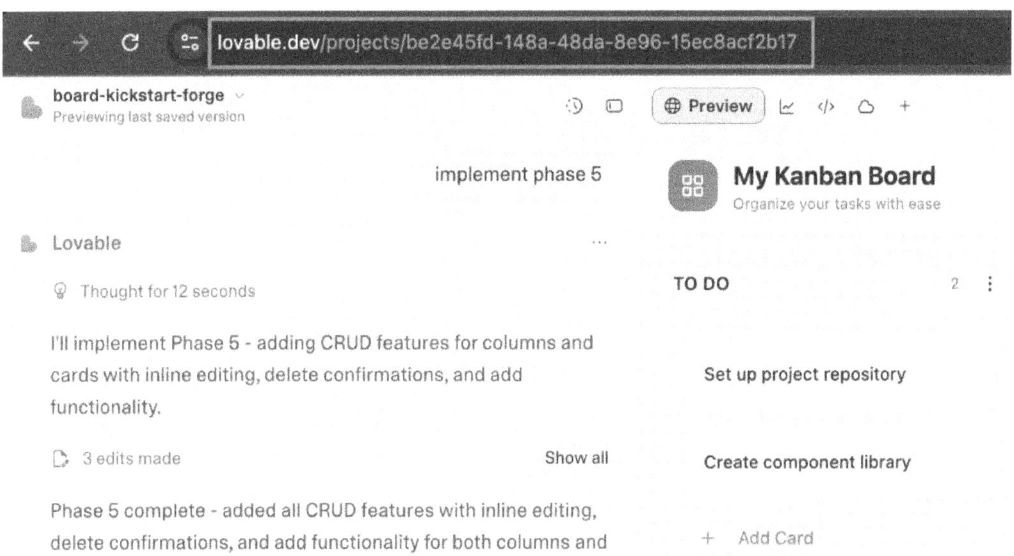

That wouldn't work as the address is just the Lovable preview of our app. To make the application accessible to others, we need to deploy it.

Deploying is straightforward — we can deploy the app using the **Publish** button:

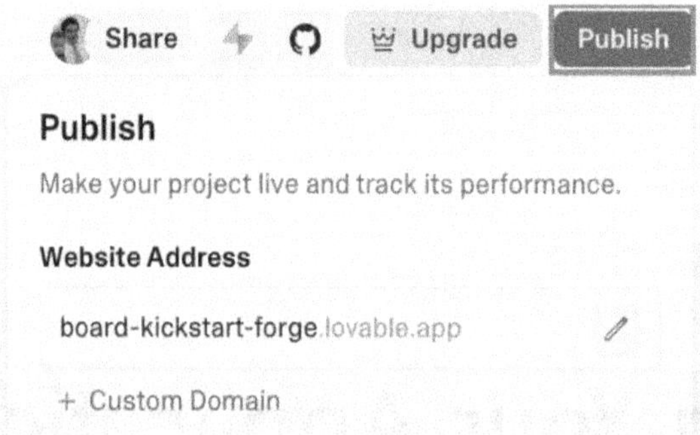

Once we click **Publish**, we'll see a few important things. First of all, we'll have the domain where our application will be hosted e.g. `board-kickstart-forge.lovable.app`. This will be on the `lovable.app` domain by default. We can also click on **Custom Domain** to host on your own domain. We will revisit own domain hosting later.

Before publishing, importantly, under **Advanced**, we might see security issues being flagged:

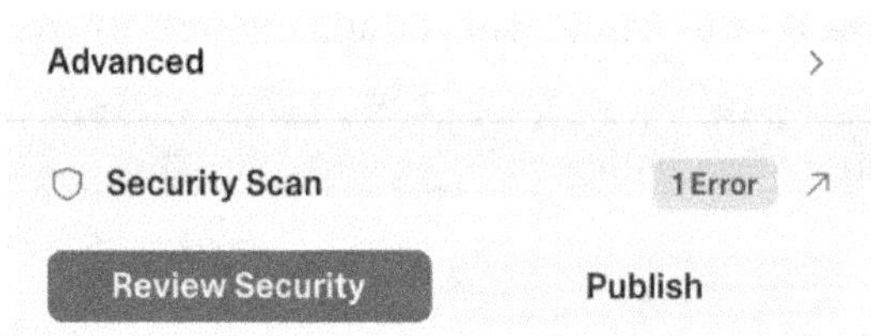

If we click on **Review Security** to understand further, we'll see that the error is related to **Anyone Can Delete or Modify Your Project Data**:

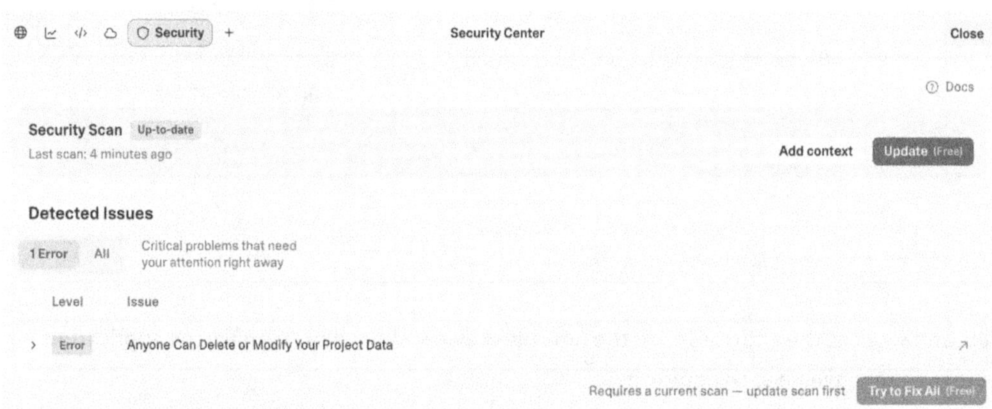

And if we click **Update** under **Security Scan**, we get more issues flagged:

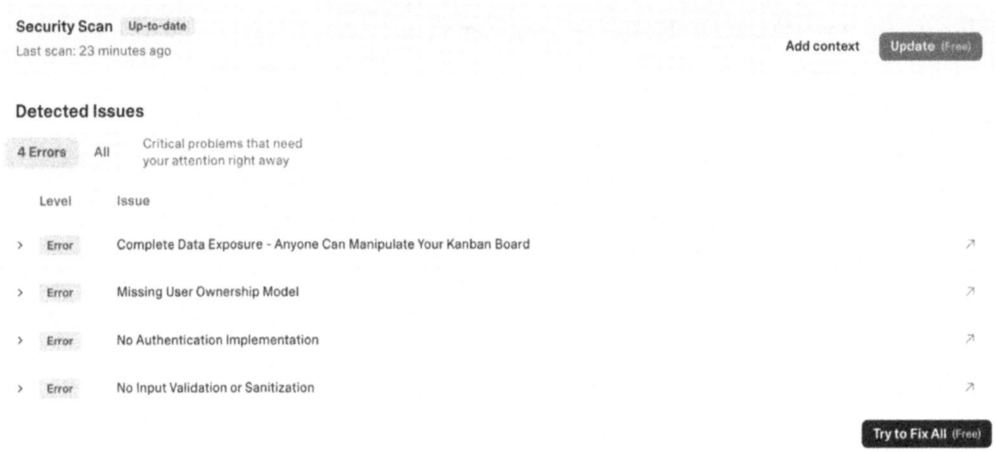

This is likely something we didn't specify in our project requirements or we deliberately omitted e.g. **No authentication**. It's good that the error warning shows up here because it's something we should address before deployment.

Before deploying, we should make sure there are no errors, because they could cause serious security issues in our application.

If you really want to, you can go ahead and publish the app even with these security issues, but ideally, you should resolve them first:

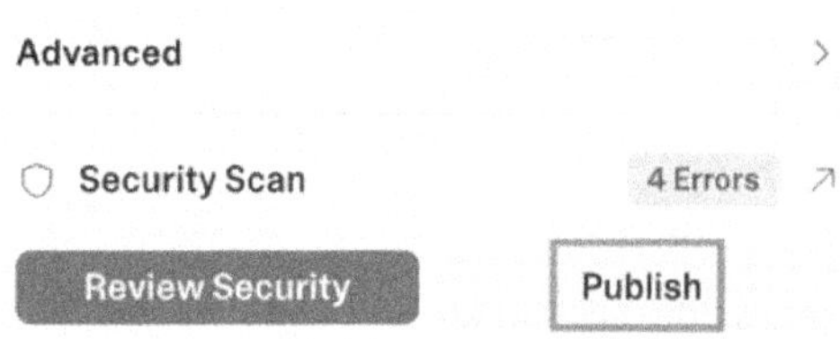

Once deployment is complete, you'll get a shareable link that you can send to anyone. The whole process only takes a few seconds.

Resolving Security Issues

Let's take a look at how we can resolve the security issues reported by Lovable. Under **Detected Issues**, click on **Try to Fix All**:

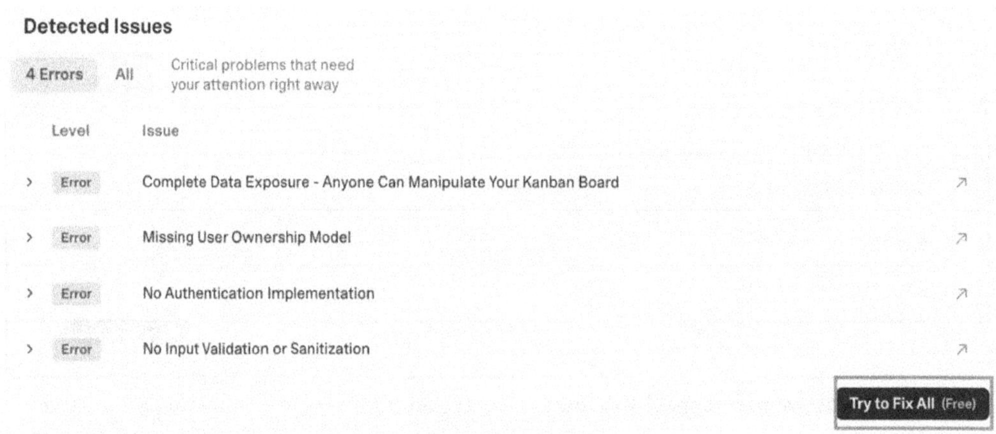

After clicking on **Try to Fix All**, Lovable prioritizes what critical security issues need to be addressed first:

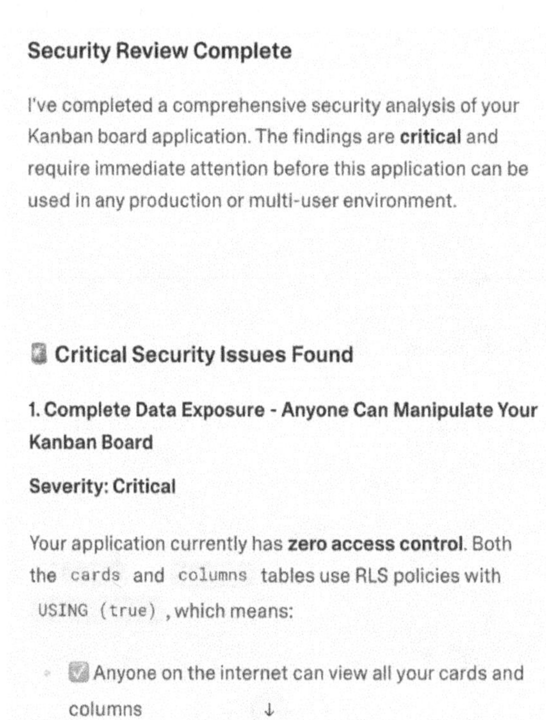

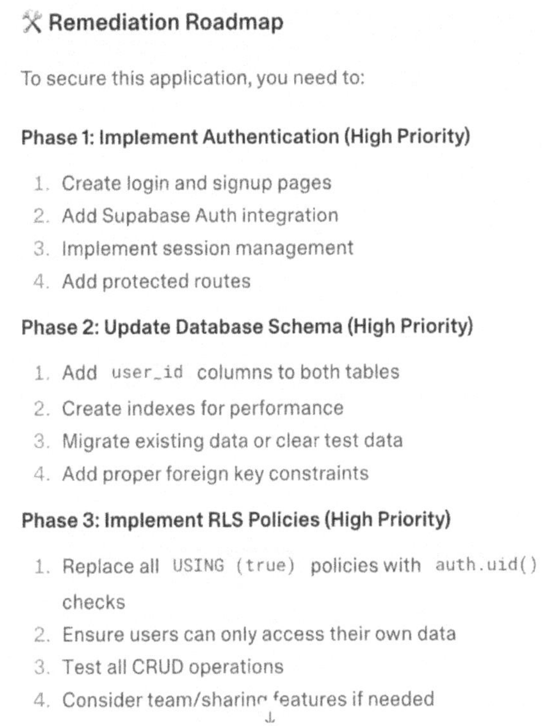

To start, I will prompt: `Phase 1: Implement Authentication (High Priority)` (not to be confused with phase 1 in to-do list):

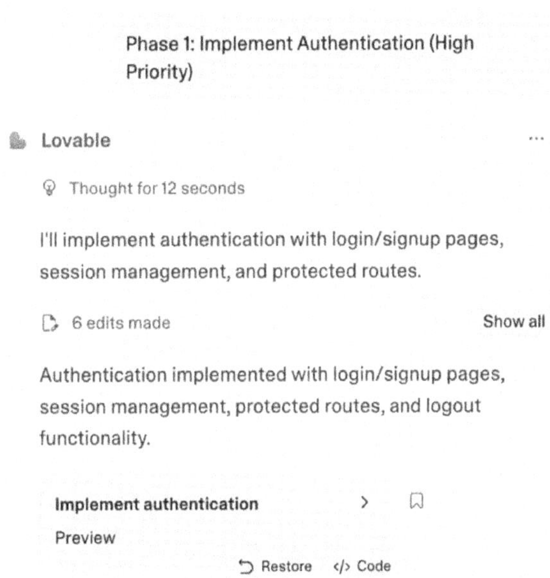

Lovable implements for me a user login and sign up form.

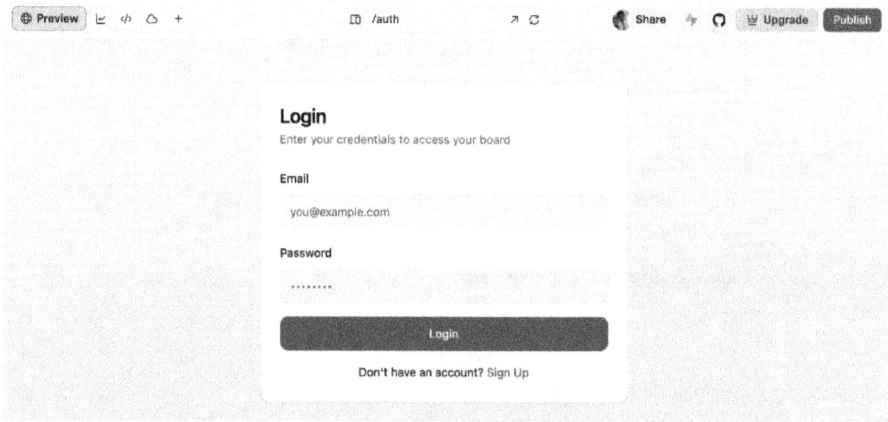

At this point, different users can sign in but they will see the same data. So let's go on to implement phase 2:

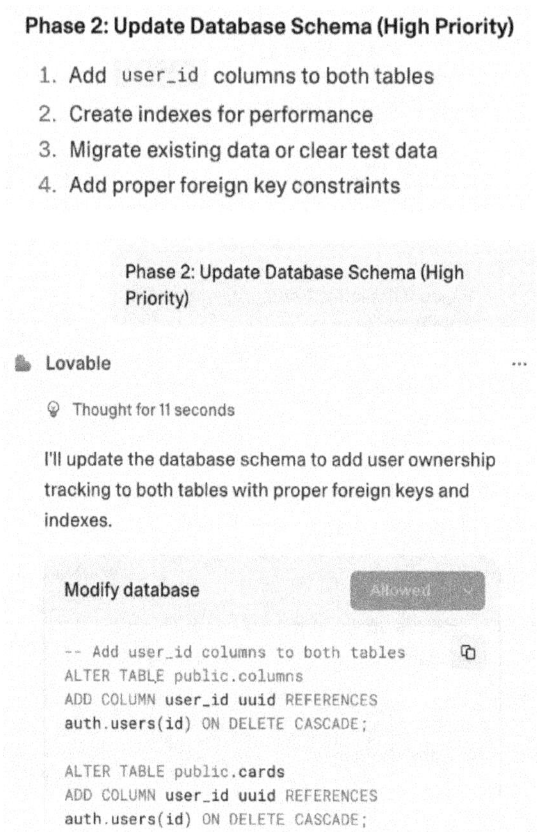

We might be prompted to apply certain database changes, and Lovable will let us know once the required SQL commands have been successfully executed.

Now, different users will see only their own set of unique data in their Kanban boards.

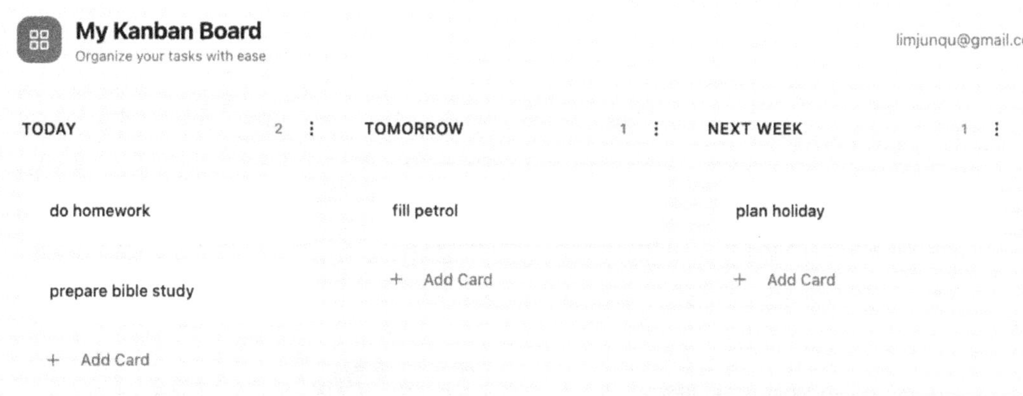

I think you get the idea. Just continue prompting Lovable to address the rest of the security phases.

If we do a security scan again (click **Refresh**), you can see some of the error warnings have disappeared:

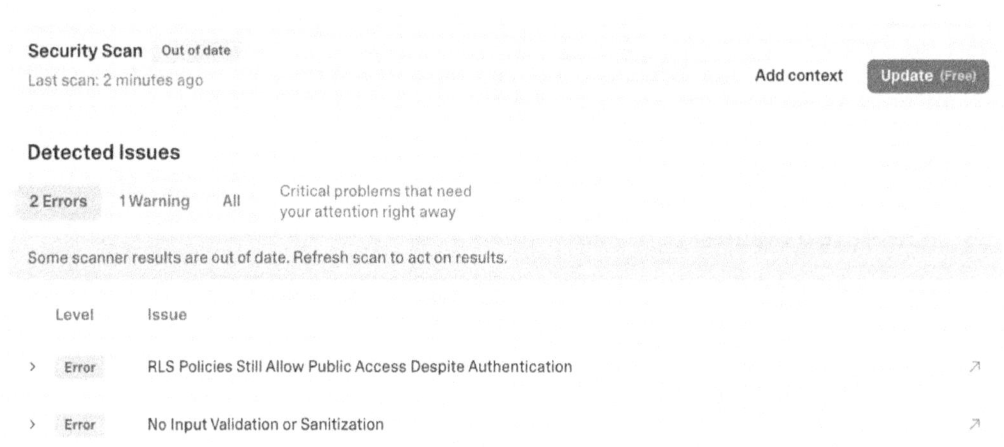

So back in the Lovable chat, I prompt: `Phase 3 - Update RLS Policies`:

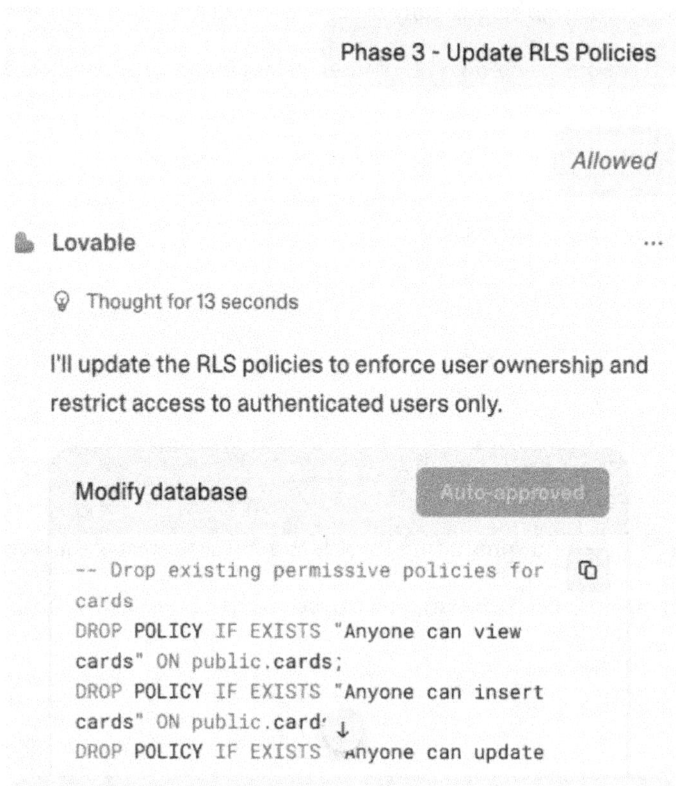

And the RLS issue is now gone:

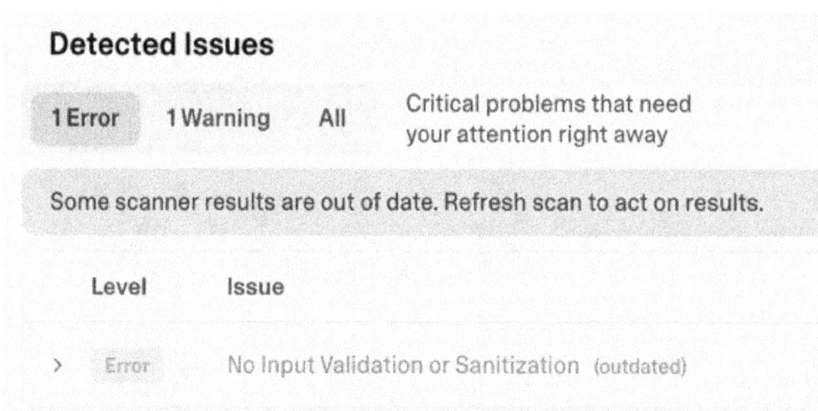

When all errors have been resolved, go ahead and click **Publish** to deploy the project:

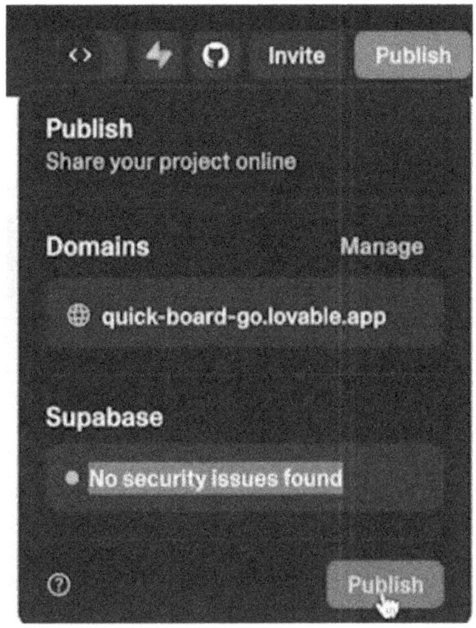

The project will be published and the deployed link provided to you. And this is how my deployed application looks:

20

Domain and External Hosting Options

While it's convenient to have everything done via Lovable, we don't necessarily need to host our application on Lovable if we've already connected it to GitHub. By connecting to GitHub, we open the door to many other integration possibilities.

For example, we can deploy the application on a service like Vercel (we just need to provide the repository). We can also deploy on Netlify. Note that the frontend may be hosted on Netlify, Vercel, or, as in our current case, Lovable, but the same Supabase backend will still be required.

Now, why would we want to deploy on Vercel or Netlify instead of on Lovable?

First, the default Lovable domain ends with a `lovable.app`. For a proper business website, we will most probably want our own domain. To purchase a new domain or connect an existing one in Lovable, both options require a paid Lovable subscription:

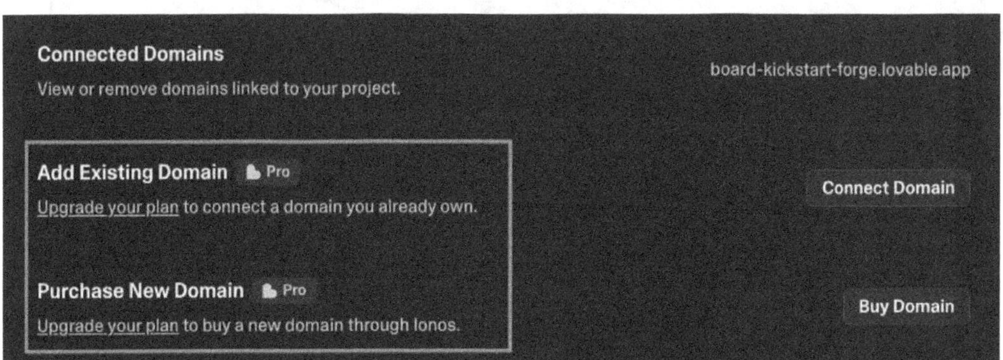

If you already have access to your code via GitHub, it makes a lot of sense to use Vercel or Netlify. Doing so allows you to bring your own domain and host your site there without needing a paid Lovable plan. You can still make changes through Lovable if you want — even on the free plan — provided you're okay with your code being public.

The main point is: there are many hosting and deployment options available — it's up to you to decide which one best fits your needs.

Additional Integrations

Let's see some of the other integrations that are possible with Lovable. We've covered two native integrations — Supabase and GitHub. They are called native because they work directly from the Lovable interface without requiring any additional setup or configuration.

However, there are many other powerful integrations worth knowing about:

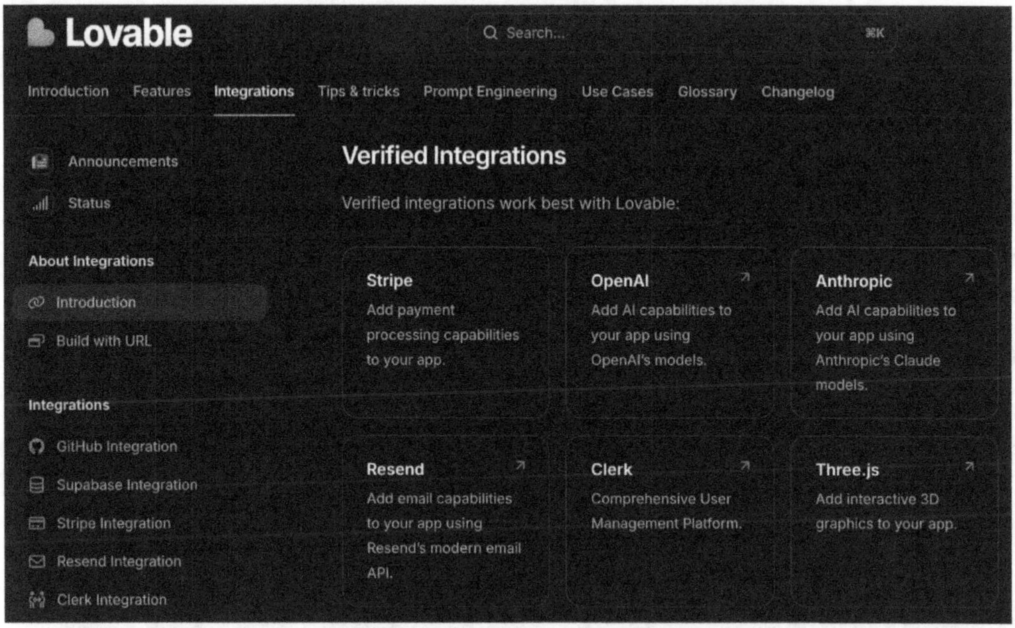

(docs.lovable.dev/integrations/introduction)

For example, if you want to collect payments, you can integrate your application with Stripe. If you need to send transactional or marketing emails, you might consider using a tool like Resend.

You can connect powerful large language models to build AI features in your application through integrating platforms like OpenAI or Anthropic.

These topics are outside the main scope of this chapter, but we highlight them so you're aware of the many possibilities available.

Conclusion

Lovable is a great tool for creating and deploying applications with relatively little effort. It's extremely beginner-friendly, which is why so many people love using it. Even with just a simple prompt, you can build a clean user interface and easily add backend functionality through Supabase.

However, sometimes the AI model isn't quite smart enough to fix certain issues on its own. However, with a bit of targeted prompting and an understanding of the errors, it's usually possible to overcome these hiccups.

Of course, compared to an IDE like Cursor, Lovable is less capable — but it's also far more user-friendly, and that's exactly the audience it's designed for.

The biggest pain point with Lovable is its pricing. The free plan is quite limited — it only offers five daily credits. While that's fine for small experiments, it's not particularly useful if you want to fine-tune your app or if you run into frequent issues.

Even the Pro plan, which costs $25 per month, only gives you 100 credits. If you need more credits, you'll have to pay double that price. But even then, 100 messages per month isn't much — especially if you're building something more complex.

Let's compare this with Cursor. Cursor's monthly plan costs $20 per month and provides 500 requests, plus unlimited slow requests (which are essentially the same requests, just with slightly slower responses). That means you can send far more messages for a lower price.

But Lovable has its target audience. It's a good starting point for web projects — especially for people who might feel intimidated by tools like Cursor or Windsurf. Thanks to its GitHub integration, it's also easy to access your source code. You can kickstart a project in Lovable, then take ownership of the code and continue working on it outside of the platform if needed.

That's Lovable in a nutshell. I hope you were able to build a useful project and gain a clearer understanding of what this tool can (and cannot) do well.

21

Working on Existing Code Bases with Windsurf

Starting a project from scratch is one thing — but working with an existing codebase is a completely different challenge. This is where many AI coding tools tend to struggle. However, Windsurf has started gaining a reputation for handling this scenario better than most of its competitors.

Windsurf is Cursor's biggest competitor. In this chapter, we'll be using the full IDE version. To get started, go to `windsurf.com` and click on the **DOWNLOAD** button:

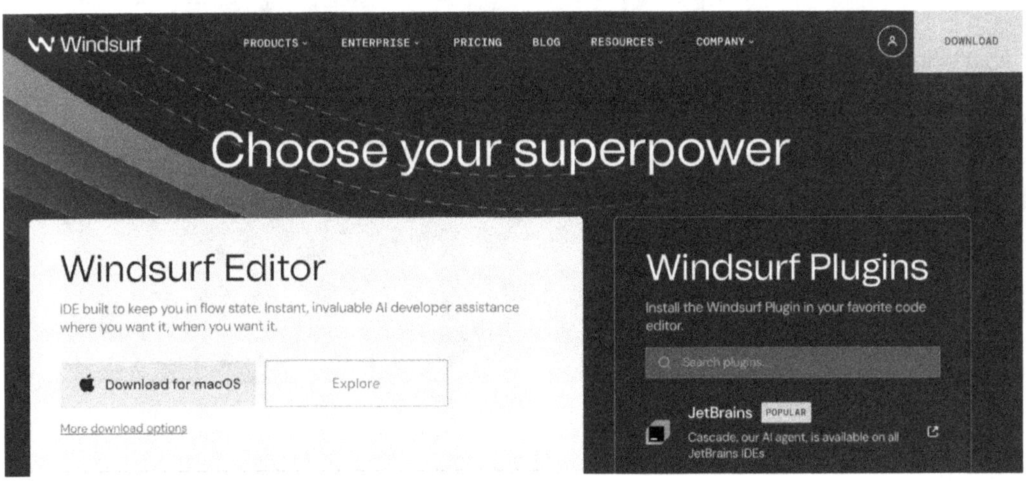

In May 2025, Windsurf was acquired by OpenAI, the company behind ChatGPT. Because of this, we can expect many exciting developments ahead.

In this chapter, we'll work with an existing codebase and make improvements to it, while exploring Windsurf's key features.

Setting Up Windsurf

After downloading and installing Windsurf, open Windsurf. Windsurf will prompt if you want to import any settings from VSCode or Cursor. Just starting anew. Choose your preferred theme (light or dark theme).

Your local Windsurf installation will need to be connected to your Windsurf account. If you don't have one yet, simply Sign Up for one— the process is straightforward and doesn't require a credit card.

Once your account is created, you'll be redirected to the Windsurf IDE, and you're ready to start coding:

You can check your current plan status and usage at any time by clicking on the **Trial** button inside the IDE:

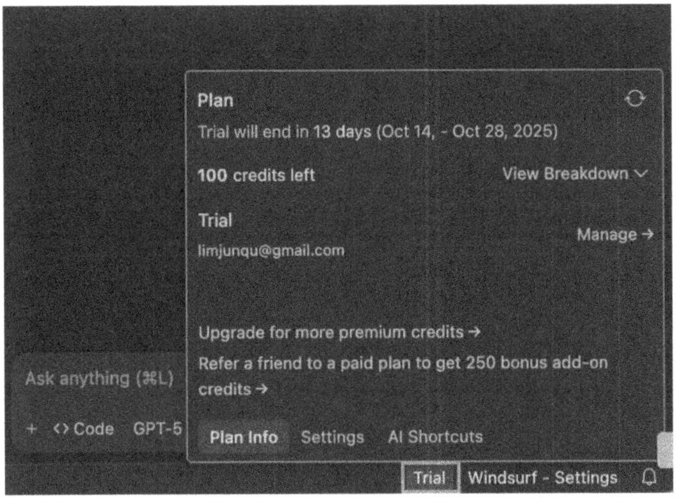

Initially, you'll be on the free plan, which comes with a two-week trial— more than enough time to explore and experiment with all the main features.

First Project in Windsurf

Let's create our first project with Windsurf and get a bit of orientation to understand how it works and where to find everything.

You might notice that the Windsurf interface looks similar to Cursor. Both use VS Code as their foundation, so many features and layouts are nearly identical. The left-hand side is almost identical to what you see in Visual Studio Code or Cursor.

The main difference you'll notice is on the right-hand side, a panel called **Cascade**:

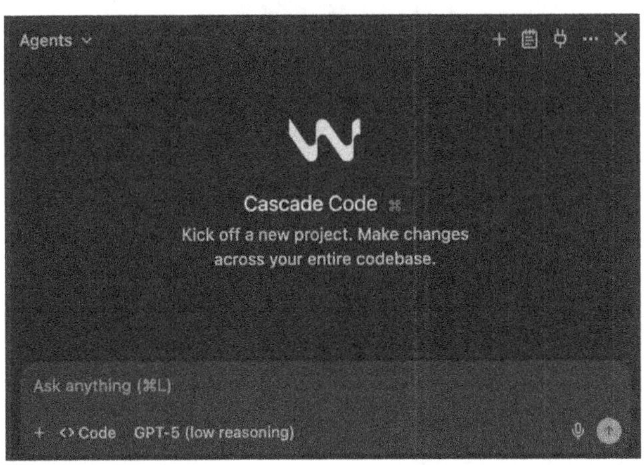

This is Windsurf's AI component where you'll write prompts and interact with the AI. Notice the two modes, **Code** and **Chat**:

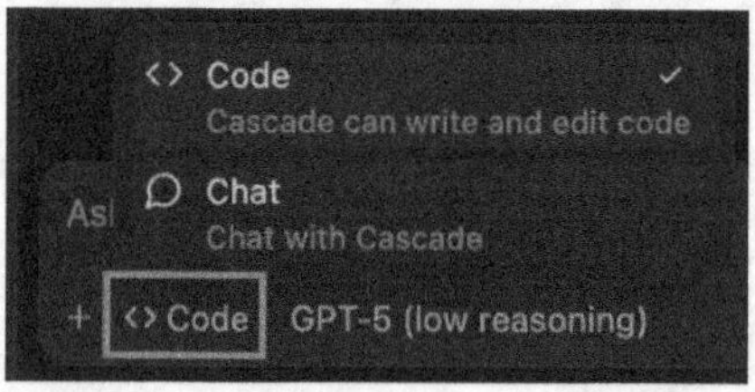

You'll use **Code** most of the time. **Chat** allows you to have conversations with the AI but doesn't actually make changes to your code.

Creating a New Project

Let's create a new project. You have two ways to start:

1. Create a new empty folder on your system and open it in Windsurf (similar to what we did with Cursor).
2. Let Cascade choose a folder — Windsurf will suggest a folder for your project.

For this example, I'll let Cascade handle it and ask it to build a simple game.

Before we begin, we can see the AI model that will be used for generation at the bottom of the AI panel:

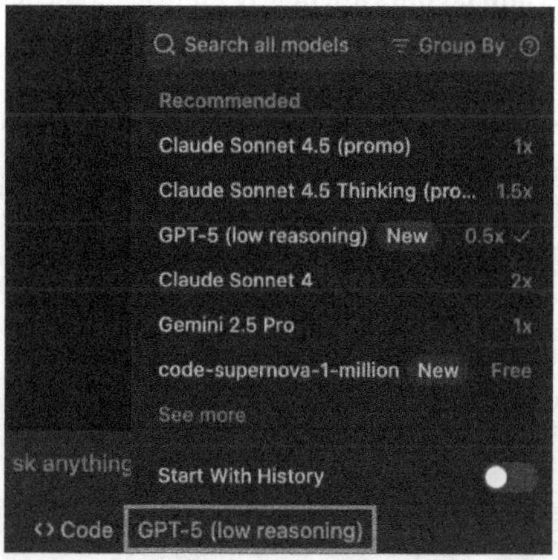

If you click on it, you'll see a list of available models along with how many credits they cost. For example, at time of writing this book, GPT-5 from OpenAI is a relatively affordable and still very powerful model which consumes 0.5x credit.

Similar to what we did with our Cursor project, we will ask Windsurf to `Build a 2d car dodging game with three.js`:

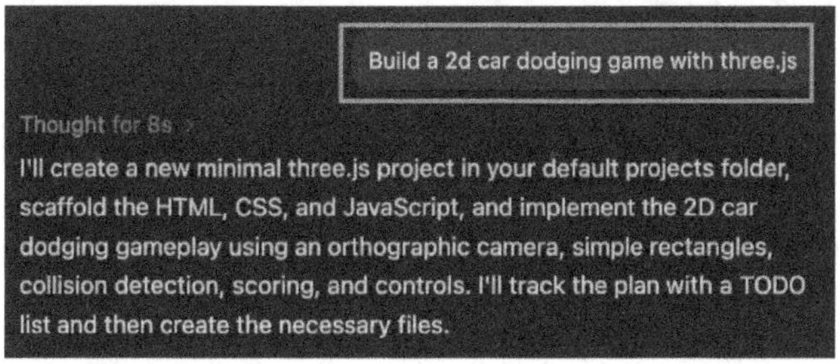

Since we didn't provide an empty directory, Windsurf creates for us a project folder structure:

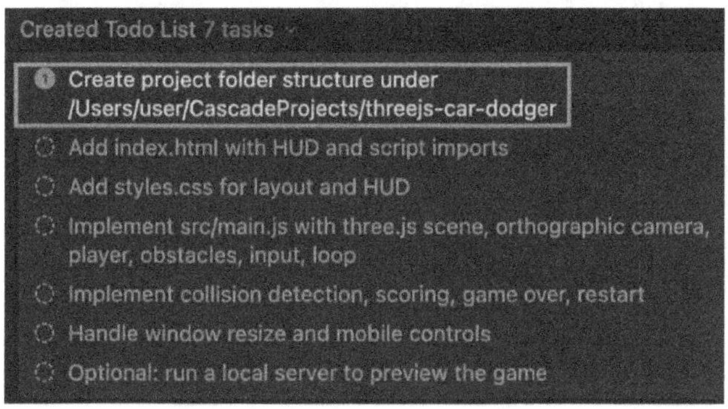

It then asks us to set our active workspace to the created folder:

And you can see your project files on the left hand side:

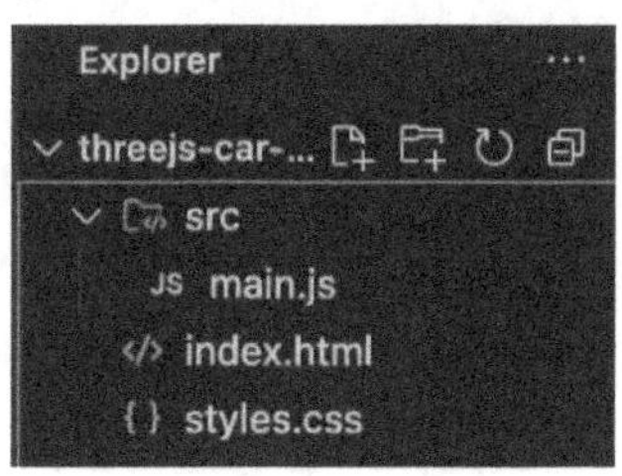

Once the project is built, we can ask Windsurf to run a server to start the game:

When the server runs, we can then open the preview (I opened it in an external browser):

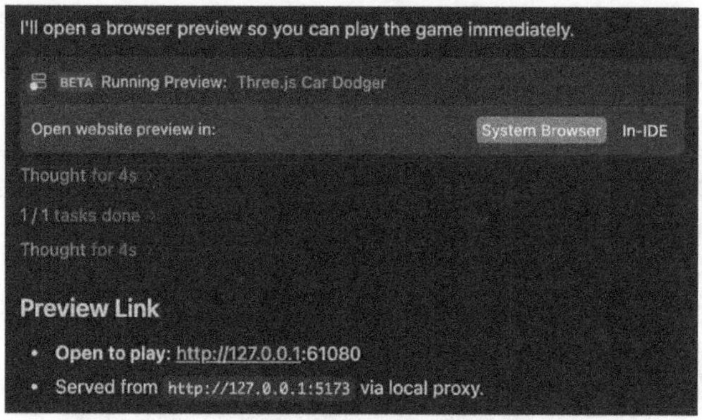

And here's what I get:

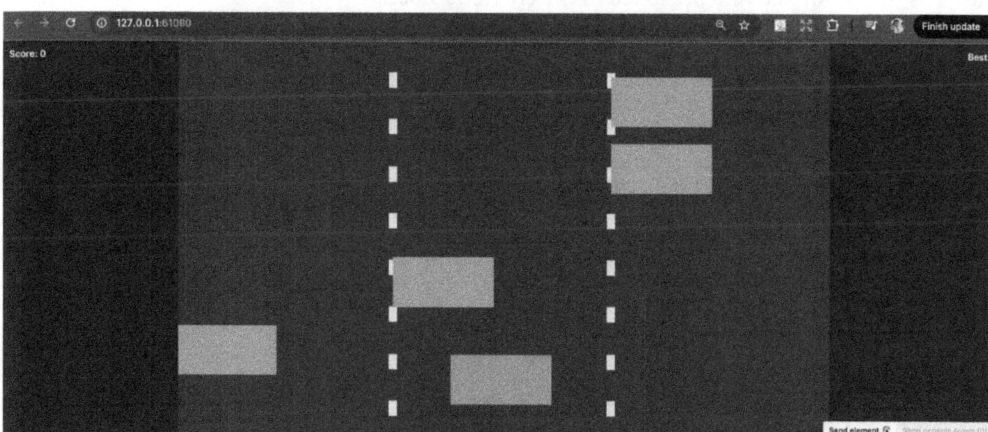

We can move the car around but the score didn't increment when I passed a red block. But that's acceptable for a first attempt. To have more features implemented, it will require more follow up prompting.

This is the general workflow for starting a project in Windsurf.

22

Analyzing an Existing Code Base

Let's put Windsurf to the test by asking it to work on an existing project. That existing project is a Kanban board app that I've built using Lovable in the previous chapter (but it can be any code base). It is not necessary that you complete the previous chapter first (in case you skipped directly to this chapter).

In the Kanban board app, you can add tasks, move them around, or delete them altogether. Much of the functionality has been built. But we would like to add features like:

- Add due dates for cards.
- Add column reordering.

This repository is stored on GitHub. We have a specifications document and also a to-do list for this project.

First, let's clone this repository locally and start working on it. We can do so in Windsurf. In Windsurf, close the existing folder that's open, and from the menu, choose **Clone Repository**:

We'll clone it from GitHub using the GitHub extension:

Select it, and hit **Copy & Continue to GitHub**:

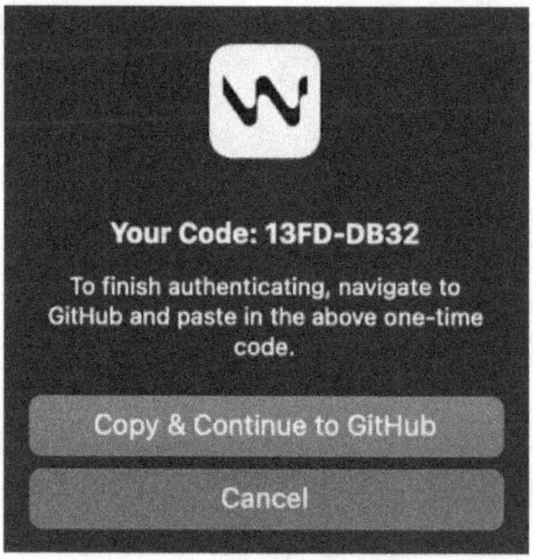

Go to GitHub, and select **Continue**:

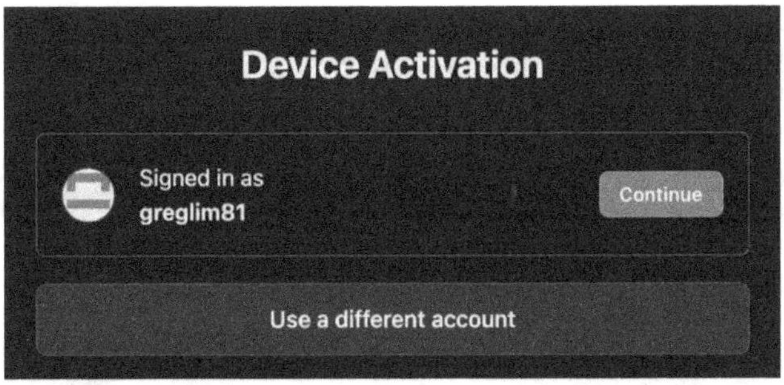

Paste the one-time code displayed inside Windsurf and **Authorize Exafunction**:

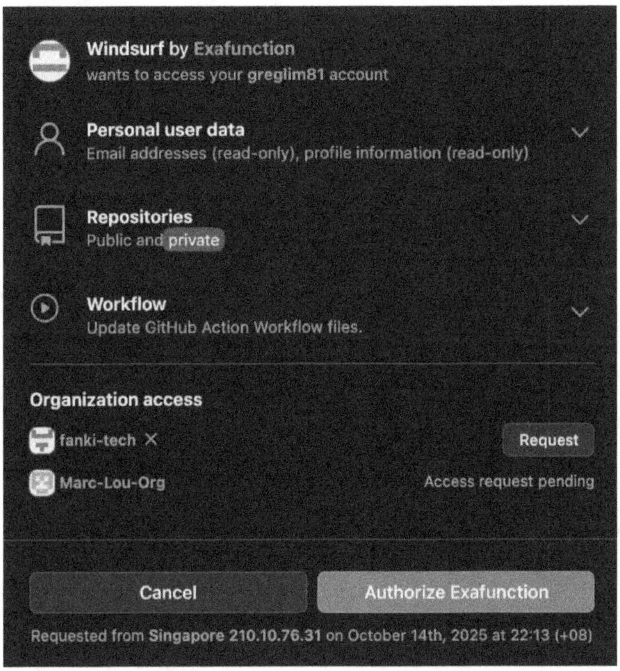

Now we're all set!

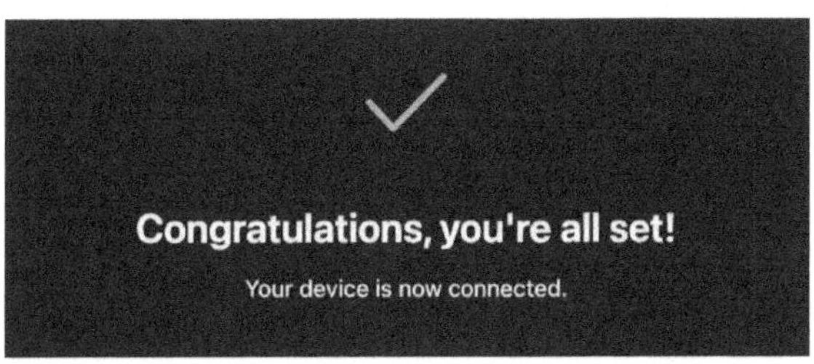

We can close this tab, go back to Windsurf, and we should see the available repositories:

I'll select **board-kickstart-forge**, choose **CascadeProjects** as the destination, and open it:

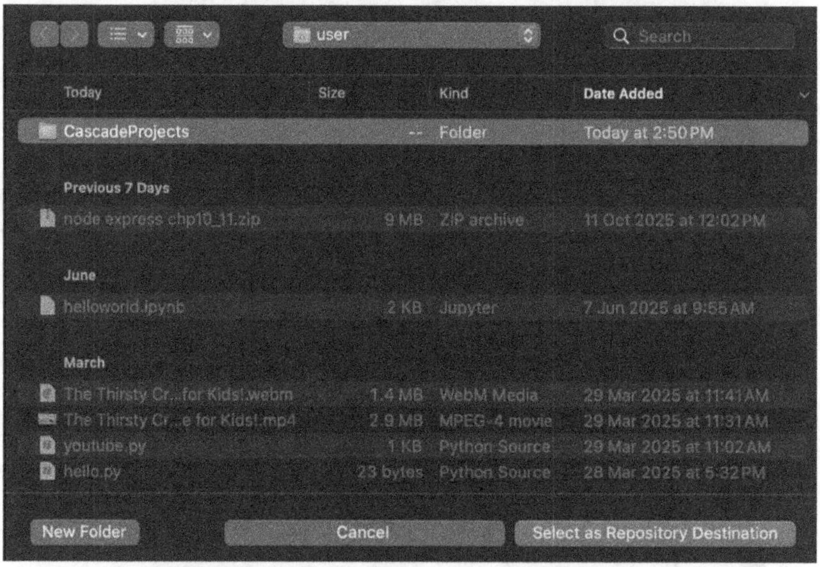

We'll trust all the files inside the **CascadeProjects** folder:

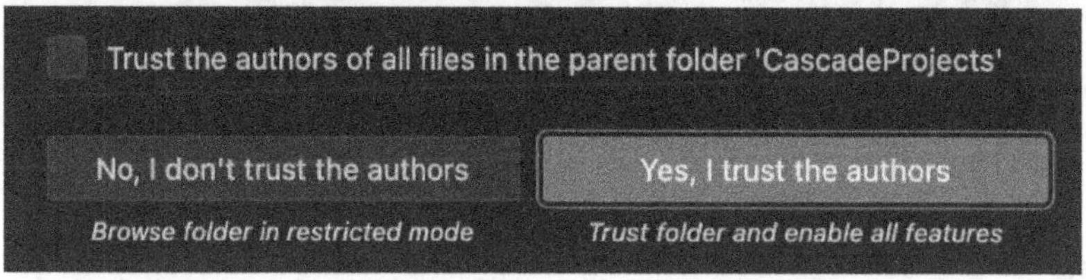

On the left-hand side, you'll now see the code that we have:

Now, Windsurf doesn't yet know anything about this codebase. So it doesn't make much sense to start making changes right away.

We need to add the specifications and the to-do list. Create a `docs` folder, and inside it, add two new files:

- `requirements.md`
- `todo.md`

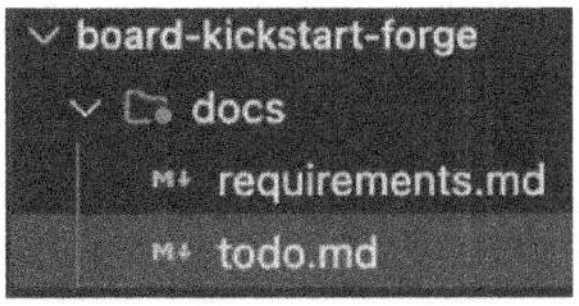

We created the specifications and the to-do list when creating the Kanban board back in the Lovable section. If you didn't go through the Lovable section, no worries. Contact `support@i-ducate.com` to get the specifications and to-do list files.

To get the specifications, we'll go to **Settings** in Lovable and copy over the necessary information:

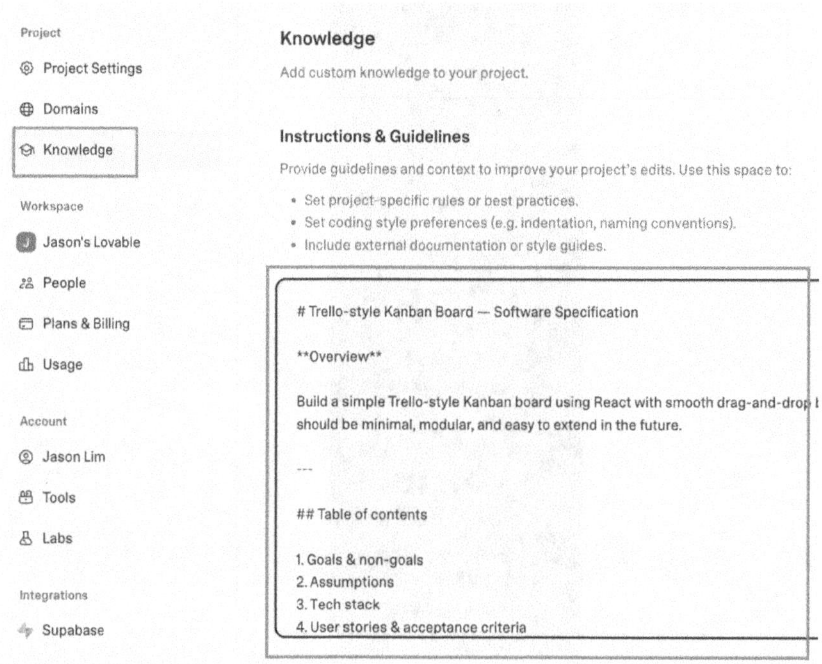

And paste it into `requirements.md`:

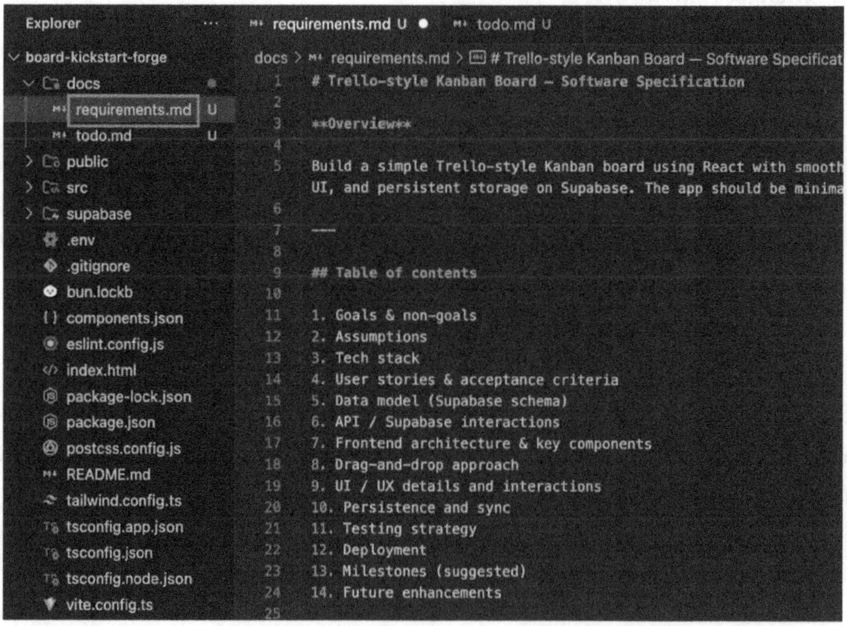

Take note only to copy till the **End of specification** section (first box below):

```
---

**End of specification**
```

```
# Trello-style Kanban Board — Development To-Do List

This to-do list breaks down the project into small, logical develo

---

## 🏗 Phase 1 — Setup & Environment

* [ ] Initialize project with **React + TypeScript** using Vite.
* [ ] Install dependencies:
```

Copy the rest of the to-do list portion (second box above) into `todo.md`:

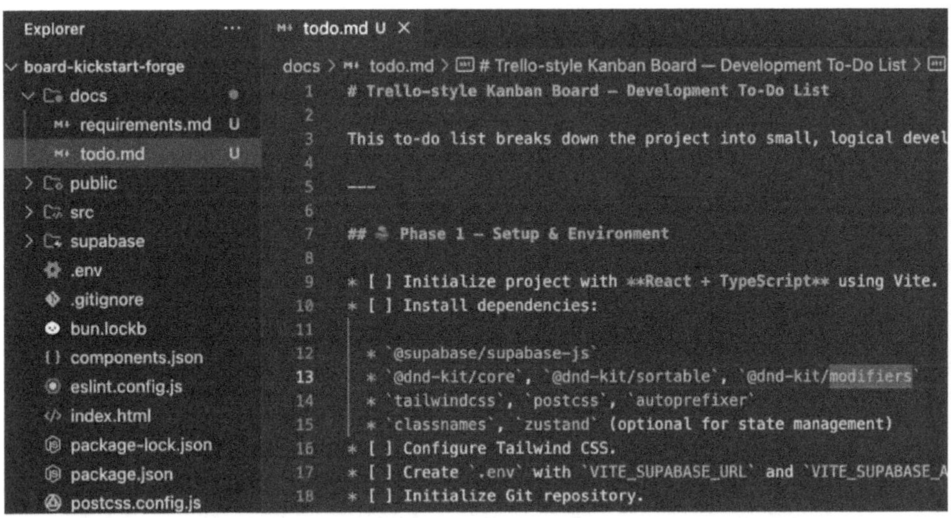

Having those set up, it's time for the fun part. We will prompt Windsurf to analyze this codebase to better understand what's been built and what still needs to be done.

Here's the instruction:

```
Analyze the current codebase. Identify which features have already been
implemented according to @todo.md and which are still pending. Update @
todo.md accordingly by marking completed tasks as done. @requirements.md"
```

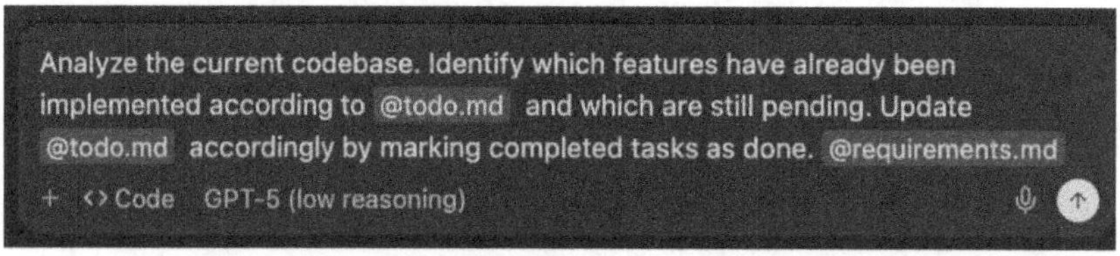

Note the referencing of files `@todo.md` and `@requirements.md` so that Windsurf knows exactly where to look.

Send the prompt and Windsurf should analyze our code base and then update the to-do file.

We can review what's been updated:

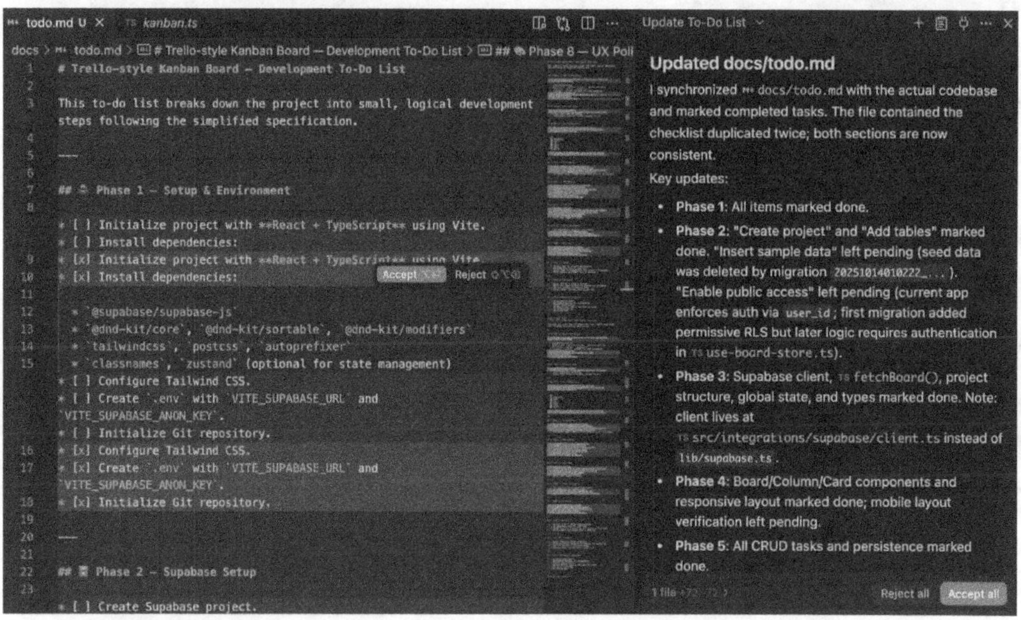

In `todo.md`, anything in red has been removed, and anything in green has been added or changed.

You'll notice that several tasks now have an **x** next to them — meaning they're marked as done.

```
## Phase 2 – Supabase Setup

* [ ] Create Supabase project.
* [ ] Add `columns` and `cards` tables according to the schema.
* [x] Create Supabase project.
* [x] Add `columns` and `cards` tables according to the schema.
* [ ] Insert sample data for testing.
* [ ] Enable public access for testing (optional for v1).
```

For example, the setup seems to be completed. Basic CRUD features and column management also appears to have been done:

```
## Phase 5 – CRUD Features

* [ ] Implement **Add Column** functionality.
* [ ] Implement **Rename Column** inline.
* [ ] Implement **Delete Column** with confirmation.
* [ ] Implement **Add Card** inside column.
* [ ] Implement **Edit Card** title inline.
* [ ] Implement **Delete Card**.
* [ ] Persist all changes to Supabase.
* [x] Implement **Add Column** functionality.
* [x] Implement **Rename Column** inline.
* [x] Implement **Delete Column** with confirmation.
* [x] Implement **Add Card** inside column.
* [x] Implement **Edit Card** title inline.
* [x] Implement **Delete Card**.
* [x] Persist all changes to Supabase.

---

## Phase 6 – Drag & Drop

* [ ] Integrate `dnd-kit`.
* [ ] Enable drag-and-drop for cards within and across columns.
* [ ] Update card `position` and `column_id` on drop.
* [ ] Implement local optimistic updates.
* [ ] Persist reordering to Supabase.
* [x] Integrate `dnd-kit`.
* [x] Enable drag-and-drop for cards within and across columns.
* [x] Update card `position` and `column_id` on drop.
* [x] Implement local optimistic updates.
* [x] Persist reordering to Supabase.                Accept  Reject
```

So quite a few things are already in place. It's not perfect, but this is a solid starting point. Now Windsurf understands the context of the project, and we can start working on the remaining features.

23

Adding Features

We're going to put Windsurf to the test by working on some features that haven't yet been implemented in this project. But first, let's start the project and ask Windsurf to simply `run the application`:

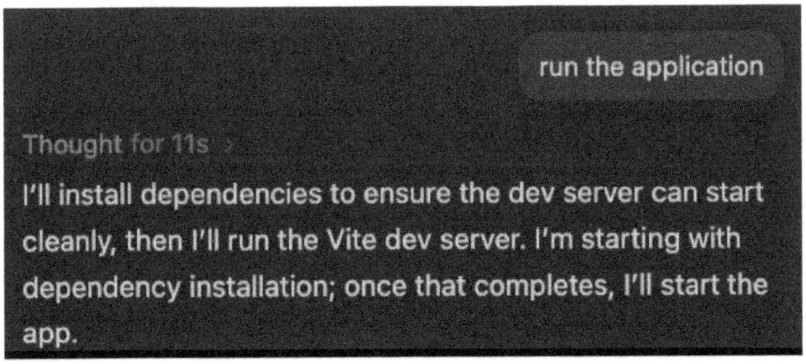

When we do that, it figures out that the dependencies aren't installed — so we'll need to install them first. Windsurf will then guide us to re-run our dev server:

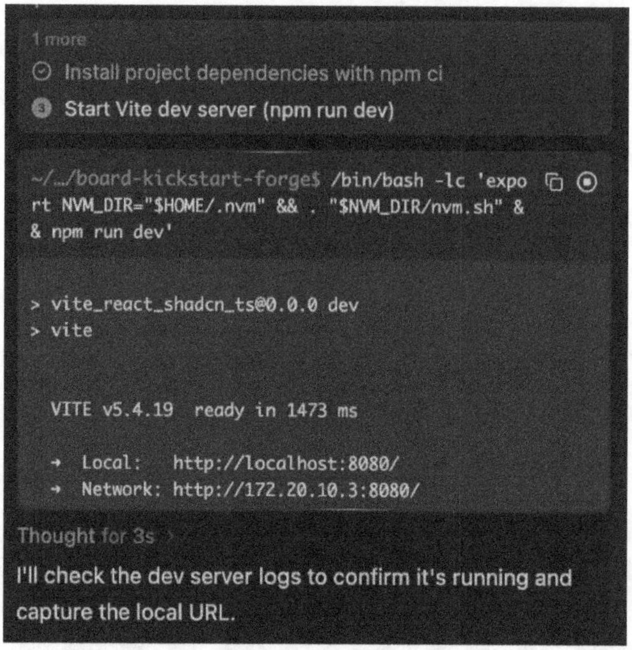

We can open our app via the provided URL, e.g. `localhost:8080` in a browser:

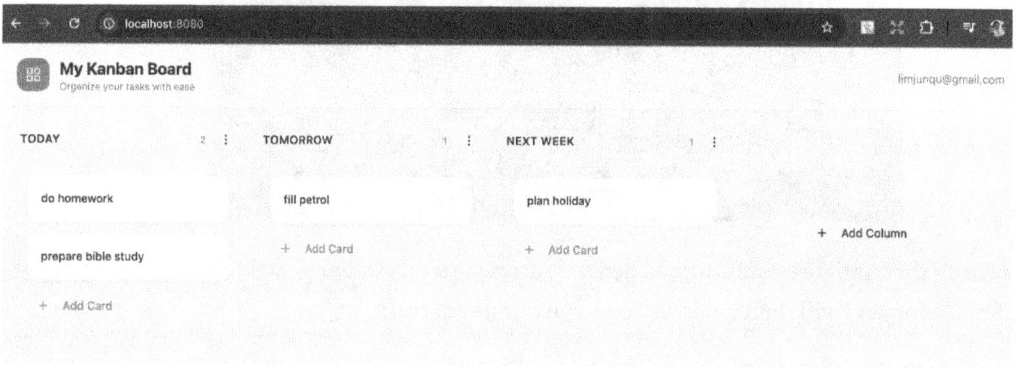

The app looks good. You can try adding, rearranging, deleting, modifying tasks to see that the app is working properly.

Now let's take a look at the to-do list and figure out what still needs to be done. For example, under `Future Enhancements` there's due dates for cards and column reordering not implemented yet:

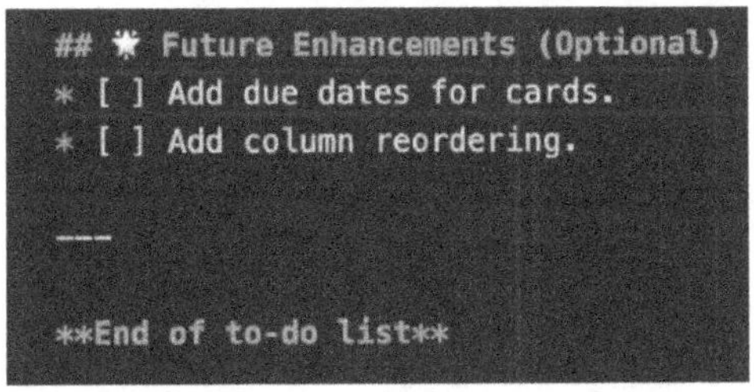

So we can say, `Implement the future enchancements in @todo.md`:

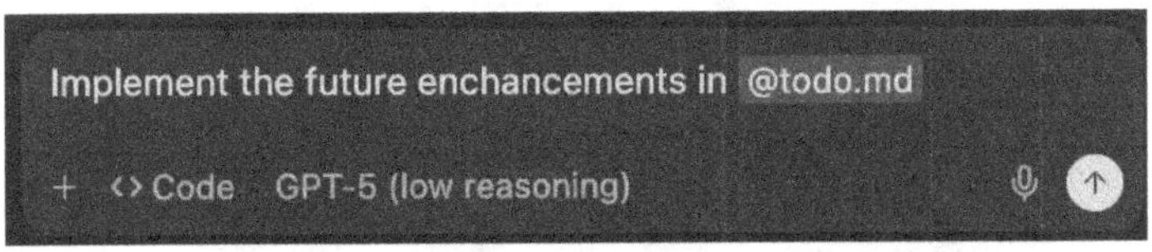

We reference `todo.md` for more accurate results. Windsurf goes ahead and implements the feature:

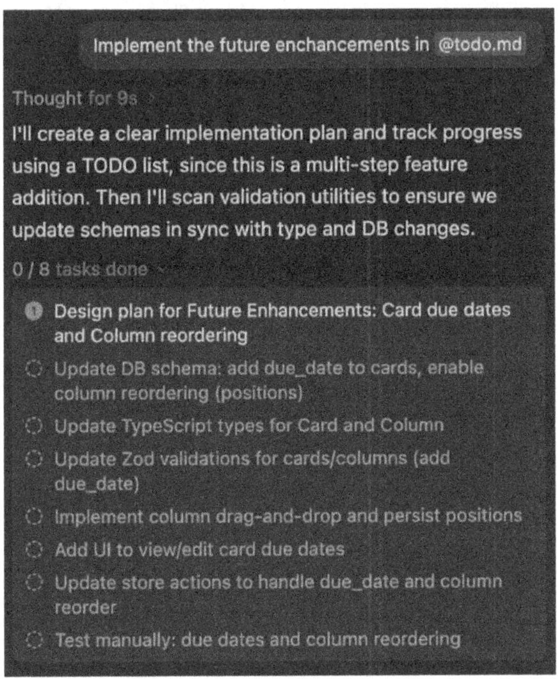

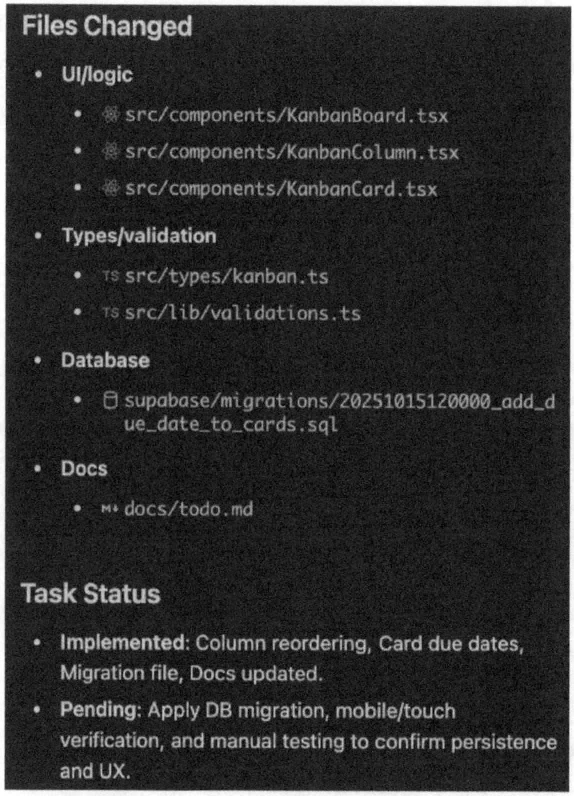

When Windsurf is done, let's check the app to confirm. In my case, both features are still not working.

So I'll first address the re-ordering of columns: `When i reorder the columns, the columns snap back into their original position. But after refreshing the page, the columns are reordered.`

```
I want the columns reordered even without refreshing the page.
```

We let Windsurf fix the issue:

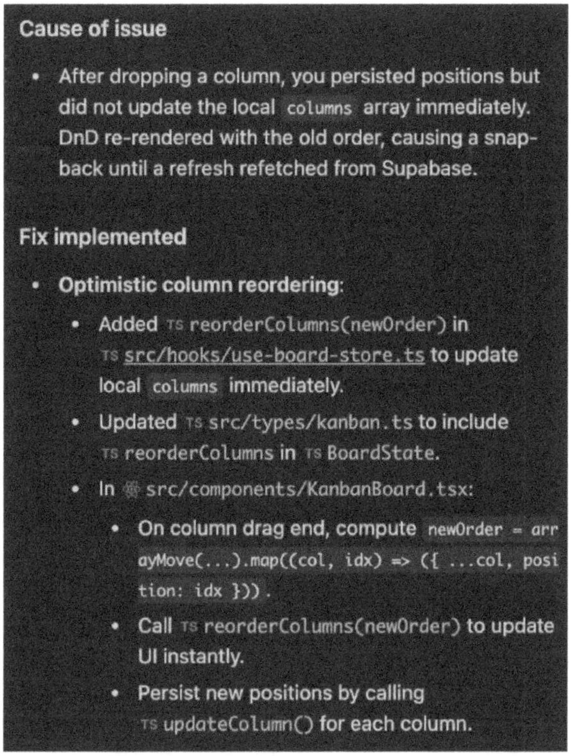

And if we reorder the columns now, they get ordered without having to refresh the page:

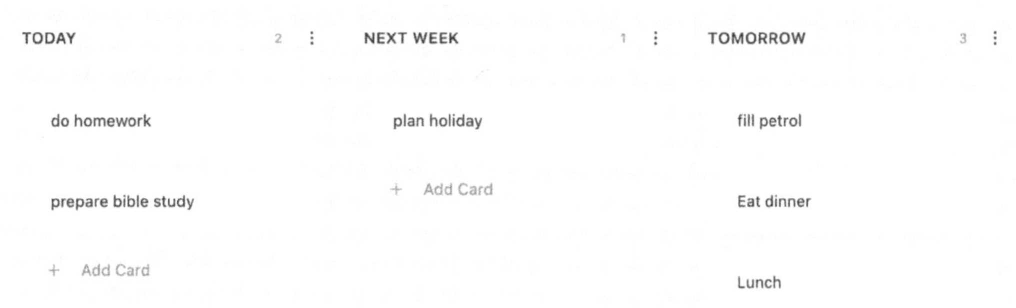

So we can confirm that the columns reordering functionality is indeed working.

I will let you give your own prompts to Windsurf to rectify any outstanding issues you face, since you might have a different one from mine. But you get the idea!

24

Windsurf Rules

The agent from Windsurf Cascade is already quite powerful, but to better adapt it to our needs and preferences, you can specify some rules. This is a more advanced feature and it's not for everyone.

But if you notice that the AI is doing something you don't like repeatedly and you want to change that behavior permanently (instead of constantly correcting it in the chat), then it makes sense to add some rules.

You can find this feature in **Windsurf - Settings** at the bottom:

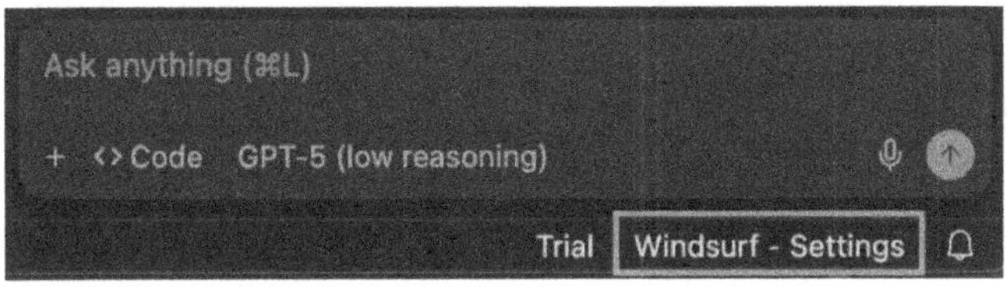

Under **Customizations**, select **Manage**:

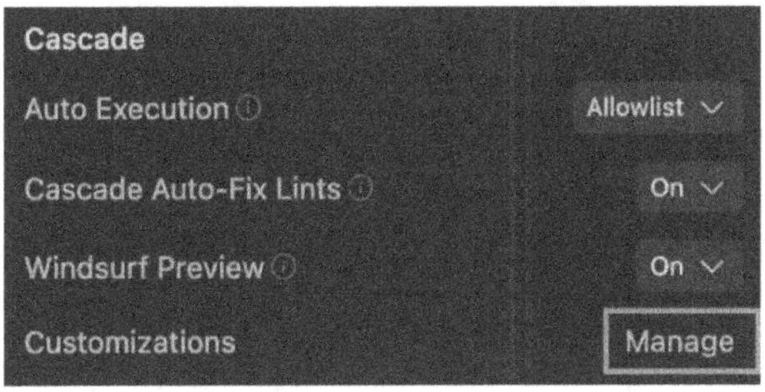

And you'll see the **Rules** section:

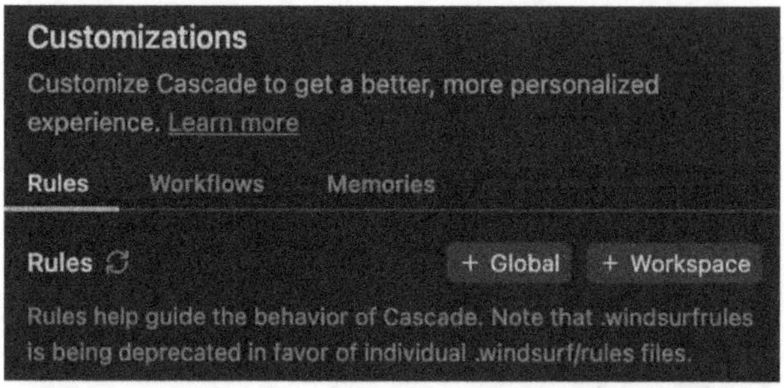

You can have **Global** rules and **Workspace** rules. Global rules apply to all your projects, while workspace rules apply only to the current project. It's up to you which one you prefer.

If you click on **Global** you'll see examples of what kind of rules you can create:

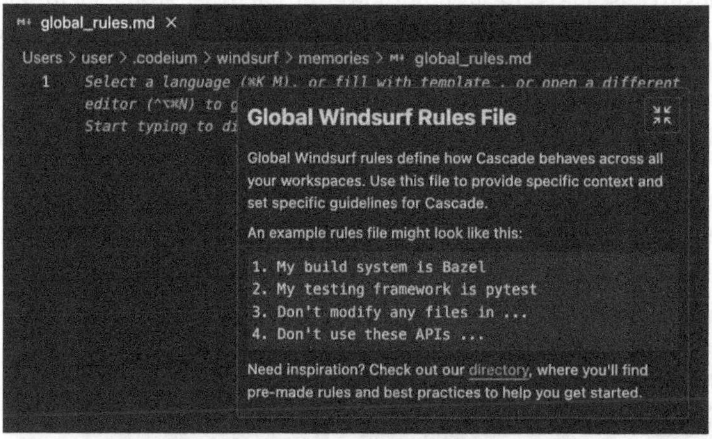

Because each project tends to have its own specific needs, I prefer **Workspace** rules over **Global** rules. And if I ever need to reuse them, I can just copy the configuration from one project to another.

So let's create a new workspace rule. Click the **+ Workspace**:

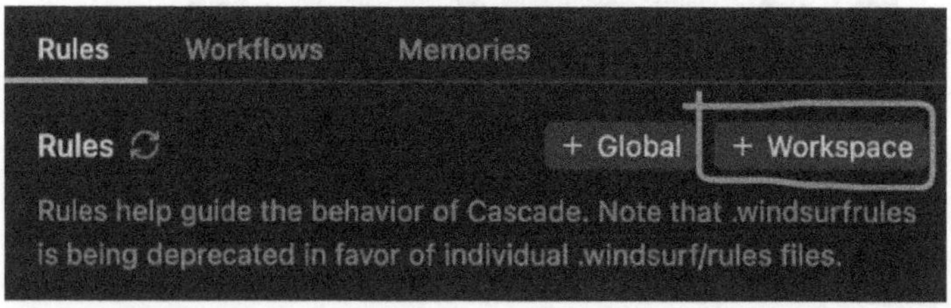

Give the rule a name — for example, `comments`.

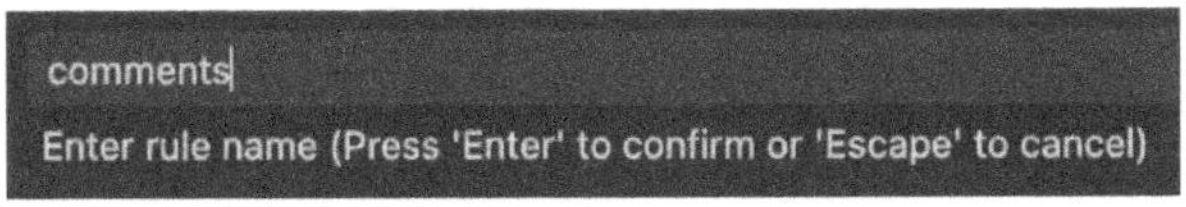

This rule will focus on writing comments for the code that's generated.

There are a few important settings here. First, **Activation Mode**. If it's set to **Manual**, we'll need to activate it manually using a shortcut:

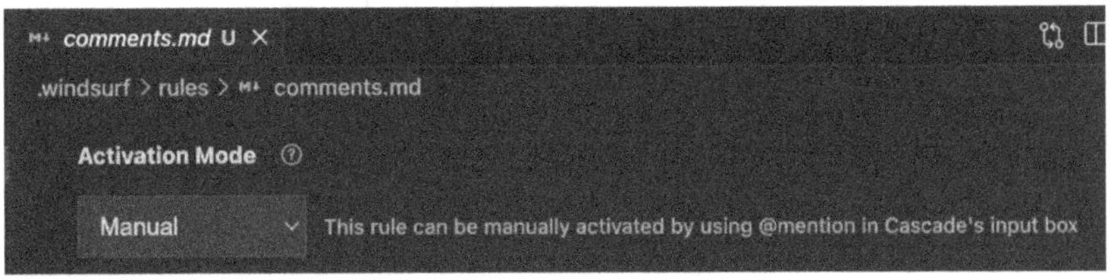

This shortcut will be available directly inside the editor.

If you want something that's always on, select **Always On** in **Activation Mode**, and in the content, specify your rule e.g. `all functions must have a one-sentence describing the function's purpose`:

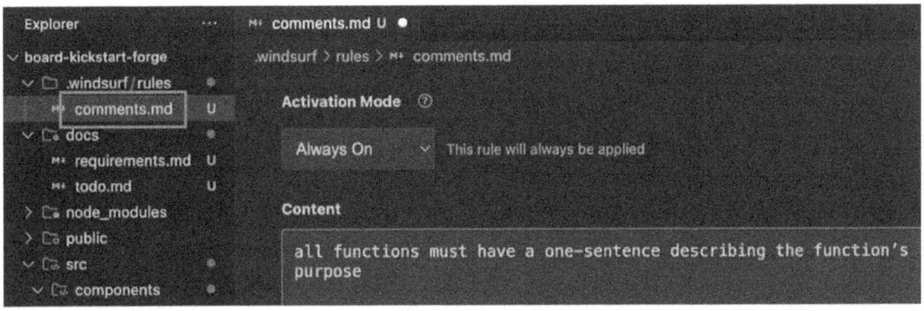

Once done, simply save it and the rule will be stored in the `.windsurf/rules` directory. This rule will now be part of the project:

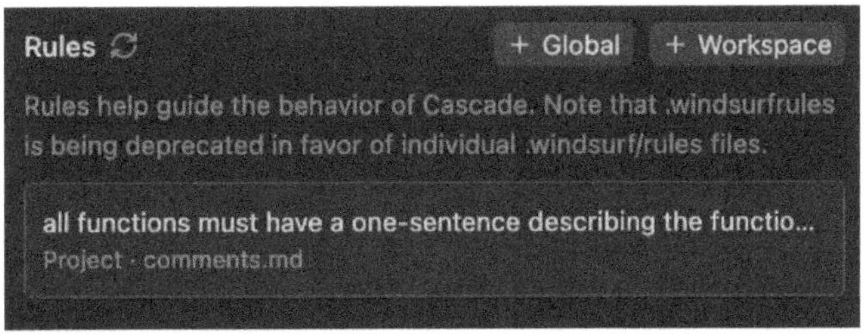

You can have multiple rule files by clicking again on **Workspace** and adding more rules. That's how you create and manage rules.

Now, in Cascade, you can also reference these rules directly within it for e.g.:

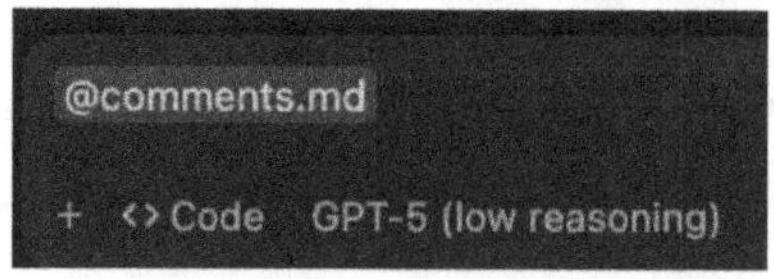

Windsurf provides a helpful resource called the Windsurf Rules Directory, which includes rule examples for different use cases — such as frontend development or general programming guidelines which you can take inspiration from to craft your own rules:

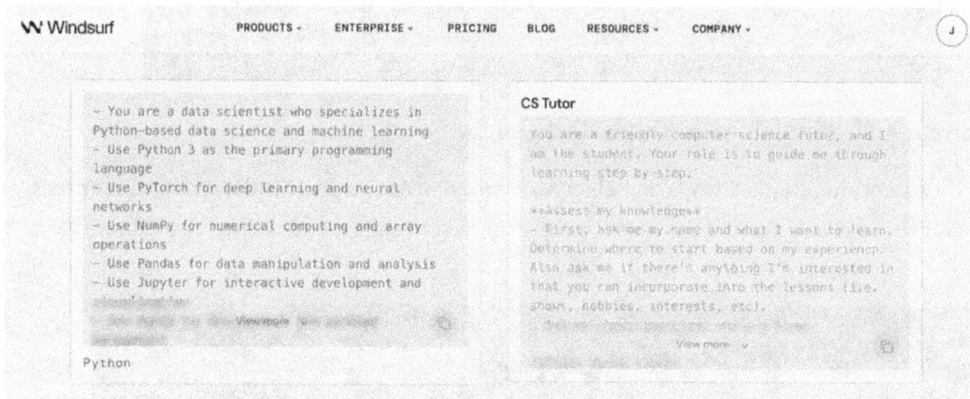

(windsurf.com/editor/directory)

For instance, you might find a rule like the below to help you understand the generated code better:

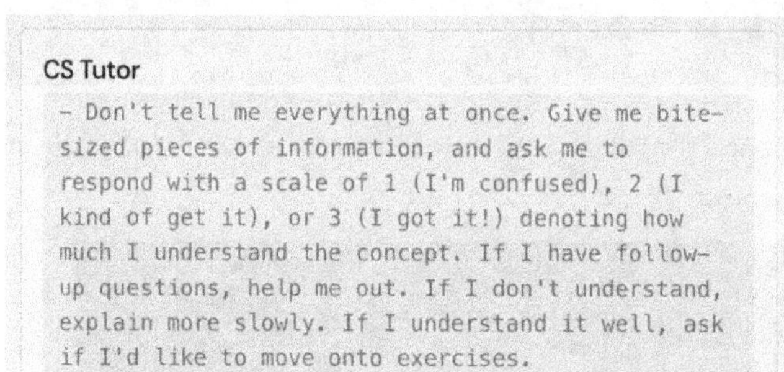

However, don't just copy every rule you see into your project. Understand what each rule does. The more rules and text you add, the harder it becomes for the model to follow them effectively. Too many unnecessary or unclear rules can actually reduce performance. So focus on using rules to correct specific behaviors you don't like — that's where they're most useful.

Finally, one more thing worth mentioning: under **Activation Mode**, you can also find **Model Decision**:

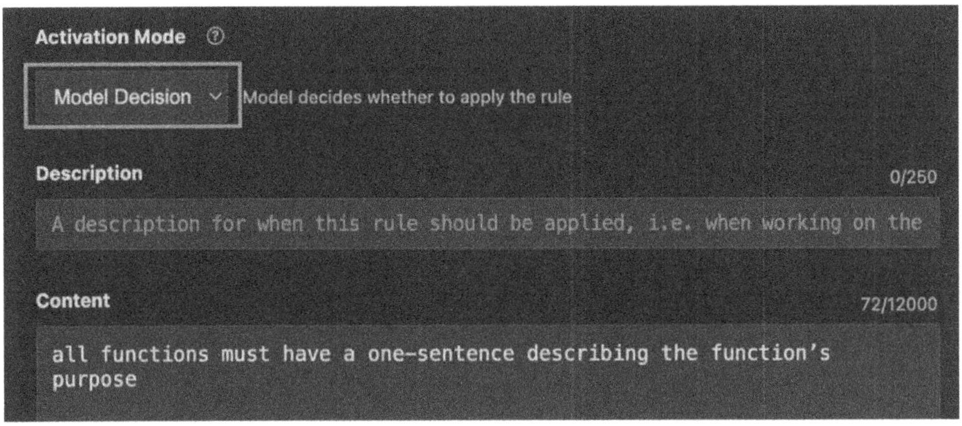

This determines whether a specific model should apply a particular rule. You can define conditions, such as:

"If you are model X, apply this rule; if not, ignore it."

That's just an example, but it shows how flexible the system can be.

In short, rules are a powerful but advanced feature. Only add the ones you truly need. Rules are simply files integrated into the IDE, making them convenient to manage.

25

Windsurf Workflows

In this chapter, we will look at an interesting functionality in Windsurf, workflows. You can find workflows in the same settings as **Rules** i.e. go to **Windsurf Settings**, under **Customizations**, click **Manage**:

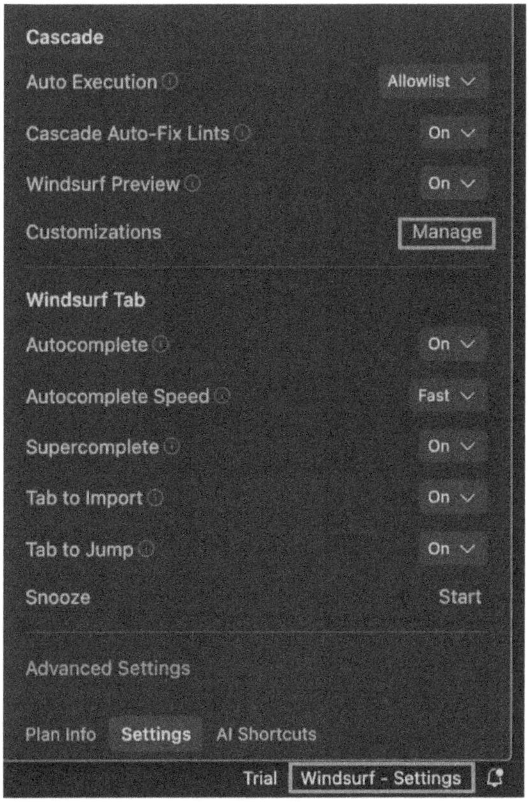

Select the **Workflows** tab:

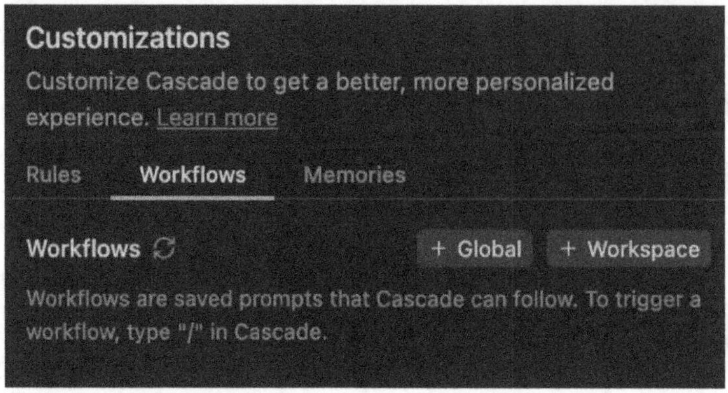

You can think of workflows like a bookmark for a set of actions you want to take. Whenever you find yourself writing the same prompt and going over a series of steps over and over, you should consider creating a workflow instead.

Let's look at a simple example. To create a workflow, click on + **Workflow** and I'm going to name the workflow `new-change`:

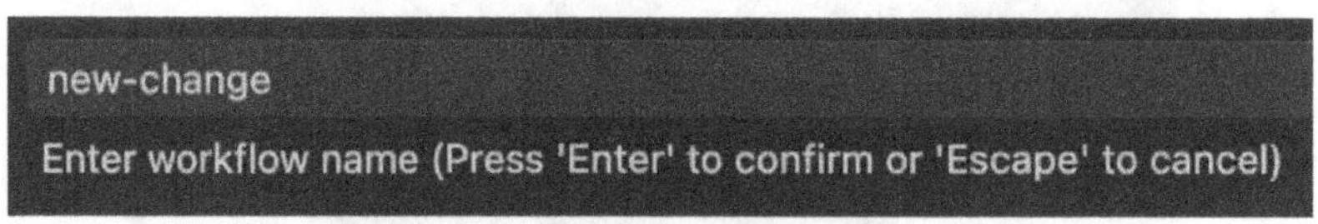

`new-change.md` will be created in the `workflows` directory:

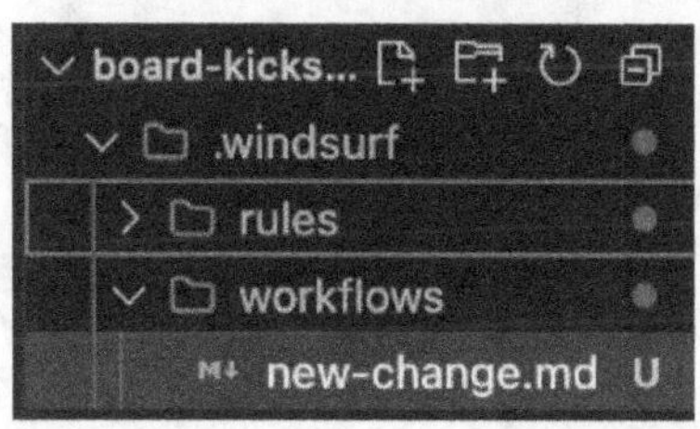

Provide a description and also the content in `new-change.md`:

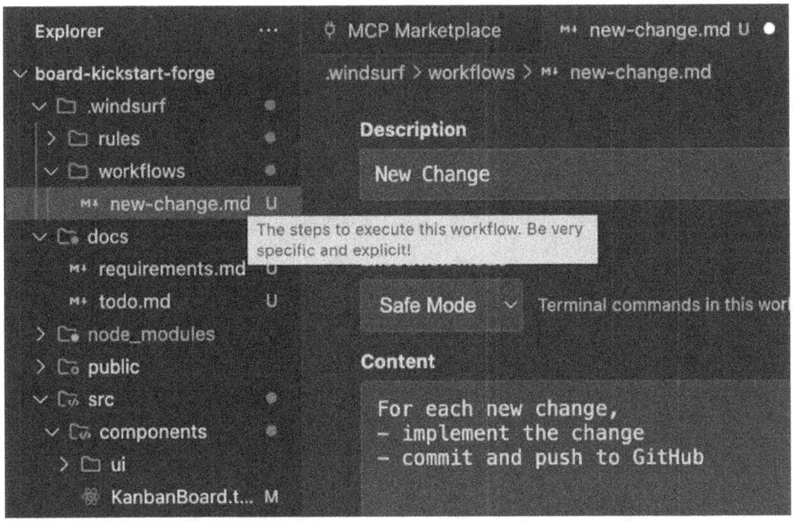

In the above workflow, I want to use it when I make new changes. For each new change, we want to implement the changes requested and also commit those changes to GitHub. Save these changes.

To call this workflow, we can do it directly from the prompt with a forward slash /, and you will see **new-change** appearing and select it:

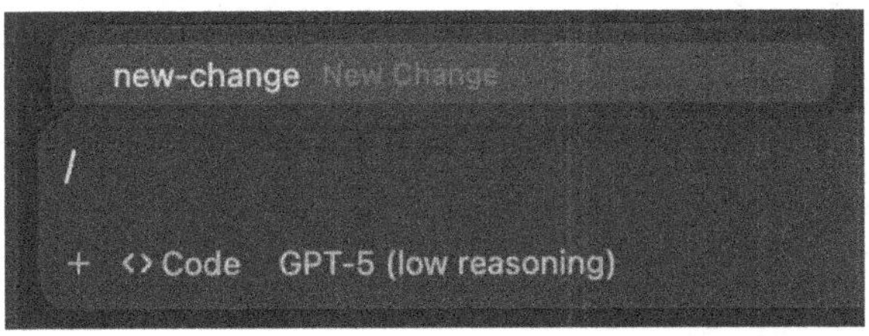

Let's now try implementing a small change. Let's change the title from **My Kanban Board** to **Greg's Board**:

We prompt:

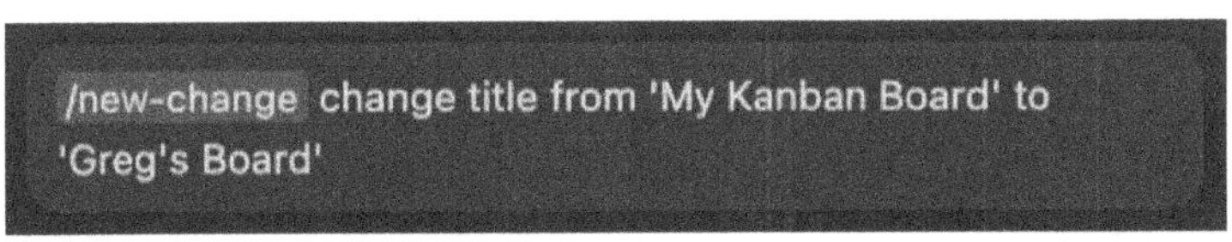

It first updates the header text and proceeds to commit and push the change to GitHub:

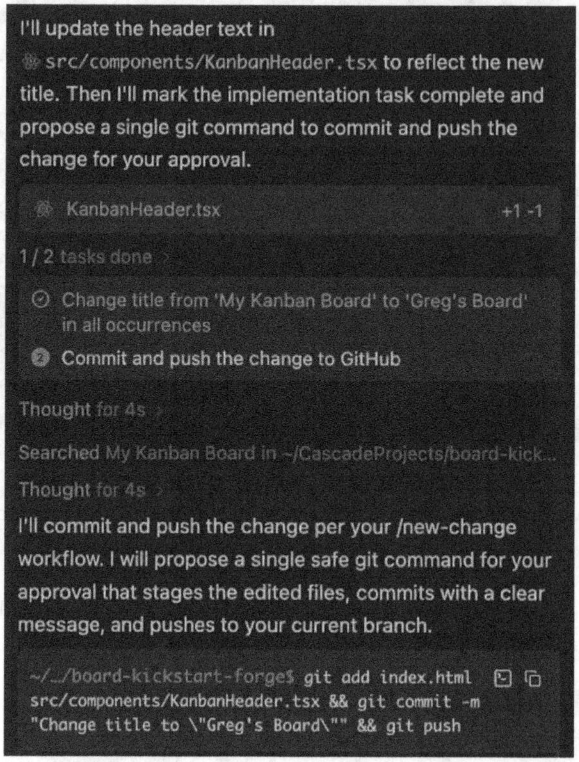

The header has been updated:

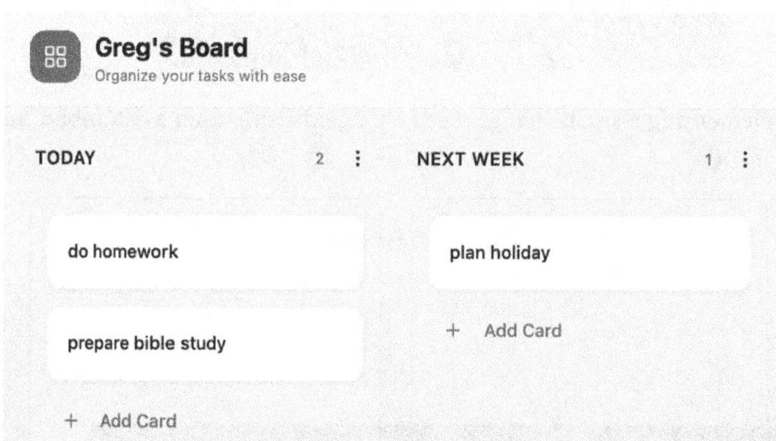

The workflow has completed:

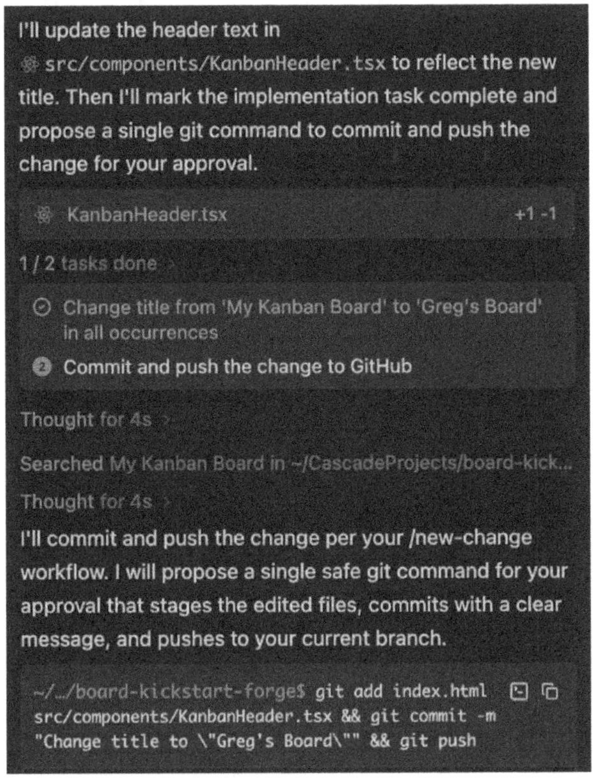

The change has been committed and pushed to GitHub. We can take a look at GitHub and see the code changes:

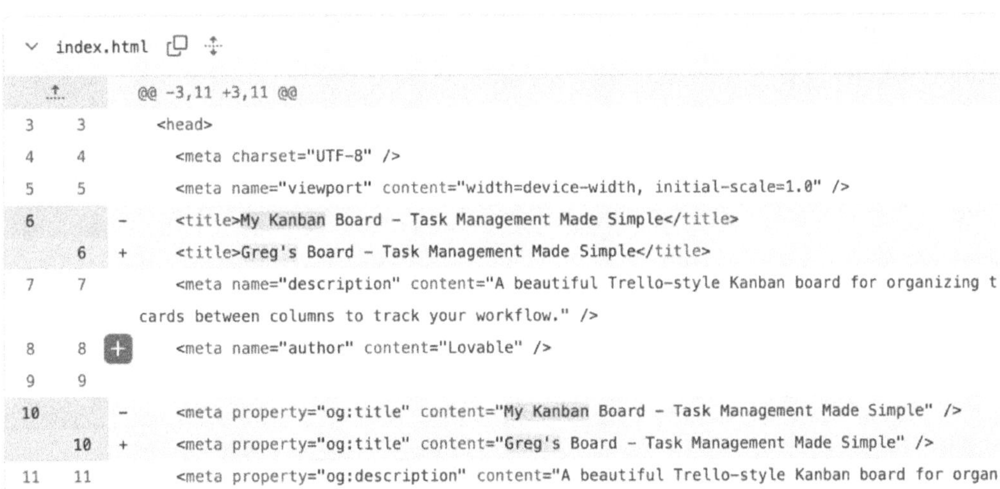

With this workflow, we now have a quick way of implementing changes, committing them and pushing them. This is the main idea of workflows. So when you find yourself going through a lot of repeating steps, you can turn it into a workflow.

26

Deploying Your Application with Windsurf

Windsurf has made deploying web applications easy. It's pretty much one prompt and one click. You can just prompt, `deploy this app`.

Windsurf has partnered up with Netlify to make deployment as seamless as possible. Behind the scenes, Windsurf analyzes all the project files, creates a production build, and then deploys to Netlify:

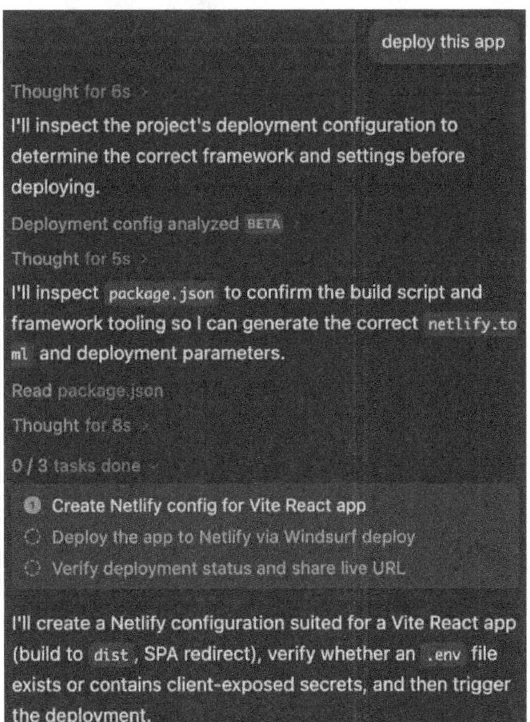

It creates a Netlify configuration file and we're going to see the **Deploy** button:

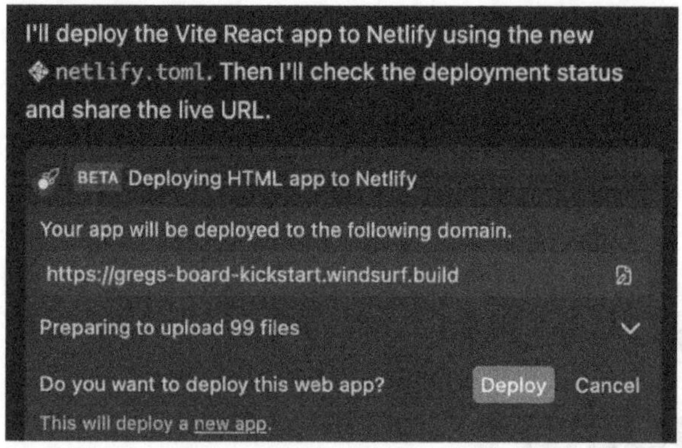

Click on **Deploy**. During the deployment, Windsurf might prompt you to log in into Netlify. The deployment process might also throw up some errors, for e.g.:

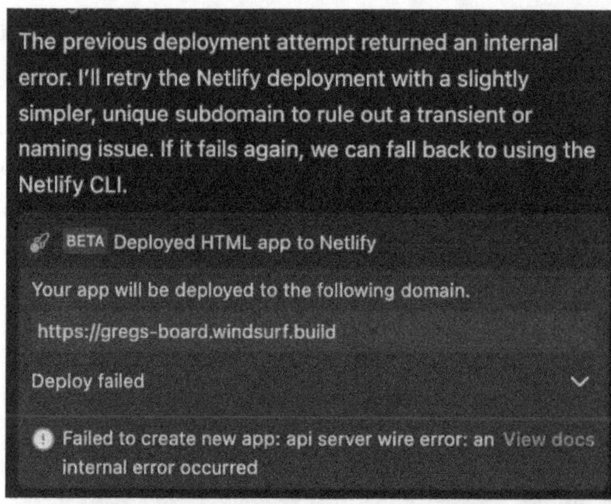

But we can let Windsurf take care of it. After some back and forth, we're going to get a deployed link:

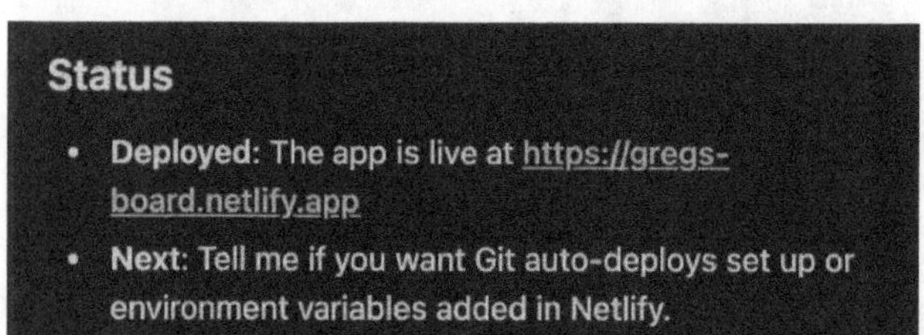

So the deployment has been completed. And our application works fine:

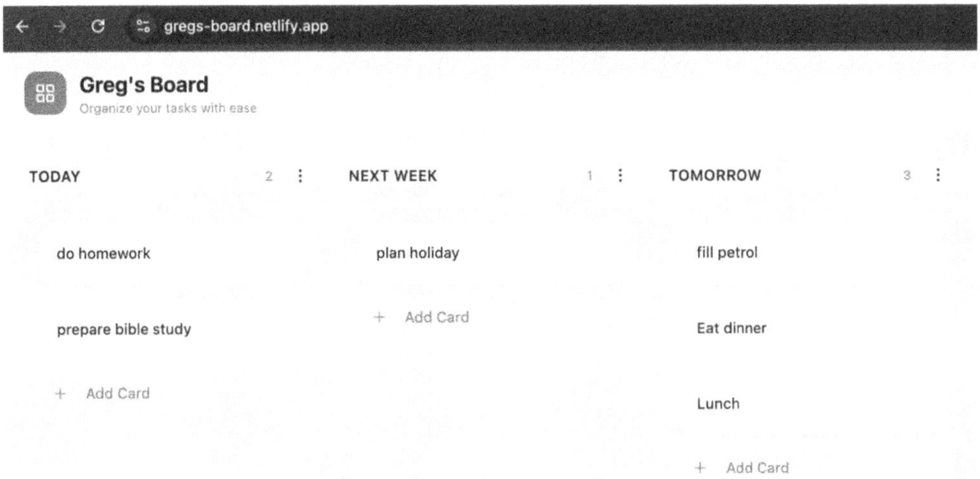

We can also go to the Netlify dashboard and see the deployment details of our app, e.g. build logs (in case there were some errors):

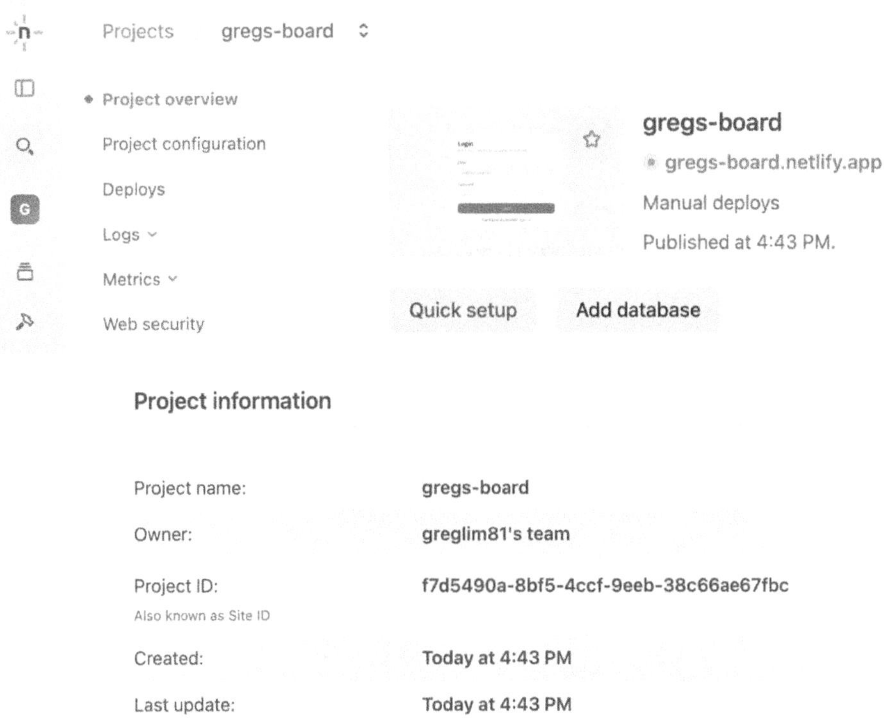

Other project info is described on the Netlify dashboard, e.g. Project ID.

I hope you see how easy it is to deploy using the Netlify integration in Windsurf. You can of course use any other provider you want and it will still be a good process.

Pricing

Windsurf provides a free plan where apart from the two-week Pro trial, you will also get 25 credits per month:

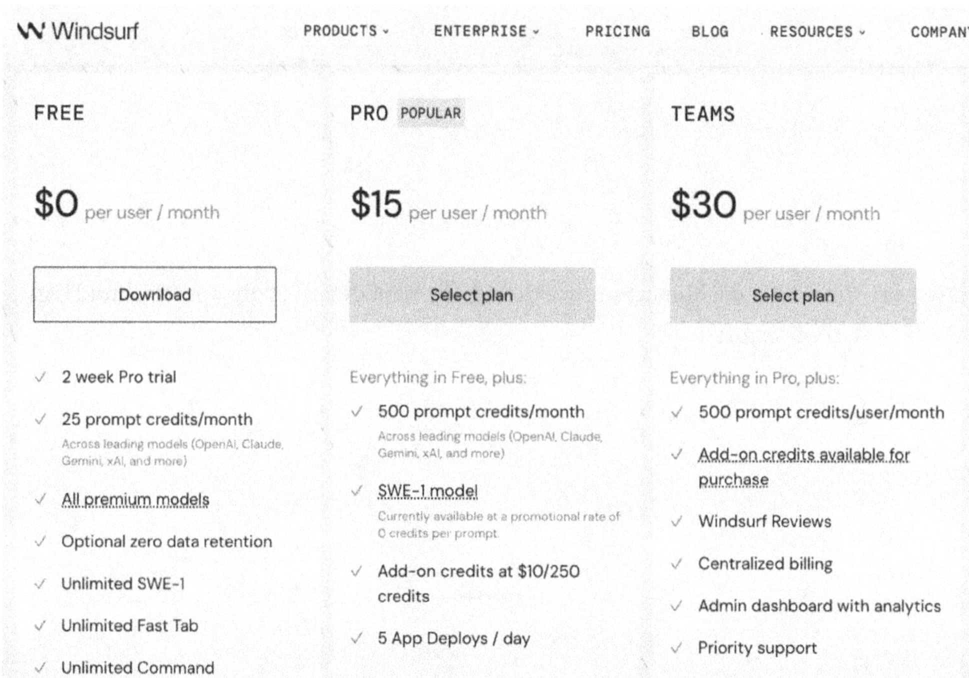

For some models, it can cost you a bit more than one credit per prompt, and for some models it can cost you less. For e.g., we can see recommended options in Cascade:

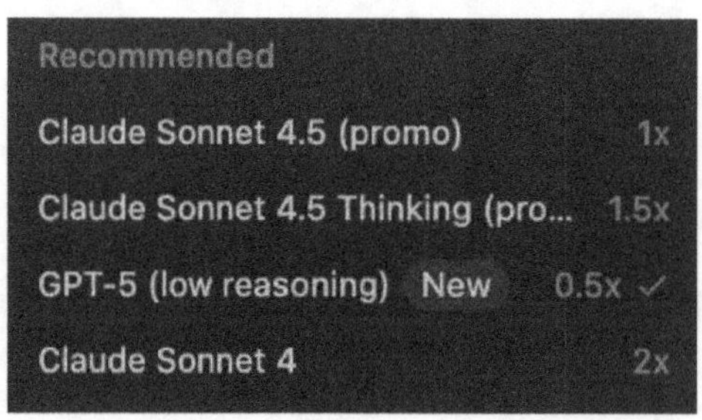

GPT-5 from OpenAI gives you two prompts per credit. If you use only this model in the free account, you essentially have 50 prompts per month. With OpenAI acquiring Windsurf, we will probably see even more preferential treatment for OpenAI's models.

If you need more, go to the Pro plan which has 500 prompt credits per month, or the equivalent of 1,000 prompt credits if you use the OpenAI GPT-5 model. Apart from this, you can also buy credits if you run out of them without having to upgrade your plan.

We're not going to go into the plans for Team and Enterprise. But the main idea is that if you're running a team or if a larger company, there are other things that you should consider.

Conclusion

This chapter gave you a hands-on introduction to Windsurf, how to use it and what its core features are.

Windsurf stands out for its ability to work effectively with existing codebases, an area where many AI tools still fall short. We explored key functionalities including AI-assisted analysis for existing projects, feature implementation, rule-based customization, automating workflows and deployments via Netlify.

The recent acquisition by OpenAI adds even more promise to Windsurf's future, especially in terms of deeper integration with top-tier models and smarter capabilities.

Final Words

AI assisted coding is a fast-changing industry right now. There's always more to learn, and for me personally, that's exciting. Whether you're an experienced developer, or just starting out, keep growing. This book is just the beginning.

Now, think about a problem you face in your day-to-day life—some task you might be able to solve through an app—and try building it with an AI assisted tool.

Hopefully, you have enjoyed this book and would like to learn more from me. I would love to get your feedback, learning what you liked and didn't for us to improve.

If you didn't like the book, or if you feel that I should have covered certain additional topics, please email us to let us know. This book can only get better thanks to readers like you.

If you like the book, I would appreciate if you could leave us an Amazon review too. Thank you and all the best for your learning journey!

Index

J

L

M

N

P

R

S

T

U

V

W

www.ingramcontent.com/pod-product-compliance
Lightning Source LLC
LaVergne TN
LVHW060036210926
848481LV00013B/3876